New Directions in Teaching English

Reimagining Teaching, Teacher Education, and Research

Edited by
Ernest Morrell and Lisa Scherff

ROWMAN & LITTLEFIELD
Lanham • Boulder • New York • London

Published by Rowman & Littlefield
A wholly owned subsidiary of The Rowman & Littlefield Publishing Group, Inc.
4501 Forbes Boulevard, Suite 200, Lanham, Maryland 20706
www.rowman.com

Unit A, Whitacre Mews, 26-34 Stannary Street, London SE11 4AB

British Library Cataloguing in Publication Information Available

Library of Congress Cataloging-in-Publication Data

New directions in teaching English : reimagining teaching, teacher education, and research / edited by Ernest Morrell and Lisa Scherff.
pages cm
Includes bibliographical references.
ISBN 978-1-61048-675-0 (hardcover : alk. paper) — ISBN 978-1-61048-676-7 (pbk. : alk. paper) — ISBN 978-1-61048-677-4 (electronic)
1. English language—Study and teaching—United States. 2. English language—Study and teaching—Social aspects. 3. English teachers—Training of—United States. I. Morrell, Ernest, 1971– editor of compilation. II. Scherff, Lisa, 1968– editor of compilation. LB1631.N358 2015 428.0071—dc23 2015007505

♾ ™ The paper used in this publication meets the minimum requirements of American National Standard for Information Sciences Permanence of Paper for Printed Library Materials, ANSI/NISO Z39.48-1992.

Printed in the United States of America

New Directions in Teaching English

To my mom and dad who have been collectively teaching schoolchildren for nearly a century and counting, and to all of the English teachers and teacher educators that I've had the pleasure of working with over the past two decades.

—Ernest Morrell

To all of the mentors—teachers, professors, and students—I have been guided by over the years. In particular, I am indebted to Carolyn Piazza, Ted Hipple, Jo Harris, Trena Paulus, Lisa Hooper, and Alan Brown.

—Lisa Scherff

Contents

Preface

Once you learn to read, you will be forever free.
—Frederick Douglass

(RE)INVENTING THE FUTURE OF LITERACY EDUCATION

Millions of Americans, like Frederick Douglass, have used literacy as a tool to empower themselves socially, politically, and economically. Academic literacy rates are positively correlated to life expectancy, educational outcomes, and earning potential. Low literacy rates are also negatively correlated to incarceration, dropout, and unemployment.

Too predictably, academic literacy achievement in schools is stratified along lines of class, race, and geography in America. Those who have less seem to receive less with respect to their literacy education. As a whole, students attending schools in the United States seem to be struggling with literacy achievement compared to peers internationally.

English educators have a tremendous role to play in re-envisioning the future of literacy education in America. They train future teachers, work with practicing teachers, conduct research in English classrooms, and observe and document powerful literacy practices that occur in non-school settings.

English educators are often also called on to advocate for sound policies and pedagogical practices at the district, state, and federal levels. Put simply, the work of English education matters, and it includes, but is not limited to, the ability to prepare the next generation of workers in which the demands for workplace literacy are greater than they've ever been.

English is a discipline that helps prepare engaged citizens who use language and literacy to speak the truth to power; English educators also help future generations appreciate the beauty of written words, be they in essays, poems, plays, novels, websites, or blogs.

More and more, English educators are moving beyond fostering an appreciation of beautiful words written by others to helping students write and distribute traditional and multimodal compositions of their own. To borrow again from Frederick Douglass, powerful English education should be an act of liberation for teacher and student alike.

While English educators are essential to informing policies and pedagogical practices that will dictate the future of literacy instruction in America, they are often fragmented in their approach to the problem. Teacher educators, literacy researchers, and classroom teachers often work in silos and are rarely in conversation with one another about how to work collaboratively to tackle the major issues of the day. Students' voices are seldom accounted for in our discussion of the present and future of our field.

To address this issue, the authors present an edited volume that integrates diverse voices from various subdisciplines, such as teacher education, urban education, multicultural education, critical cultural studies, digital media literacies, new literacy studies, and adolescent literacy to converse with university-based English educators and K–12 classroom teachers to create a dialogue about what is known about powerful literacy teaching and learning and what we will need to know in order to meet the challenges and opportunities of English education in the twenty-first century.

Introduction

Ernest Morrell and Lisa Scherff

The destiny of colored America . . . is the destiny of America.
—Frederick Douglass

WHY NOW? POWERFUL ENGLISH EDUCATION
FOR THE TWENTY-FIRST CENTURY

Students, families, communities, and neighborhoods simply cannot survive in the twenty-first century without raising academic literacy rates. Countless impoverished and historically marginalized youth will not be positioned to succeed academically until they are confident in their ability to do so and until they feel that the academic activities they are being asked to take part in are socially, culturally, and technologically relevant.

Toward these ends, these students must become the recipients of empowering literacy pedagogies that demand academic excellence, increase cultural competency (Ladson-Billings, 1995), draw on linguistic and cultural wealth (Lee, 1993; Yosso, 2005), make connections to youth culture and non-school literacies (Fisher, 2007; Morrell, 2008), treat them as transformative intellectuals (Freire, 1970), and fully realized human beings (Darder, 1991; hooks, 1995).

Given this moment so full of challenges and possibilities, English educators must ask themselves how to better engage in relevant and rigorous scholarship that will facilitate efficacious intervention into matters of educational policy and practice. How do English educators leverage this scholarship to develop practices in P–16 classrooms, preservice teacher training, and professional development that provide a new generation of teachers the confidence and the license to innovate and to connect with youth? In other words, how do we transform the scholarship that will help to transform the profession to keep it vital and vibrant in its second century?

As members of a discipline, we need to dedicate ourselves to amassing all that is known about effective teacher education, classroom instruction, and the literate lives of students and their families, and to sharing that information with a growing majority that is frustrated by the standards-testing regime, but at present sees no better alternatives. Everyday English teachers and teacher educators are creating powerful learning ecologies that need to be better supported, understood, and shared if that success is to multiply.

We simply have to do a better job of collecting information on the scores of highly effective English language arts teachers who are consistently achieving results in high-poverty, high-need schools. Of course we have to say more about what we mean by "results" or "effective." We need to expand the language of effectiveness to include more than just test results, but we cannot shy away from this task as a discipline. The answers to many of the most difficult questions in literacy education are located in these successful classrooms across the nation.

The world needs independent, free-thinking, open-minded intellectuals who can come together across multiple lines of difference to collect, process, and produce information that will help solve the most challenging problems of our time, and no discipline is more important in shaping this kind of citizen than English. If we tap into the everyday literate lives of our students; if we resource teachers and classrooms, give them sound examples of success, and provide for autonomy and voice simultaneously, we will help realize this ambitious and worthwhile goal of increasing literacy and college access for all of our students.

Powerful English education for the twenty-first century means or requires moving beyond "methods" classes to the study of local contexts and stakeholders—differentiating instruction, including envisioning, fostering, and utilizing new or hybrid spaces for teaching and learning in which lines between teachers and students are blurred in order to ensure that all students are provided with an opportunity to learn (Moje et al., 2004; Scherff & Piazza, 2008/2009; Souto-Manning, 2010).

A reimagined discipline also requires creating activities and experiences for preservice English teachers that promote critical reflection, including longer, more integrated placements (Cochran-Smith & Lytle, 2009; Fecho, 2004). Finally, transforming English education demands that we take a questioning stance regarding policies and practices, such as standards and assessments, that constrain our efforts to improve students' literacy rates (for example, Kirkland, 2010; McNeil & Valenzuela, 2001; Scherff & Piazza, 2005).

Robert Yagelski (2005) challenges English educators to address what Orr (1992) refers to as the "crisis of sustainability"; this means playing a central role in shaping the local and broader communities we want our students to live, survive, and thrive in.

Portes and Smagorinsky (2010) additionally call on English educators to go beyond normative organizational structures and practices that function to maintain the status quo. In order to do so, English educators must equally emphasize and promote the work of effective classroom teachers, research in their college and university classrooms, and investigations in the field.

A MULTI-VOICED, CRITICAL, MULTIDISCIPLINARY APPROACH

Weaving together the multiple voices of K–12 classroom teachers, teacher educators, university-based researchers, and advocates for educational justice, this co-edited volume attempts to create a comprehensive vision of critical and culturally relevant English education at the dawn of the twenty-first century across five domains: classroom teaching, teacher education, scholarship, standards and assessment, and advocacy.

This volume is multi-voiced. It includes perspectives from classroom teachers, teacher educators, and researchers in language and literacy, positioned to respond to recent changes in national conversations about literacy, learning, and assessment that have been triggered by recent events in education, such as the creation of the Common Core State Standards and the dismal performance of America's teens as measured by both national assessments and international comparisons.

These variously situated authors also recognize the rapidly changing demographics in America's schools, the changing nature of literacy in the digital age, and the increasing demands for literacy in the workplace. All of these forces combine to shape their practice and research, and their responses to these conditions are at the heart of this collective work.

This volume is critical. The authors recognize that English education does not happen in a vacuum. At all times education is a political act, and schools are embedded within a sociocultural reality that benefits some at the expense of others. As the Frederick Douglass quote reminds us, literacy has the potential to emancipate, but it can also constrain, erase, diminish, and disparage.

Therefore the approach advocated throughout many of the chapters is one of critical literacy, in which young people gain a set of skills that allow them to become more able, discerning, and empowered consumers and producers of texts (Morrell, 2008). The critical literacy framework is also one that sees as an end of education the development of students who are advocates for equity and justice. As many of the following studies take place in historically marginalized central city and rural communities, many of the students' experiences are of inequity and injustice.

The volume is also multidisciplinary. Given that we contemplate what we teach, how we teach, who we teach, and where we teach, English education has been and will continue to be connected to and within conversation with multiple fields of inquiry. Toward that end our authors engage literature studies, language studies, composition studies, and new literacy studies, but the chapters also draw upon sociology, psychology, linguistic anthropology, cultural studies, gender studies, ethnic studies, and computer science.

The thoughtful pieces included in this volume address some of the key concerns of the day, such as:

1. What does critical and culturally relevant teaching look like in America's English classrooms?
2. How do English educators prepare tomorrow's classroom teachers to be culturally sensitive and attuned to standards and achievement?
3. What are the most effective methods of investigation for the discipline of English education?
4. How do we conduct research that informs the field of English education and that also speaks to larger conversations of policy and practice?
5. How are English educators drawing on their existing knowledge base to advocate for changes in policy and practice?

It is our hope that these voices cohere in a volume that will guide our conversations on the scope and power of English education as a discipline.

ORGANIZATION OF THE BOOK

The first section, "Classroom Teaching," focuses on narratives from a diverse set of classroom teachers who have attempted to incorporate critical and culturally relevant practices into their English classes. These teachers describe what they believe to have been the successes in such an approach. How do they define success? What are the challenges they have faced with such an approach?

In chapter 1, Jerica Coffey, a high school English teacher in Southern California, offers a critical multiliteracies approach to secondary English instruction. Drawing from the diverse research literatures of critical pedagogy, new literacy studies, and the sociology of urban education, Jerica develops a socially, culturally, and technologically relevant English language arts curriculum that weaves multimodal texts and issues of immediate concern to students together with traditional academic texts like novels and plays. Jerica also offers opportunities for students to share their sophisticated multimodal productions with the wider world, thereby developing their academic self-esteem, sense of agency, and critical awareness, while also reinforcing the importance of literacy education to their academic and social futures.

In chapter 2, "Cultural Relevance in the Modern Language Arts Classroom," Jose Paco Fiallos presents powerful examples of how English teachers can increase relevance and motivation by connecting their classroom practice to the lives of students. By asking key questions that gauge students' interest and making efforts to help students find individual and personal meaning in literary texts, Jose was able to transform his practice and make reading and writing more relevant and meaningful to his students. In this chapter he shares both his voyage as a beginning teacher and the new practices that emerged as a result of a change in focus to his students' interests and needs.

"English Education, Pedagogy, and Literacy Acquisition in an Era of Participatory Media" (chapter 3) by Antero Garcia describes a study that took place in a ninth-grade English classroom in which iPods were given to all students in an effort to research the potential of mobile media within an English classroom. Antero employs what he calls a *wireless critical pedagogy* that is intended to enable high school students attending a historically underperforming city school to become informed and capable media producers. This chapter reflects on the changing nature of literacy in the twenty-first century, and it addresses both the challenges and opportunities that accompany the uses of mobile media devices in a central city English classroom.

In chapter 4, "Toward a Literacy Continuum," Latrise P. Johnson and Maisha T. Winn consider the literate lives of three African American male youth, examining how their literacy learning and participation in high school influenced their literate identities. The authors address two essential questions: In what ways can literacy teaching and learning contribute to the making of literate identities of these young black men? What can we learn from these youth that will prepare all youth for meaningful literacy participation beyond high school English classrooms?

In "Black and Latina/o Youth Communicative Repertoires in Urban English Language Arts Classrooms" (chapter 5), author Danny C. Martinez presents a one-year ethnographic study of the regularities and variances in the language practices of Black and Latina/o youth in urban English language arts classrooms. Danny identifies multiple linguistic competencies that youth possess that are often not taken up by English language arts teachers. While these repertoires have the potential to increase students' confidence and connection to classroom discourse, they are often discounted or even dismissed from formal classroom discourse. Mr. Martinez argues that refocusing our gaze to understanding, appreciating, and incorporating the multiple linguistic repertoires of students will increase engagement and academic achievement.

The second section, "Teacher Education," presents accounts from English educators who have attempted to transform their methods classes to help prepare more powerful English teachers for today's diverse classrooms. Veteran English educators representing diverse geographical and socioeconomic institutional contexts reflect on the ways that they as individual faculty, and collectively as English education programs, have gone beyond preparing English educators and moved to "powerful" English education. Some of the questions that they considered include: What assignments, both set in and outside of class, have had a positive impact on their students' growth as English teachers? What challenges have they faced in making the changes they felt were needed in their classes and programs? Finally, what types of evidence are teacher educators using to measure the impact of their programs on the profession?

In chapter 6, "Service Learning in Third Spaces: Transforming Preservice English Teachers," Lisa Scherff presents information from a summer program that brings high school students and preservice teachers together, through service learning, to read and discuss young adult literature and other texts. Lisa argues that service learning initiatives in literacy teacher education can provide teaching and learning experiences that are equally and mutually beneficial for K–12 students and preservice literacy teachers.

In chapter 7, "English Teacher Education for Rural Social Spaces" Leslie S. Rush shares her experiences as the only English educator in the state of Wyoming and the challenges its rural nature presents for English teacher education. Leslie pushes English educators to embrace the importance of focusing more intently on rural educational issues. She also shares practices that are employed to develop critical and reflective practitioners in her English education program at the University of Wyoming. The chapter concludes by offering some recommendations for English teacher educators in rural settings, always acknowledging that each rural setting presents its own constellation of the challenges and affordances of rural education.

Chapter 8 deals explicitly with the question: How can assignments with socially just foci cultivate critical preservice English teachers for *social justice* in the twenty-first century? In "Learning from Equity Audits: Powerful Social Justice in English Education for the Twenty-First Century," sj Miller prompts the field of English education to consider what preservice teachers can learn from using equity audits in their field placements to assess the absence and/or inclusion of social justice.

The final section, "Scholarship and Advocacy," presents theoretical and research narratives from teacher educators whose scholarship and advocacy work addresses some of the most pertinent and pressing issues facing English education in the twenty-first century. Specifically, scholars share how their research challenges the status quo and breaks new ground in English education. What aspects of English education research do they see as most relevant for addressing the literacy issues of the twenty-first century and beyond?

Chapters 9 and 10 both consider critical and culturally relevant English education in the digital age. In chapter 9, "Critical Engagement through Digital Media Production: A Nexus of Practice" Cynthia Lewis and Lauren Causey explore students' uses of digital tools in an English classroom that was part of a Digital Media (DigMe) Studies program, a collaboration between a local university and a large historically underachieving central city high school. Cynthia and Lauren show how a classroom focused on student engagement, critical inquiry, and digital media production engages and inspires students to become empowered producers of traditional and multimodal texts in an ethnic and socioeconomically diverse school.

"Being literate and being digitally literate," argues Troy Hicks, "if they ever were separate, are now one and the same." In chapter 10, "(Digital) Literacy Advocacy: A Rationale for Creating Shifts in Policy, Infrastructure, and Instruction," Hicks argues that English teachers, who have always been advocates for equal access to texts, must now become advocates for students and their digital literacies. He provides teachers, who must accept that technology is part of their jobs as literacy educators, with resources to assist them with the ever-changing technological/instructional tools.

The authors of chapter 11 believe that the English classroom is a particularly suitable place to learn how such power relationships work: teachers can encourage students to consider how authors of texts use words in particular ways to stir up emotions; to highlight particular ideas about situations, individuals, or groups of people; and to manipulate others. In "'Don't Say Gay': Using Action Research to Interrogate Language Use in the English Classroom," Susan L. Groenke and Judson C. Laughter explore the relationship between an English education program and a former intern's journey to employing the language of social justice in her own English classroom. The first part of their chapter explores an action research seminar offered at their university. They take readers through the journey of the class, which begins with personal histories and transitions into developing a research question and executing a study. The second part of the chapter explores one intern's struggle to change a culture of homophobia in her English classroom.

Patricia Lambert Stock, author of our final chapter, has spent much of the past twenty years exploring the value of practitioner research. In "Practitioner Research in English Education," she examines a teacher inquiry workshop (TIW) that is at the heart of the invitational summer institutes of the National Writing Project (NWP), a highly acclaimed, forty-year-old professional development project to draw attention to several kinds of multimethod research that those of us who think of ourselves as practitioner researchers in English education have been developing and applying to beneficial effect for the last half century.

One of the constants in this world is change. As change occurs in the field of literacy education, it brings both challenges and opportunities. The rapid transformations in the nature of literacy practice, the demographic composition of America's classrooms, and the increasing demands for literacy in the workplace have created both anxious and exciting moments for the profession. Some of these changes may allow us to connect more powerfully with students and communities, as several of our authors suggest. Other changes may threaten a focus on literacy as a civic tool, or they may constrain the creative interactions between teachers and students that is a hallmark of the discipline. What will ultimately come of these changes should be largely influenced by those who practice in the field as P–16 educators, teacher educators, and educational researchers.

Together as a growing and dynamic field we must work together to face our most pressing challenges, and to ask and answer our most pressing questions: As English educators, how do we engage in relevant and rigorous scholarship that will facilitate our intervention into matters of educational policy? How do we develop powerful P–16 practices, preservice teacher education programs, and models of teacher development that give a new generation of teachers the confidence and the license to innovate and to connect with youth?

Our hope is that collectively the following chapters provide the insight, guidance, and inspiration that we need to reinvent the future of our discipline.

REFERENCES

Cochran-Smith, M., & Lytle, S. L. (2009). *Inquiry as stance: Practitioner research for the next generation.* New York, N.Y.: Teachers College Press.

Darder, A. (1991). *Culture and power in the classroom: A critical foundation for bilingual education.* Westport, Conn.: Bergin & Garvey.

Fecho, B. (2004). *Is this English? Race, language, and culture in the classroom.* New York, N.Y.: Teachers College Press.

Fisher, M. (2007). *Writing in rhythm: Spoken word poetry in urban classrooms.* New York, N.Y.: Teachers College Press.

Freire, P. (1970). *Pedagogy of the oppressed.* New York, N.Y.: Continuum.

hooks, b. (1995). *Teaching to transgress: Education as the practice of freedom.* New York, N.Y.: Routledge.

Kirkland, D. (2010). English(es) in urban contexts: Politics, pluralism, and possibilities. *English Education, 42,* 293–306.

Ladson-Billings, G. (1995). *The dreamkeepers: Successful teachers of African-American children.* San Francisco, Calif.: Jossey-Bass.

Lee, C. (1993). *Signifying as a scaffold for literary interpretation: The pedagogical implications of an African-American discourse genre.* Urbana, Ill.: National Council of Teachers of English.

McNeil, L., & Valenzuela, A. (2001). The harmful impact of the TAAS system of testing in Texas: Beneath the accountability rhetoric. In G. Orfield & M. L. Kornhaber (Eds.), *Raising standards or raising barriers? Inequality and high-stakes testing in public education* (pp. 127–50). New York, N.Y.: Century Foundation Press.

Moje, E. B., Ciechanowki, K. M., Kramer, K., Ellis, L., Carrillo, R., & Collazo, T. (2004). Working toward third space in content area literacy: An examination of everyday funds of knowledge and discourse. *Reading Research Quarterly, 39* (1), 38–70.

Morrell, E. (2008). *Critical literacy and urban youth: Pedagogies of access, dissent, and liberation.* New York, N.Y.: Routledge.

Orr, D. W. (1992). *Ecological literacy: Education and the transition to a postmodern world.* Albany, N.Y.: SUNY Press.

Portes, P. R., & Smagorinsky, P. (2010). Static structures, changing demographics: Educating teachers for shifting populations in stable schools. *English Education, 42,* 236–47.

Scherff, L., & Piazza, C. (2005). The more things change the more they stay the same: A survey of high school students' writing experiences. *Research in the Teaching of English, 39,* 271–304.

Scherff, L., & Piazza, C. L. (2008/2009). Why now, more than ever, we need to talk about opportunity to learn. *Journal of Adolescent & Adult Literacy, 52,* 343–52.

Souto-Manning, M. (2010). Teaching English learners: Building on cultural and linguistic strengths. *English Education, 42,* 248–62.

Yagelski, R. P. (2005). Stasis and change: English education and the crisis of sustainability. *English Education, 37,* 262–71.

Yosso, T. (2005). Whose culture has capital? A critical race theory discussion of community cultural wealth. *Race, Ethnicity, and Education, 8* (1), 69–91.

1

Classroom Teaching

Chapter One

Preparing to Serve Your People

Critical Multiliteracies Pedagogy
in a Secondary English Classroom

Jerica Coffey

> You pursued learning because this was how you asserted yourself as a free person, how you claimed your humanity. You pursued learning so you could work for the racial uplift, for the liberation of your people. You pursued education so you could prepare yourself to lead your people.
> —Theresa Perry, *Young Gifted and Black*, p. 11

"Miss, are we really going to change the world?" It was a sincere question posed to me as I was driving a group of students home from a leadership retreat in the Bay Area, and Ana's question echoed the sentiment of many youth that day who wanted to believe they were engaged in learning that could truly impact their community and school. After four days of reading, discussing, and critically examining youth-led social and political movements, defining leadership and examining the root causes of the lack of youth leadership in our school, and developing a plan to take action, these twenty youth from June Jordan School for Equity (JJSE), where I taught for five years, left the retreat energized and ready to work for change. Ana's question reflected both the critical hopes and doubts of young people witnessed daily in the classroom.

Convincing them that literacy can be a tool to fight for justice is no small task, particularly when their material conditions reflect the accumulation of generations of political, economic, and social dispossession. Under these conditions it is important not to peddle a false hope (Duncan-Andrade, 2009) that reflects the dominant narrative students have been fed their entire lives about working hard to get out of the 'hood. Nevertheless, at the retreat the goal was to historicize movements and situate literacy for communities of color as a practice of freedom when used as a tool to organize and empower communities. So instead of responding to Ana by saying "It's up to you," I said with confidence, "Our people always have, and we always will."

Spaces outside of school like the ones described above were important to experience as a literacy teacher for several reasons. First, they provided firsthand knowledge of the power of critical literacy practices in authentic contexts. Second, the power of these experiences in spaces organizing with youth outside of school reflected Ira Shor's (1999) definition of a critical literacy that challenges the status quo in an effort to discover alternative paths for self- and social development.

This kind of literacy—words rethinking worlds, self-dissenting in society—connects the political and the personal, the public and the private, the global and the local, and the economic and the pedagogical for rethinking our lives and for promoting justice in place of inequity (Shor, 1999, p. 1). For years, district mandates and restrictive policies surrounding narrow notions of assessment, such as standardized testing, dictated what happened in my classroom.

Unfortunately, it seemed that powerful experiences like the first annual JJSE student leadership retreat were spaces that could only be created outside of the limits of a classroom, no matter how moving the level of engagement and commitment they elicited from students to use learning as a tool for changing the community. The idea of teaching for the long haul without bringing the power of those spaces into the fold of my everyday teaching practice became unimaginable.

The disengagement and resistance to a culturally irrelevant curriculum exhibited by many students was simply too much to bear, and academic failure was not a viable option for an educator committed to equity and justice. While it did not happen overnight, several powerful experiences organizing with youth outside of the classroom, like the one described above, helped reframe the purpose of English education for myself and for my students.

With the move out of the false binaries of "engagement or rigor" and "developing civically engaged youth or teaching to the test" that prevented the development of new approaches, my teaching was transformed. Following a commitment to bring these worlds together, student learning and engagement increased dramatically, and eleven years later I am still as passionate as ever about my work for the classroom.

CRITICAL MULTILITERACIES FOR THE URBAN CONTEXT

In its position statement on twenty-first-century literacies, National Council of Teachers of English (NCTE) proposes a definition of literacy for the twenty-first century as follows:

> As society and technology change, so does literacy. Because technology has increased the intensity and complexity of literate environments, the twenty-first century demands that a literate person possess a wide range of abilities and competencies; many literacies. (NCTE, 2008)

When I read these words for the first time, they resonated with personal experiences from twelve years of classroom teaching: my students are becoming increasingly literate in new technologies and media that should be used as a bridge to deeper learning in the classroom.

While much scholarship points to the need for a multiliteracies (New London Group, 1996) approach to English instruction for all students to be prepared for the multimodal, high-tech globalized world, the realities on the ground, for those of us working in schools with students and communities that have been historically, politically, and economically dispossessed, the structural limitations to developing this pedagogy are daunting to say the least.

At my current high school in Watts, merit-based pay is being instituted, even further entrenching a competition model that rewards narrow notions of literacy instruction and that places additional constraints on the work of English teachers. This chapter, therefore, begins with an intimate understanding of the daily challenges for those teachers who feel committed to expanding notions of literacy across the content areas.

We live in a world in which proficiency with the tools of technology and critical media consumption are essential for citizens to fully participate in our society in meaningful ways, so it is necessary for educators to push back in whatever ways we can and maintain a pedagogy grounded in the belief that being literate in today's world requires much more than traditional reading and writing. Students must learn to build relationships with others in diverse contexts, to pose and solve problems collaboratively and cross-culturally, and to create, critique, analyze, and evaluate multimedia texts. Additionally, all of the aforementioned must happen in authentic contexts.

The pressure to move away from situating student learning in authentic contexts is very real and should be acknowledged. When a school's fidelity is based on a test score and when increasingly one's efficacy as a teacher is tied to a test score, these seductively powerful forces lead many in the profession to opt out of engaging students in collaborative projects that take time and energy to produce, defaulting on a test-prep curriculum because this is the instruction rewarded in our current high-stakes testing reality.

Nevertheless, in this system, in what ways is it possible to develop a multiliteracies pedagogy that develops students as readers, writers, and co-creators of multimedia texts for the purpose of critically engaging with the world around them? Furthermore, for a population that has been economically, politically, and socially marginalized, like the children in Watts and southeast San Francisco, what technology would deepen their engagement in writing and reading for the purpose of creating change in their community?

The idea of twenty-first-century literacies has taken firm root in English education both in teacher preparation and via the Common Core State Standards (CCSS) that are playing out in classrooms across the country. This movement is important because it forces us to expand notions of literacy and to begin thinking about students as practicing multiliteracies before they come to our classrooms. However, our field must begin to define for itself what powerful multiliteracies teaching looks like for dispossessed urban youth. The next section of this chapter is an attempt to do so.

CRITICAL MULTILITERACIES PEDAGOGY AS A PRACTICE OF FREEDOM

In *Young Gifted and Black,* Theresa Perry (2003) argues that if we are to deal with the dilemma of schooling when working with students for whom there is no logical or predictable relationship between education and access in the social, educational, or economic realms of our society, we must ask ourselves these questions:

> Why should one make an effort to excel in school if one cannot predict when and under what circumstances learning will be valued, seen, acknowledged? Why should one focus on learning in school if that learning does not have the capacity to affect, inform, or alter one's perception or one's status as a member of an oppressed group? (p. 11)

These questions are critical for English teachers in urban schools to consider, as they ponder an important aspect of the teaching of literacy that is rarely discussed—that is, the importance of how one frames the *purpose* of literacy for one's students. It became necessary to address Perry's questions in a meaningful way with the students in order to help them understand the power of literacy in their lives and commit to challenging texts, rigorous research, and academic writing.

Students should leave the classroom knowing that for their communities, literacy has always been an integral part of the struggle for liberation. It is a legacy for them to own. From slaves risking their lives to learn how to read, to the Freedom Schools of the 1960s and the digital multimedia movements of the current day, it must be made clear to students that all struggles for change are deeply grounded in literacy practices. When students have clarity that literacy has been and continues to be a life-or-death struggle in our communities, they often rise to the challenge and embrace their education in powerful and meaningful ways.

Of course, this philosophy of literacy learning is not something you just put in your syllabus, explain on the first day, and keep written on a big poster on a classroom wall. It is a philosophy that must be experienced, interrogated, and developed through everything from the curriculum you design, to the novels, films, and projects you assign to students. In other words, it is a philosophy that we must *live* each day with our students. Following is an outline of two teaching units that are part of a year-long learning cycle to do just that.

In the first week of school, several key lessons allow me to frame these ideas and develop in students a clear sense of purpose for their literacy learning. This first, week-long mini-unit is called *Becoming a Warrior-Scholar*. Drawing from history and popular culture, this unit engages students in writing and discussing powerful examples of people of color who use literacy as a practice of freedom, a way to assert their humanity, and to struggle for justice for their community.

The unit begins by asking students to make a Venn diagram to compare and contrast the differences between a warrior and a scholar. In small groups, students discuss their comparisons and then share them during a whole-class discussion. Every year, students develop and debate very nuanced aspects of what it means to be a scholar and what it means to be a warrior.

A discussion of self-discipline versus blindly taking orders is always rich and comes organically from their own thinking. Knowledge as a weapon for self-defense is almost always a theme brought up in each group, and one that is built on throughout the year. No matter what students say at this point, there is a rich conversation developing about the purpose of education that we are creating as a community.

Next, three clips are shown from the films *Hurricane* and *The New Karate Kid*, and from an interview of Tupac Shakur. The class also reads an excerpt of an interview with Comandante Ramona, a key female leader in the Zapatista Army for National Liberation (EZLN), published in *Doble Jornada* (Perez & Castellanos, 1994), in which she articulates the role of language and learning in indigenous women's liberation struggles.

These examples are chosen carefully; each serves the purpose of adding complexity and depth to the way students understand the role of literacy and learning in their lives. In "Reading in Their Own Interests: Teaching Five Levels of Analysis to US Students of Color in Urban Communities" teacher-researcher Patrick Camangian (2013) argues for engaging students in five levels of analysis to foster a critical reading of texts and move beyond "limiting our reading instruction to surface level understandings of texts [that] does not awaken students' social consciousness as much as it stifles their abilities to think."

Students are asked to engage these levels of analysis while making sense of the various texts:

1. **Explicit**: What important things did students hear, see, or read? This thinking is always summative, factual, or unarguable.
2. **Implicit**: Reading between the lines, what is the text's suggestive meaning?
3. **Interpretation**: What do students believe about what text? What is their emotional response?
4. **Theoretical**: What philosophical understandings can we bring to the text?
5. **Application**: Now what? How can we apply what we learn to our lives?

At this point, as it is the beginning of the year, students can handle the first three levels of analysis, so the lesson walks through the thinking processes to help them synthesize their thinking into a vision statement at the end of class. It begins with the narrative of Rubin-Hurricane Carter, a professional boxer who was wrongfully convicted of a triple homicide in 1966 and not exonerated until 1985. His case is a compelling example of using literacy as a practice of freedom.

Much of the film's introduction is narrated from Carter's autobiography, which he wrote in prison in 1974. Through his autobiography *The 16th Round: From Number 1 Contender to Number 45472,* Carter tells the story of becoming a warrior-scholar, developing self-discipline, reading, and maintaining physical health as a practice of freedom. In 1980, the autobiography received the attention of a young man whose guardians would eventually assist in overturning his conviction. In this way, Carter literally wrote himself into freedom.

The second clip is from the film *The New Karate Kid*. While lacking any explicit social critique, there are important lessons about the purpose of sacrificing for the sake of learning that are important for students to examine. In the clip, the main character, Dre, learns the essence of a self-defense practice: discipline, attitude, commitment, and heart. Many of the students loved the new version of the film, which revised the "wax-on, wax-off" scene to a "jacket-on-jacket-off" scene. The protagonist, played by Jaden Smith, is training to defend himself by putting his jacket on and off of a wooden pole. At first Dre cannot see the purpose in this seemingly benign activity and eventually breaks down with frustration, almost giving up.

Shortly after his breakdown, Mr. Han, Dre's teacher, shows Dre that when he applies his skills to another context, his self-discipline and practice allow him to defend himself against his oppressor.

Without fail, this scene always generates a critical conversation with students about attitude toward and commitment to something challenging. All year, the course will be asking students to commit to stretching themselves, making personal sacrifices, and engaging with texts that may be harder than they have ever been asked to deal with before. So this is an important conversation that will recur all year to remind students to embrace the challenge of rigorous reading and writing when, inevitably, things get tough.

Finally, the analysis and discussion of films concludes with an interview of Tupac (1999) in which he encourages young people to critically analyze their experiences. In this short, ten-minute clip, he discusses his views on everything from the prison industrial complex to the military industrial complex and urges young gang members to turn their self-destructive energies into community-productive energies.

There is a pause for discussion at the point in the film when Tupac directly addresses the young men in our communities trying to live the corporate dream of Thug Life by saying, "If you're so hard, if you're so tough, let's start a revolution." The class interrogates this comment at length and adds student interpretations of it in the process of developing a collective definition of warrior-scholars. This phase of the unit culminates with an excerpt of a 1994 interview with Comandante Ramona—modern Mexico's most powerful example of indigenous leadership. Before reading the interview, students are shown an image of this tiny indigenous woman with her embroidered native huipil blouse and all but her eyes masked by the typical Zapatista face covering. They learn that Comandante Ramona played a key role in helping the Zapatistas take control of one of southern Mexico's most important cities, demanding greater rights for the indigenous people of Mexico, and resisting Mexico's involvement in the North American Free Trade Agreement (NAFTA).

While gravely ill with kidney disease, she defied a government ban traveling from the jungles of Chiapas to Mexico City and established a National Indigenous Congress, risking arrest and death to unify indigenous groups and demand that the local and federal Mexican authorities respect the human and social rights of indigenous people. In this interview, Ramona encourages women to get involved in organized struggle for the dignity of their communities and articulates that part of the organized struggle is learning from books.

After students are done with independent thinking and analysis, they go back to their groups and discuss their interpretation and implicit analysis of each text. Then they are asked to create an extended definition of the concept of a warrior-scholar that is a definition they can commit to living up to while taking the class. Below are some examples of how students made meaning of this week-long unit and the definitions they constructed in both the tenth- and twelfth-grade English classes: one tenth-grade student, Isaac (all names are pseudonyms to protect participants), wrote:

> A warrior-scholar is someone that learns from people in history's mistakes, fights for their community, and fights for their rights. They are street smart, relentless, and someone who fights under a sense of justice, not afraid to live in reality.

Isaac's comment about not being afraid to live in reality shows that he realizes the importance of his learning being grounded in his existential condition. It also shows a critical awareness that some of us are afraid to live in reality because reality is painful. This becomes an important point of discussion later in the year, when we study the role of media in shaping our perceptions of the world. Jasmine, a twelfth-grader, wrote:

> A warrior-scholar is someone who gets together and fights against others not fights between themselves. Using physical and mental sacrifices. It's someone who uses knowledge as their weapon to defend their community. Somebody that is determined and that is a leader. They're the change that the world wants to see. If you were a warrior-scholar you would protect your community instead of going against it.

Jessica's definition highlighted something central to the reality of students in our school—horizontal violence. This is violence that Freire (2006) defines as the result of the oppressed not being able to lash out against their oppressor and internalizing negative beliefs about their own community. Jessica's definition proved rich for opening up a discussion about why this type of violence happens frequently in our school and on the streets of our community and why a warrior-scholar would not condone or engage in this behavior. Guadalupe, Gersan, Mario, and Jesus came up with the following definition collectively:

> Someone who is well educated. That knows what he/she talking about; and someone that defend themselves through their words as in speeches or protests and that shows leadership. They speak up for their rights and they aim for success no matter what stands in their way. A warrior-scholar is aware of what they are fighting for.

It is true that these students do not live up to these visions for their literacy learning every day. However, when these are the identities that they are constructing in the first four days of class, students are clear about the *purpose* of their literacy learning and can answer Perry's questions for themselves. In making meaning of the unit the students are demonstrating their capacity to engage in what Aronowitz and Giroux (1993) define as critical literacy, a practice that:

> demonstrates modes of critique that illuminate how, in some cases, knowledge serves very specific economic, political and social interests. Moreover, critical literacy would function as a theoretical tool to help students and others develop a critical relationship to their own knowledge. (p. 127)

While it is important for students to understand the way knowledge is used to serve the interests of dominant groups, they must also understand that their knowledge can serve their own economic, social, and political interests as well. The mini-unit described above is part of a year-long struggle to keep students engaged in their own knowledge creation through various literacy practices. It has become an integral part of my practice because of the way in which students begin to internalize the identity of warrior-scholars—a critical component of building their academic identity around literacy as a practice of freedom.

LANGUAGE, IDEOLOGY, AND POWER

Morrell (2008) challenges notions of language arts teaching as a politically neutral endeavor and instead argues for our English classrooms to be sites of critical language studies. He asserts that "allowing students to make sense of the ideological nature of language in the US could go a long way to promote navigational strategies and cross-cultural understanding while also increasing language and literacy skills" (p. 87).

Once the students are armed with a newly developed clarity about the purpose of language learning, the course builds on the warrior-scholar mini-unit described in the second section of this chapter, with a unit of study that integrates both the traditional content of a high school English classroom and media literacy. According to NCTE's (2008) definition of twenty-first-century literacies, literate students in the twenty-first century can create, critique, analyze, and evaluate multimedia texts.

This unit's lessons and assessments bring together both a critique of popular media, a recommended author for the Advanced Placement English Literature course, Luis Valdez, who wrote the play *Zoot Suit*, and student-generated film projects. In brief, *Zoot Suit* is a play that offers excellent examples of the challenges marginalized groups face when they try to form identities resistant to hegemony and use culture as a form of resistance.

Set in 1940s Los Angeles, the play outlines the injustices Chicano youth and other youth of color faced at the hands of institutions like the media, which fueled racially motivated violence that erupted into what historians call the Zoot Suit Riots. A historically situated topic, how institutions like the media work to criminalize and dehumanize communities of color, holds deep relevance to my students' lives today as youth that live in South Central Los Angeles and Watts.

Using the play and a reader filled with primary sources from the time period that are readily available online, students are asked to closely examine the rhetoric of newspapers like the *Los Angeles Times* and draw parallels between the language used to describe youth of color in our city in the 1940s during World War II and images and characterizations of youth in popular films such as *Down for Life, Boys in the Hood*, and *Freedom Writers*.

The goal is for students to discover for themselves the archetypes of youth of color from their community that grip the public imagination and interrogate their function and purpose in the society in which we live. As argued in *Pedagogies of Difference: Rethinking Education for Social Change*:

> How men and women act in the world is largely related to how they perceive themselves in the world, and thus we understand that the existent potential to transform . . . will remain unrealized if we fail to appropriately perceive and develop a critical consciousness of this condition and its possible undoing. (Tejada, Espinoza, & Gutierrez, 2003, p. 18)

From violent and callous gang bangers to single teen mothers abandoned by their parents, students quickly see how the same ideas about who they are play out over and over again, creating a static, one-dimensional vision of their identity that has real-world consequences. The play and primary sources allow students to historically situate this knowledge and understand how these race-based stereotypes are exploited over time.

Zoot Suit is an excellent dramatic text that deals effectively with racialized stereotypes in the media and allows students to use traditional literary analysis to unpack the way hegemony works in popular media and its consequences for people in our communities. Knowing that academic literacy is a core goal in every unit, before producing their own multimedia texts speaking back to issues they feel are incorrectly dealt with in the media, students write a traditional literary analysis essay that is also a social critique. The prompt that they respond to is as follows:

> According to Luis Valdez in *Zoot Suit*, what conflicts do marginalized groups face in trying to form an identity resistant to hegemony? What literary devices does Valdez employ to convey this message? How is this relevant to society today?

It is important to include here the essay students write because powerful multiliteracies pedagogy in urban communities of color must be a skillful weaving of new literacies such as digital and media literacy with traditional literacies that will help students navigate and change society's institutions. Student essays reveal their ability to negotiate these multiple literacies in the same piece of writing.

> Jaquelinne: The media only shows one side of the story. In scene two of *Zoot Suit,* a play that shows how Mexican youth were criminalized, and how the press dehumanizes Mexican youth. Using language like "zoot suited goons" and "Mexican Baby-Gangsters," the media picks on Zoot Suiters because of the way they dress (38). This supports my opinion because the press did not say the zoot suiters are just expressing themselves through their clothes. Another example is during the Iraq war. In February 2003, there were 390 interviews endorsing the war. Only three made the war sound like it was a bad idea. They made it seem like everyone wanted to go to war but in reality most people opposed the invasion. (Excerpt from Jaquelinne's essay, October 28, 2011)

Jaquelinne's essay responds to the prompt with examples from the text and connects the text to her critique of the media's treatment of the invasion of Iraq. She is showing the ability to read both the text and the world in which she lives. She is also showing her knowledge of important language to name phenomena happening in the media, such as criminalization and dehumanization.

Rigoberta's conclusion to her essay made similar powerful connections:

> Although this took place in the 1940's, we can still witness the way the dominant culture still fights to maintain power today. For instance, ethnic studies have been outlawed [in Arizona] and it is illegal for Chicano youth to learn their own culture, history and roots. The law SB2281 prohibits the Chicano or Mexican-American classes that were actually increasing high school graduation rates in the Latin American community. The removal of these classes is a modern form of cultural genocide. These youth are being stripped from an education that is rightfully theirs. . . . The Zoot Suit play allows us to live in a time period that has been forgotten, but unfortunately history repeats itself, and is doing so this very moment in Arizona. Knowing our history and past events can help us identify methods that worked and methods that did not work to fight back injustices. Historic literature can help us unravel the workings of our society and critically analyze the hegemonic structures in our current society. (Excerpt from Rigoberta's essay, November 7, 2011)

Rigoberta's response is powerful because the class did not discuss the struggle over ethnic studies in Arizona. When asked why she made this connection, she responded that she had seen the film *Precious Knowledge* recently and it made her think about what was happening in the play.

Duncan-Andrade and Morrell (2008) argue that the ability to deconstruct dominant texts is not enough for critical English education; students must also develop the skills to create their own critical texts that can be used in the struggle for social justice. For communities not allowed access to dominant institutions like the media, it is important that English education allows students to "talk back" to these institutions and shape for themselves the messages about how they are moving from being objectified by the media to becoming creators of media in their own community's interests.

To this end, a final goal for this unit is for students to use their critical media literacies to develop their own media. In collaborative groups, students choose a topic they feel the media silence or ignore that is impacting youth in their community, and in small groups develop, from script and storyboard to editing, a film that "talks back" to the issue. Some students choose to dramatize the issue, and some choose to employ documentary-style interviews to convey their message. Topics range from violence and homophobia to rumors and stereotypes.

All groups perform research on their topic to inform their work and integrate this research into their films to blend more traditional research with digital media skills. Moreover, by this point in the unit, students have carefully examined how media sources use language to persuade, so they come up with their own "counter-slogans" that send a strong message about the topic to persuade their audience.

This year, a group trying to speak back to homophobia being promoted in churches used the slogan, "I didn't choose to be gay. I was born this way. I'm blessed." Whatever the message, the importance of this project is for students to empower their language and digital media skills to engage in the world in a meaningful way.

Those who think that a film project is superfluous in an English curriculum should think about the skills involved in writing a screenplay. Students must apply what they have learned about characterization, mood, tone, and rhetorical devices to construct a quality screenplay and get a message across. Asking students to perform these tasks for an authentic audience (those who view their films) makes them much more competent at analyzing these aspects of an author's craft the next time we want them to deal with a challenging canonical text.

IMPLICATIONS AND CHALLENGES OF A CRITICAL MULTILITERACIES PEDAGOGY

Not surprisingly, even with an extensive and expanding body of research on the power of a multiliteracies pedagogy, including critical literacies, policies on the ground in our schools remain disconnected from work researchers conduct in the field. State-mandated tests that are believed to prove a teacher's efficacy do not reflect the reality of twenty-first century literacy demands.

This disconnect creates a disastrous chasm between urban schools that serve poor working-class youth of color and more affluent schools in which student literacies are usually developed in ways that integrate multiple literacies into English education (Anyon, 2006; Finn, 1999). Urban schools trying to raise test scores more often than not will promote a strict teach-to-the-test regimen of traditional reading and writing rewarded on high-stakes tests and inevitably undervalue a range of other literacies that make a young person prepared to participate effectively in today's high-tech, globalized world and in today's democracy as critical consumers and producers of information.

How then should English teachers in urban schools approach a critical multiliteracies pedagogy? Those who teach in high-poverty schools, in which narrow ideologies of literacy reign, can prove the importance of a critical multiliteracies pedagogy by investigating their own practices using approaches like those outlined earlier and becoming careful researchers of their own curriculum and pedagogy.

We must do this in collaboration with others, taking control of our own professional learning spaces. The abilities to create the curriculum described here and to articulate and deeply examine its impact on student learning were developed via participation in several teacher inquiry groups—each with its own goals and foci, but all committed to improving access to powerful literacies in communities like Watts and southeast San Francisco.

Engaging in collaborative inquiry is one way to develop expertise in how new literacy approaches can be mapped onto traditional academic literacies and justify spending two weeks on a film project when state testing is around the corner. Clearly, as teachers experiment with new approaches to literacy instruction, we must remain committed to getting feedback from our peers, as well as producing rigorous results demonstrated by student work that integrates these multiple ways of reading, writing, and re-creating the world.

Lastly, while research in the field of English education has supported classroom teachers with a clear vision of twenty-first-century literacy, we still need to define twenty-first century literacy for the dispossessed and disenfranchised. What does the pedagogy of the oppressed look like in the twenty-first century? How does it integrate multiliteracies approaches differently to meet the needs of students for whom, as Perry (2003) defines, there is no logical relationship between effort and outcome in the social, political, and economic realms of our society?

Teachers in urban schools need to begin answering this question for themselves and inserting their voices into the larger district, state, and national conversations happening about the discipline. To do otherwise will maintain the status quo and further disempower our students from the kind of literacy education they need in order to become powerful participants in creating a more just and equitable world.

REFERENCES

Anyon, J. (2006). Social class, school knowledge, and the hidden curriculum revisited. In W. Lois & G. Dimitriadis (Eds.), *The new sociology of knowledge* (pp. 37–46). New York, N.Y.: Routledge.

Aronowitz, S., & Giroux, H. (1993). *Education under siege.* Westport, Conn.: Greenwood Publishing Group.

Camangian, P. R. (2013). Reading in their own interests: Teaching five levels of analysis to US students of color in urban communities. *International Journal of Multicultural Education, 15* (2), 1–16.

Duncan-Andrade, J. (2009). Note to educators: Hope required when growing roses in concrete. *Harvard Educational Review, 79* (2), 181–94.

Duncan-Andrade, J. & Morrell, E. (2008). *The art of critical pedagogy: Possibilities for moving from theory to practice in urban schools.* New York, N.Y.: Peter Lang.

Finn, P. (1999). *Literacy with an attitude: Educating working-class children in their own self-interest.* Albany, N.Y.: SUNY Press.

Freire, P. (2006). *Pedagogy of the oppressed.* New York, N.Y.: Continuum International Publishing Group.

Morrell, E. (2008). *Critical literacy and urban youth: Pedagogies of access, dissent, and liberation.* New York, N.Y.: Teachers College Press.

National Council of Teachers of English. (2008). The NCTE definition of 21st century literacies. Retrieved from http://www.ncte.org/positions/statements/21stcentdefinition.

The New London Group. (1996). A pedagogy of multiliteracies: Designing social futures. *Harvard Educational Review, 66* (1), 60–93.

Perez, M. U., & Castellanos, L. (1994, March 7). Do not leave us alone! Interview with Comandante Ramona. Originally published in *Double Jornada.*

Perry, T. (2003). Freedom for literacy and literacy for freedom: The African American philosophy of education. In T. Perry, C. Steele, & A. Hilliard (Eds.), *Young gifted and black: Promoting high achievement in African-American students* (pp. 11–51). Boston, Mass.: Beacon Press.

Shor, I. (1999). What is critical literacy? *The Journal of Pedagogy, Pluralism, and Practice, 4.* Retrieved from http://www.lesley.edu/journals/jppp/4/shor.html.

Tejada, C., Espinoza, M., & Gutierrez, K. (2003). "Towards a decolonizing pedagogy: Social Justice Reconsidered." In P. Trifonas (Ed.), *Pedagogies of difference: Rethinking education for social change* (pp. 9–39). New York, N.Y.: Routledge Falmer.

Chapter Two

Cultural Relevance in the Modern Language Arts Classroom

Jose Paco Fiallos

Jose (Paco) came to the teaching profession young and with little classroom experience other than what he acquired in his own time in public schools. While he idealized teaching as a profession due to the profound impact many of his own teachers had on him, and had often considered becoming a teacher, his path to the profession was indirect.

Like many other teachers, Paco graduated having studied literature and writing, but had not received any teacher training by the time he applied for positions at several schools. He was twenty-two when he greeted his first class, guided only by the teachers idealized in his memory. Those first days were difficult as Paco tried to emulate the things his teachers had done daily with seemingly little effort.

The experience of those early days greatly shaped the teacher that Paco would become. He had the common experience of so many early career educators: assigned to teach five sections of general-level tenth-grade English. The assumption that general or regular students, those not tracked into honors, I.B., or AP courses, are primarily in those classes due to behavioral issues does not really address the nature of most general classes.

What Paco quickly learned is that the population of general-level English represents the most diverse group of students on any campus. In those five classes were students of vastly varying ethnicity and culture, learning ability and interests, in addition to students with learning disabilities and language barriers. Paco came to class with the naive expectation that his love and excitement for literature, tied with his expertise, enthusiasm, and fresh ideas, would be enough to engage any student. This was fed, again, by his own high school experiences. He reflects, "What I failed to remember was that I was never part of a general-level class; and in my own honors or advanced courses, when the love of literature was not enough to motivate, the ever-present GPA race tended to keep students in line."

The issue of motivation was one of the first major hurdles Paco encountered as an English teacher. Of course, motivation is directly tied to relevance. What is the relevance of literature that is not representative of the students? So much of the canon, especially that of a tenth-grade world literature curriculum, is old, white, and male.

Unfortunately, Paco lacked many of the tools, primarily experience and training, to help students make personal meaning from the texts they studied. That is not to say that there were not successes. One of the greatest joys that Paco found is that students are desperate to meet the expectations of their teachers, so long as those expectations are reasonable and the teacher is willing to put in just as much work. Looking back, both he and his students probably worked too hard that year.

The work of teaching is not just what occurs when a teacher is guiding students through whatever task they are presently engaged in. In fact, that time accounts for a rather small piece of the "teaching" pie. What so few people outside of the profession know is how so much of what professional educators have to manage behind the scenes before, after, and even during class while they teach is managing things other than actually teaching. It was all of those other aspects of the profession that Paco was truly unprepared for in his first year.

From planning, all the way from lesson to unit; to learning how to use the technology, when technology is present and functional; to interacting with parents, students, and administrators professionally and constructively, especially when in conflict; to learning, understanding, and implementing all the standards in preparation for the world of high-stakes assessments; to keeping up with current research and the implementation of best practices through effective professional development; and finally, to effective time management, especially as it relates to grading, planning, and the ability to maintain a personal life outside of school.

While those issues are raised in teacher training programs, nothing can really prepare novice teachers for the continuous juggling necessary to be a successful teacher. This explains the extremely high attrition rate for early career teachers.

Paco often refers to his first year of teaching as the worst year of his life. He was unprepared to cope with the often-conflicting needs of being in the classroom, noting "I was inexperienced in managing a classroom; I was largely untrained in best practices; and I did not know how to manage time so that my professional life often bled into personal time. But I also learned that I loved being with students and the learning exchange that takes place from the moment they take their seats."

Those key minutes between bells, when the students are in their desks, are when teachers have the opportunity to share their expertise, hear students' ideas and help students frame questions and build answers, and listen to them as they commune with our cultural past; those are the minutes that keep teachers coming back every year. When each day throws its countless obstacles in Paco's and his students' way, there are always the moments of success that balance out the scales.

Paco also refers to his first year teaching as the best of his life because the experiences he gained, both successes and failures, cemented his long-held desire to be a teacher. That year established a benchmark to which Paco could compare each future year, and also showed him that being an English teacher is so much more than talking about literature. While the things heretofore described address the struggles of an early career teacher, it is the "so much more" where the ideas of relevance in students' lives and cultural awareness can begin to come into play.

Again, Paco looks at his early practices as they were shaped by his own experience as a high school student. Because he was primarily in advanced English classes, Paco's exposure to teaching styles was fairly limited. A high-performing, self-motivated group of students need to be led to language arts studies in a much different way than a lower-performing, more diverse group. Likewise, English teachers also need to consider what additional language skills students bring with them to class beyond formal reading and writing.

"Many teachers are guilty of setting a learning goal that is not only beyond the grasp of students, but also neglects to allow students to bridge that ability gap through the use of the students' own experiences and knowledge." When Paco made this realization, he felt he started to become a teacher.

It started by getting over the frustration that his students seemed to just not get it; that no matter how many different ways he presented the literature that he loved and was so passionate about, students would not give more than a casual acceptance of the next required assignment. It was followed by the simplest of questions: What are *you* interested in? This is a question Paco realizes "I should have been asking this every day, it should have been guiding my practice. This is one of the keys to being an effective teacher. On the first day ask students 'What are you interested in?'"

He goes on to note

> This devaluing of who my students were was one of the worst mistakes I made as a beginning teacher, and one of the main hurdles to being relevant in the lives of students. Why should I expect students to produce quality work, let alone enjoy the process, if I don't show them first that the work they produce matters to me, and second, that the work is a meaningful step toward a greater

understanding of the subject material. I had built a barrier between my students and me by envisioning myself as separate from the learning process.

In teaching relevance is meaning making; it is answering not only the question "What does this mean?" but, equally important, "What does this mean to me?" Teachers of literature and writing constantly have to ask themselves: Why do I love these words and why don't my kids? Teachers must break down the barriers between themselves and their students and talk about who they are, what they are interested in, and what they love about words.

All students may not be able to read and write formally with the same level of understanding and complexity, but all students have experience in deciphering information and then fitting that information into the framework of their world. The past two decades have seen the adoption of technology, from the Internet to cell phones, at incredible rates. With that technology has come the ubiquity of instant access to information of any level of credibility.

It is a simpleminded conclusion for anyone to summarily label a student illiterate because they do not pass a standardized test when those tests ignore an entire range of skills that the modern era has created in the information age.

Paco observed students experience difficulty with formal reading and writing when dealing with texts in class. They might read a passage but then not gain much beyond superficial traits of the text, or students might have an idea that they want to express in an essay, but then do not give adequate development or support to the idea, either because they don't know how, or because they don't see the purpose.

He also observed those same students able to express themselves eloquently with great detail when dealing with personal matters, able to perform a complex series of web searches to find a very specific piece of information, or plan a social engagement with multiple people in moments through the use of their cell phone.

These are not the traditional forms of literacy that current standards address and test for, but it is hardly accurate to say that students who can perform all of these complex tasks are illiterate. All of these examples require lingual clarity, dexterity, and most importantly to modern students, efficiency that an "illiterate" student simply could not utilize.

This idea of lingual efficiency is one that becomes a barrier to many modern students. People living in the modern world have adapted to the rapid flow of information, always ready at their fingertips, by minimizing the number of words needed to convey a specific message. Whether considering text messaging, Facebook status updates, or posts to Twitter, communication has shifted in favor of easy-to-digest mini-messages.

Even journalism reflects this shift to efficiency with many turning to less formal sources of news, like blogs or other social media tools, for their updates, and the newspaper has largely fallen out of use. Recently, when doing a writing activity in which students were to write a letter to a person of their choosing, several students raised the question of purpose. "Why would I take the time to write a letter when I could just text or email or even call them to tell them what I want to tell them?" they asked.

For many, the responses of "because the process is important," "because it makes it more personal," or "because when you write by hand you tend to write more and better" simply did not hold water.

The drawn-out nature of language arts studies, the analysis of longer texts, the writing and revision process, is foreign, and it is so because the skills that modern life has demanded students to develop are largely ignored and often shunned in traditional classrooms. We do not need to do away with essays and novels. But relevance does demand that we take the amazing abilities that our students come to us with and use them in order to help get lagging students better equipped to handle the demands that traditional language arts requires.

In addition to a world that moves faster than ever before, modern students live in a world that is more interconnected and culturally diverse than ever. Old concepts of race and ethnicity are changing as America's population changes. Hispanics now represent the largest minority group in the United States, and whites are projected to no longer be the majority group in the United States by 2042, according to the 2010 U.S. census. This is already the reality in numerous states. Yet the traditional literature canon is not reflective of this diversifying population.

Teachers and administrators around the country are advocating for greater cultural representation in the classroom, yet there is little support in that regard. As a teacher of minority background, Paco sees the need and importance of teaching literature that is not only timeless, but also timely. Rather than abandon the classics as they have been presented for generations, it is necessary to augment the canon with examples of literature from authors as diverse as our nation's population. "I have often considered the irony of the tenth-grade world literature curriculum that I teach, which is mostly written from the outsider's perspective of western culture *about* other cultures, rather than from a member of the culture itself."

Culture is not just the result of origins, of race or ethnicity. All aspects of students' cultures impact who they are as individuals. From musical tastes to recreational interests to style and fashion choices and social groups, all of the choices that everyone makes in their daily lives establish a complete identity that students should be encouraged to express in classes, to be aware of who they are, so that when they examine literature they can find a personal meaning by comparing personal experience with the characters' and writers' experiences.

Students should be encouraged to explore their personal identities so that not only can they analyze text according to the interpretation of the teacher, but also augment that through the collective interpretations of the class in order to build countless levels of individual and personal meaning.

Cultural relevance begins with personal expression. Paco sees this as a very important part of teachers' classrooms. "Students enter my classroom and find pieces of who I am all over the place. On my walls students see posters for favorite films, pieces of art that I love, and portraits of favorite authors. On my bookshelves they see a collection of my own books that they may borrow. Near my desk they see photos of family, friends, and pets, my teaching certification, my diplomas, and cork boards with photos of past students."

One of the activities that Paco recommends is to have students on the first day of school look around the classroom and find one thing that catches their eye or otherwise interests them, and ask the teacher a question about it. After they write this question down, the teacher then has them write one interesting fact about them. This helps the teacher distinguish them from each other as he or she gets to know who they are.

According to Paco, nearly the entire period is spent answering questions and learning their personal facts so that by the end, even if he knows only one thing about each of them, they all have a fairly good idea of who he is and understand through the process that he is open to them and that the reciprocal is encouraged.

The students get to take the time to know him and each other as individuals, all with diverse interests and backgrounds, but all equally valuable. This style of personal inquiry, of learning about people as individuals and examining the things that make them individual, as well as that things are shared, is what guides relevant learning. Finding commonality provides the safe jumping point from which students can examine the unfamiliar.

Relevance is further fostered when the skills that students possess outside of class are valued rather than shunned. Low-performing students, often labeled and tracked for much of their school experience, are deterred from making learning gains, first because they are genuinely facing difficulties performing tasks that teachers have repeatedly expected them to be able to accomplish, and second because they come to believe that they are indeed illiterate or that they possess none of the skills required in a language arts class.

Rather than fault a student for skills they possess, Paco highlights the differences between formal and informal situations, and encourages them to carry over those skills in informal tasks. Classroom discussions, personal writing opportunities, arts and crafts, presentations, research projects, and multimedia activities, among many others, all provide students with opportunities to utilize their strengths in situations in which less formal communication is acceptable. Students understand that informal is not the same as ungraded.

All of these activities are accompanied by scoring rubrics that guide the students through the process by which Paco grades their work. Because these activities are so diverse, from Internet research to musical presentations, most students encounter a task for which they are adept.

Through the guidance of the rubrics and the encouragement of interest-guided work, students are able to begin collecting successes and build confidence in their abilities. With the nature of informal activities established, bridges to the more formal, traditional reading and writing activities can begin to be built, or informal and formal exercises can be blended together.

"The blending of formal and informal work," Paco writes, "is often where I find the most success with my classes." He developed a non-fiction writing unit that combines students' personal tastes with the collecting of music, informal writing through the use of personal narrative, and formal writing through expository essay. The premise of the unit is that students will create autobiographical soundtracks.

A pre-writing activity has students break down their life or a specific era of their life according to key events or experiences. They then begin to pair those experiences with songs that they associate with those events or that are thematically linked to the experience, ending up with at least ten songs/events. The next step is to write brief (100 to 150 words) personal narratives about those important experiences and events in their lives.

"I encourage students to experiment with writing styles at this stage, and offer suggestions of trying narrative poetry, stream of consciousness writing, or some other non-traditional writing style; but I also encourage them to write in a way that makes them feel comfortable and that is appropriate to the story being told." By the end of this step, the students will have at least ten personal narratives linked with songs. The next stage is a formal writing activity in which students explain the themes present within their soundtrack, the process of pairing stories and music, and the overall effect music has had on their life.

While students tend to get excited about this project, the part that they generally enjoy the most is the last stage in which they get to tie all the pieces together in an actual song booklet. Paper and other art supplies are used over several class periods, allowing students to assemble the various components of this project into a booklet like one would find in a purchased album, including song lyrics, their personal stories, and the formal essay serving as an introduction to the album.

Paco gives extra credit to those students who go further and actually burn copies of their songs. The end products are as diverse as the students, with some presenting very muted booklets, dominated by black-and-white text, while others develop elaborate collages or layered images of personal photos to match their writing.

This style of blended project does several things to establish relevance. It primarily allows students to express themselves according to their own identity using their own voices. It also develops the writing process by using multiple stages of planning, writing, and revising.

Because it is project oriented and built of several stages, it provides continuity over a period of time, breaking the routine of single-day activities with little carryover. It allows students to become familiar with both formal and informal writing situations, and to understand the appropriate situations for each.

Finally, it helps students to understand the non-fiction genre, in this case memoir, in the context of their own experiences. As students develop their own writing, the class also examines various canonical pieces of non-fiction writing, so that both literature analysis and self-reflection happen simultaneously.

Relevance is for students to have guidance, a clear-cut set of goals, to get them started, but the freedom and autonomy to express themselves within those set guidelines. In addition, students should have the opportunity to shift between types of tasks regularly. But the real key to cultural relevance is the shifting between analysis and personal reflection, the process by which students take someone else's work and begin to see themselves in it.

But how do teachers, particularly younger teachers, come to know this? "My first year was that very routine of day-by-day read a little, write a little, answer a few questions, and then move on to the next story," Paco reflects.

"When the memories of my high school teachers failed me, I turned to whatever I could find in the textbook without thought to building connections or developing themes over time. I thought that if I couldn't make them love literature, at least I could get them to do some work. And of course this failed me; even I did not have any personal stake in the outcomes."

Over time, as he gained experience, Paco began to experiment more in his lesson planning. "By my second year I had the vague outlines of lessons and units like the ones I have mentioned. But more significant to me as a professional, I had begun to receive the training and professional development that backed up the things that I was learning to do by instinct and intuition."

Much of teachers' first-year training focuses on the basics of classroom management and the general ethics and guidelines by which teachers operate. But it is the professional development focusing on cultural relevance and changing dynamics in the classroom that really helps teachers hone their craft. Paco surrounded himself by teachers who had honed their craft to an art and, more importantly, were willing to share some their wisdom.

Effective professional development and the willingness to get out of the classroom and into the rooms of other teachers is what will make new teachers better at their craft.

This is the last major piece of culturally relevant teaching. It is impossible for individual teachers to know everything about what is going on around the country. But effective teacher training and learning opportunities presented by knowledgeable professionals brings the changes in our culture, the technology, the latest research, the freshest experiences, to the largest audience. Without these opportunities, teachers cannot grow.

Teaching is not an easy job. It is demanding, it is exhausting, and it is stressful. There are times, especially in the modern social and political environment, that this profession seems to be losing its own struggle for relevance in the United States. But what keeps Paco coming back is the knowledge that "at the start of every year I will have a new set of children to meet, to learn about, and to share experiences with. It is knowing that our culture is shifting, and that to remain relevant, I have to shift with it. It is no longer the truth that teachers are respected simply for being who and what they are."

Language arts is the most important of the subjects in school because all other subjects depend on language to communicate their ideas. If students cannon learn to make meaning from text, then how can they make any other meaning? Language arts is universal in that text is universal. Whether that text is a book, a newspaper, a film, or an advertisement, the ability to connect the audience to the text and build meaning is what makes learning possible. The texts are changing, and cultural relevance demands that teachers like Paco adopt the new in order to connect students to the old. Then they can connect to anything.

Chapter Three

English Education, Pedagogy, and Literacy Acquisition in an Era of Participatory Media

Antero Garcia

On a naturally warm day in May, a set of iPod Touches[1] are distributed to the seventeen ninth-grade students in the period three English classroom at South Central High School (a pseudonym, as are all student names in this chapter). Together with their teacher, they were going to journey into co-created research focused on the possibilities of mobile media devices like iPods within formal learning environments; though I designed the structures for this exploration, I told my students that their insight would help me frame the classroom practice.

With significant challenges related to student practices with mobile media in many classrooms, it was with some apprehension that I designed a framework for the use of iPods in my classroom. As experience with mobile devices in the classroom in previous years had been sometimes vexing, there was some uncertainty about the possibility of creating more opportunities for distraction and disruption.

Like a new teacher stepping into the classroom for the first time, I felt that uncertainty about whether I would be able to *control* the classroom. A review of notes from this opening day reveals a consciousness of how these concerns reflect a very traditional relationship with students: concerns stemming from unwillingness to cede the teacher's assumed power via the wireless tools this study utilized. Though this project began by looking for ways to transform learning *with* technology, there was some realization that such a transformation would significantly change the classroom dynamic with the students.

Several hours later, after finishing work at school and heading to the grocery store at 4:04, a text message came through (see figure 3.1). Holden's text was only the beginning in a series of disruptive and troublesome events that affected our class engagement with iPods for English education. However, while there are significant areas of educational policy and pedagogy that need to be addressed, mobile media ultimately offer several opportunities for critical English education.

This chapter examines the ways students used cell phones in a secondary English classroom to develop a framework for critical pedagogy in an age of participatory culture. To do this, it looks at how these students and the teacher established a space for critical use of mobile media in an English language arts classroom, the implementation of strategies for using mobile devices as part of critical pedagogy, and the pragmatic challenges of encour-

Figure 3.1. Holden's Text

aging and relying on daily use of mobile media in core content area classrooms.

Through differentiation of academic practices and socialization of the classroom community—as is discussed in this chapter—mobile devices can help reinvigorate a critical pedagogy of English education for the twenty-first century. Considering the specific ways mobile devices can build toward a critical pedagogy within the digital classroom, however, it is also important to ponder the challenges one might encounter.

Mobile devices and participatory media more generally are contentious topics within the field of education (Collins & Halverson, 2009); some individuals indicate mobile devices are valid, necessary tools for equitable education, while a claim from teachers at South Central High School is that they distract students from academic learning. Recognizing the views of both sides of this debate, this chapter acknowledges that mobile devices are both tools for engagement and devices that distract; the context is dependent on the learning environment, issues of trust, and teacher pedagogy.

By noting both opportunities and challenges experienced while using mobile media in one English classroom, this chapter outlines ways that mobile media can positively impact English education and disrupt traditional learning practices that may not be suited for the "shape-shifting portfolio people" we are educating today (Gee, 2004).

ABOUT THE STUDY

Located in the heart of Los Angeles, South Central High School is one of the oldest public high schools in the city. With a student population of approximately 3,400 during the time of this study, South Central High School was also one of the largest in the city. Its demographics mirrored those of its surrounding community: 83 percent Latino, 15 percent black, and 2 percent multiracial, with an English Language Learner group that makes up 39 percent of the students. Eighty-seven percent of the students received free or reduced lunch (CBEDS, 2010).

The percentage of students that graduated from South Central High School is 35, and the majority of these students did not graduate with the courses needed to be eligible to enroll in most four-year universities (UCLA IDEA, 2010).

All participant and place names have been changed in this study. South Central High School was chosen as a pseudonym not only as a signal of the general geographic location in which this school and this study are immersed, but also to validate the counter-narrative of cultural prosperity that persists in urban Los Angeles. Due to historical depictions of poverty, violence, and squalor in films, music, and news headlines, the community of

South Central Los Angeles has, for the past several years, been in a state of flux.

In a deliberate effort to erase a cultural past of uprising, resistance, and negative press through renaming the community, mainstream media and the governing agencies of Los Angeles now refer to the community as "South Los Angeles." However, despite the flooding of "South Los Angeles" messaging in media, my students never refer to this community as anything but "South Central."

To this end, the author spent eight years as a teacher at South Central High School, first working with ELL and twelfth-grade students, and later voluntarily focusing on ninth graders—the grade most likely to drop out at the school based on locally collected data.

While there is a growing field of research that looks at how learning has significantly changed as a result of shifts in cultural media engagement (Thomas & Brown, 2011; Davidson, 2011; Ito et al., 2009), the realities within many classrooms reflect pedagogical practice that ignores these developments (Frey & Fisher, 2008). In discussing the pragmatic challenges and possibilities of mobile media in the following pages, this narrative focuses on the author's own experiences as a classroom teacher. The empirical research includes analysis of students' critical textual production (Morrell, 2008) and inductively analyzed daily fieldnotes.

TOWARD A FRAMEWORK FOR WIRELESS CRITICAL PEDAGOGY

To understand how mobile media can be tools to guide twenty-first-century critical pedagogy, an understanding of what mobile devices offer in the classroom is necessary. At the same time, it is necessary to look at how critical pedagogy is also in a process of changing. Though this study is informed by the tenets outlined by Paulo Freire decades ago, the contexts of his pedagogy working with adults in Brazil are vastly different from work with ninth graders at South Central High School.

Instead of merely applying a foundational pedagogy developed for a vastly different context, this wireless critical pedagogy looks to build toward opportunities for student empowerment, access to career-preparing skill sets, and distribution of youth counter-narrative within my own school community. Within this vision of a modern critical pedagogy, mobile devices offer a pragmatic means for differentiation and for socialization.

By helping to develop empowered identities via the mobile opportunities of differentiation and socialization, these devices can foment "conscientization"—a critical consciousness of the social and political elements of one's world and the ability to act upon these elements (Freire, 1970). Following is a framework for a wireless critical pedagogy that outlines specific ways that these mobile devices may be harnessed in classrooms not just academically, but for the purpose of developing critical consciousness and supporting youth literacies.

Differentiation through mobile devices means personalizing learning experiences for students in numerous ways. Most classrooms would benefit from differentiation tools included on most mobile devices, including:

- **Audio engagement with texts**: This signals a shift in classrooms from privileging only print media.
- **Varied opportunities for textual production**: Producing images, video reflections, interviews, and text messages vary the way "work" looked within the classroom.
- **Graphic organizers and supports**: Previously discussed use of mind-maps, for instance, supports students in thinking systemically and making connections across personal experiences and academic curriculum.
- **Continual, formative assessment of student learning**: Asking students to respond to text messages while in class enabled the instructor to quickly gauge individual student learning and engagement and revise lesson plans and instruction based on responses students sent and feedback they provided.
- **Potential to explore resources and independent checking for understanding**: Through online searches and peer collaboration, resources to further the scope of student research and investigation ballooned. Likewise, metacognitive reflection on the learning practices were multimodal and varied; students were able to mindmap, record, photograph, write, and text their experiences, highlights, and challenges within the classroom, taking greater ownership and responsibility for the onus of critical research within an English classroom.

Recognizing the many ways that student learning experiences were differentiated, iPods and other mobile devices are tailored to provide individual learning modifications for each student.

Further, mobile devices in the classroom helped enrich in-class community and extend this community beyond the confines of the school bell. It also extended learning beyond the realm of the classroom walls. As such, here are several ways that mobile media devices act as tools for socialization:

- **Enable communication between mobile users**: Peer-to-peer communication meant collaboration on work for class took place at home, over the weekend, and sometimes during lunch periods.
- **Signal student dispositions and identity practices**: The ways that students personalize their devices as discussed at the beginning of this chap-

ter allow students to acknowledge and work with each other in ways that authenticate student performances of identity.

- **Foster learning opportunities beyond the walls of the classroom**: Students interviewed community members through text and chat applications, called local businesses for opinions, and documented their community through photography and documentary production.
- **Bridge in-class experiences with civic opportunities for learning**: Mobile devices allow for opportunities for students to increase ways of developing service learning both in and out of schools (see Middaugh et al., 2012).
- **Develop technical literacies**: Through increasing student confidence with mobile media apps and digital textual production, students begin to see themselves as a community of researchers, utilizing technology to increase advocacy.

In looking at the examples of socialization and differentiation, it is worth reflecting how these activities, within the active classroom mirror, shift cultural interaction with media. The classroom becomes a space of possibility, driven by peer motivation, and is a physical representation of a passionate affinity space (Gee 2004; 2011). iPods—in my classroom context, other mobile devices for others—afford students the opportunity to engage more humanely within an institution that may have treated them otherwise.

For example, in building a contemporary critical pedagogy with these wireless tools, it is important to recognize that these devices help educators engender empowered identities in youth. Through connecting the personalized tools that already have youth-invested cultural capital to the classroom learning experience, wireless tools help make the classroom, sometimes perceived as uninviting, a space of familiarity.

Culturally relevant curriculum, in a wireless critical pedagogy, is not simply the media used for youth engagement—the texts, films, music, and artifacts brought in the classroom. Instead, the *medium* is a critical component of a culturally responsive approach to engagement—iPods are a youth-validated tool that is now harnessed within this critical pedagogy. Similarly, this critical pedagogy becomes one that is student centered in its implementation.

As tools that offer a direct connection to the teacher through calling, texting, and emailing, mobile devices help further positive relationships and mentorship. They emphasize a teacher response to students—creating content, posing questions, and building theory, students share their work with each other and the teacher, who then provides feedback, suggestions, and critique.

While these are ways that mobile devices facilitate relational development within classrooms, they do so under the guidance of deliberate pedagogical decisions; it is the combination of technology and teacher pedagogy that drive a student-centered wireless classroom.

In addition, technical literacies harnessed for critical purposes also contribute to this critical pedagogy framework. Students in the class utilized Quick Response (QR) codes to create, publish, and distribute counter-narratives throughout the school (Garcia, 2012). Though the production of these codes could have been framed as rote and procedural, the technical literacies are couched within the explicit purpose.

In developing the ways students used QR codes as part of the class gameplay, the framework-oriented applications and components common on mobile media devices (like the QR reading app) are tools of critical pedagogy. Technical literacies like these propel English classrooms to reimagine the kinds of work conducted within them. By ensuring that imaginative work comingles with the pragmatics of execution, technical literacies are at the fulcrum of ensuring the relevancy of English education in an era in which humanities and liberal arts are frequently challenged as productive spaces.

Additionally, the possibilities of community and civic engagement that these tools offer signal how a wireless critical pedagogy may leverage participatory media tools to reach *across* the boundaries between school and community to comingle the location of the student learning experience both physically and virtually.

That is, students can both physically interact and document learning in schools and communities and connect to individuals through mobile tools for virtual communication, interaction, and provocation. As these devices shifted classroom interaction from teacher-centered to student-centered interaction, so too does a wireless critical pedagogy shift the onus of research questions and direction to the shoulders of students.

The tools for both independence and community-driven research and engagement act as the fulcrum for a critical pedagogy in the shifting culture of mobile and participatory media. A wireless critical pedagogy focuses not on teacher-mandated instruction, but on the *needs* and interests of the classroom community developed collectively. This critical pedagogy leverages wireless tools to build humanizing relationships within the classroom and to also extend the reaches of this classroom into the surrounding community.

Looking at the many ways that mobile media can amplify student agency, voice, and community within traditional classrooms, these devices can be utilized in ways that challenge dominant power structures in schools. However, in doing so, an agreement between teachers and students must be reached.

Table 3.1 outlines several of the key tenets of a wireless critical pedagogy. Though not exhaustive, this chart offers ways for educators to reflect on their own practice and in what ways it may instantiate wireless critical pedagogy. Further, as participatory culture (Jenkins, 2008; Jenkins et al., 2009) continues to funnel into classroom practices, learning frameworks like "Connected Learning" (Garcia, 2014; Ito et al., 2013) find parallel tenets in their theories of educational growth.

Though many of the tenets listed come from existing pedagogical traditions (and typically conform to traditional understandings of critical pedagogy), they are noted as ways a critical pedagogy may better respond to the cultural shifts that participatory media have brought to bear on classrooms and schools.

While encouraging forms of mobile media use within the classroom, together with the students we created boundaries and ways to utilize these devices. Initially, we sought small areas where these phones could augment traditional classroom structures. The Internet in the school isn't working again? That's fine, students spent time using their devices to look up information on the California Basic Educational Data System, Wikipedia, and the Los Angeles Unified School District Report Card database in order to compare inequities within their school.

Students began searching for various resources online with some initial teacher facilitation of sites for research. Two of the students, Katherine and Holden, bookmarked these suggested sites along with sites they encountered through their own online information searches. Likewise, Holden, pressing the two buttons on the iPod simultaneously, would take screenshots of relevant information instead of writing it down.

When prompted, these students explained their strategies to the rest of the class. Highlighting student research practices emerge like this—simple components such as bookmarking data, taking screenshots of pertinent information—helps students reinvent new critical practice with mobile devices within the school.

However, as mobile media devices become prevalent, forcing mobile media use into the marginal spaces of traditional pedagogy is problematic. The numerous limitations and disruptions already discussed signal the ways that South Central High School and the vast majority of public schools are operating in modes that do not contend with the very different landscape of learning and engagement in which students—not to mention the global economy—are immersed.

MOBILE PEDAGOGY AND ORIENTING
THE TEACHING PROFESSION

Prior to a widespread embrace of phones, iPods, and other noise-producing, distraction-causing devices in schools, teachers and administrators need to reassess classroom instruction in an era of participatory pedagogy. As research emphasizes the recent shifts from primarily consuming media to pro-

Table 3.1. Key Tenets of Wireless Critical Pedagogy

Student Centered	• Student interest, knowledge, and perspective drive content and production. • Youth-guided research acts as a component of wireless critical pedagogy, not as a separate pedagogical approach.
Empowered Identities	• As mobile devices can allow students to document, share, and amplify their expertise, they can act as tools for Freire's (1970) concept of "conscientization." • Likewise, adjusting the activities within classrooms to situate student learning within various roles shifts how students perceive and interpret class work and its relevance in the "real world."
Community Driven and Responsive	• In conjunction with youth-driven research practices, work within classroom contexts speaks to and focuses on community needs and concerns. • Critical educators can help bridge in-class learning with the expertise, opportunities, and challenges that are faced beyond the school boundaries; through digital tools, visits, and role-play, alternate voices help bolster student interaction within their communities.
Culturally Relevant	• Though mobile devices can be seen as ubiquitously embraced as part of youth cultural practice, bringing these devices into classrooms changes the context of how they are perceived. Simply "using phones" in a classroom is not culturally relevant. • Applying youth cultural practices, including student personalization of mobile devices and fluidity of social and academic time within classrooms, responds to and builds upon the ways mobile devices are interpreted in youth social interactions.
Critical Technical and Academic Literacies	• Classroom learning still places focus on academic literacies and technical skills. However, these are applied within purposeful contexts. Students produce academic texts and develop technically complex media in order to advocate, inform, persuade, and ignite discussion amongst an audience. • While students still write and produce research reports, persuasive essays and other content expected within traditional classrooms, this work can look different: a student's essay may be a persuasive memo written to (and actually given to) the city council; a research report may be turned into an edited segment of a Wikipedia entry; a response to a literary text may become a blog post to engage in public-driven discourse.

| **Not Reliant on Technology** | • Though this pedagogy is responsive to cultural shifts as a result of participatory media tools like mobile devices, it does not require expensive technology. |
| | • A wireless critical pedagogy is a revitalization of critical pedagogy for the twenty-first century, not simply utilizing digital tools within a classroom. As such, educators need to look beyond specific tools and apps, focusing on incorporating the cultural practices of participatory culture for critical education. |

ducing and remixing media (see Jenkins, 2008), ways that students engage with media and literature in classrooms and beyond is shifting. In particular, an era of participatory pedagogy needs to continually challenge ways that mobile media policies and on-campus technology still maintain socioeconomic disparities (Morrell & Garcia, 2013; Jenkins, et al., 2009).

The role that teachers play in fomenting an attitudinal shift toward mobile media in schools needs to be recognized. In designing a curriculum that revolves around mobile media use in the classroom for this study, there was an explicit focus on utilizing features and applications that were intuitive and already largely in use by a mobile generation (Lenhart, 2009; Lenhart et al., 2010).

In looking at the basic functions that are featured on most mobile devices, we ensured a universality of applicable use in most classrooms across the United States. While this approach looks at the digital tools available, it is also focused on the kinds of dispositions these tools are orienting America's workforce; though global laborers rely on mobile media (Ling & Horst, 2011), schools like South Central High School treat the devices like unnecessary toys.

We focused on the most basic features of mobile devices with two explicit goals in mind. Within the classroom for this study, a primary aim was to ensure student familiarity, comfort, and confidence with how these devices were used. Based on an analysis of student social practices with mobile media devices, it became evident that basic functions like texting, listening to music, and creating photos and videos were regularly utilized by youth.

At the same time, a goal that extended beyond the scope of this study was to alleviate teacher discomfort with utilizing these devices. In working with peers at South Central High School and at two different teacher education programs, introducing new technology and sets of tools into classrooms was generally received with trepidation. An area of my research considers how using very basic attributes of mobile media devices might make them more readily adaptable by other teachers after this study was completed.

My earlier works discuss the way that even the phrasing of "new media" dissuades many educators from adopting tools for a critical mobile pedagogy, stating that, "without redefining the terms we are using to describe these tools and student work, digital technologies can actually be perceived as a cult-like sub-genre of the stuff teachers use; it can be looked on with bemusement by a critical mass of teachers as a pedagogical circus sideshow" (Garcia, 2011).

Teacher use of new media is largely relegated to an ancillary, optional activity. A lack of confidence with understanding and using a seemingly complicated feature of a mobile device would be an easy reason for a teacher to shun a pedagogy that includes mobile media practices. If teachers merely have to understand how to text, photograph, and scan images with a phone (often practices teachers are regularly engaged in), the transfer of this study's curriculum becomes a more possible enterprise.

The burgeoning research on mobile media, as described in this chapter, signals that teacher preparation and professional development need to focus on mobile media dispositions and adaptation in classrooms rather than on preparing teachers to utilize specific tools.

MOBILE DISRUPTION: SPACE, TIME, AND TEXT

As a teacher, the word "disruption" usually signals a problem within the classroom. Entire preservice classes are shaped around managing classroom "disruptions." In this context, they are to be avoided at all costs. However, outside of the classroom, when discussing developments in technology, a "disruption" is often seen as positive.

A disruptive device—like a smart phone or iPod—changes the ways society interacts, behaves, and produces work. It disrupts culture in ways that produce and reframe forms of knowledge. As such, globalized economies are disrupted by the potential of digital media in positive ways. Nearly everyone is interacting or working in ways that are mitigated by mobile devices, except for most public schools.

Digital devices like phones function as literacy tools that disrupt in several different ways simultaneously. They bisect the possibility of textual construction by time, place, form, and context. Communication can now be disrupted by both place and time—students were encouraged to text class updates to their absent teacher when a substitute was present. Similarly, in past experiences working with social networks (Garcia, 2008), conversations do not need to happen in physical space; a conversation on a service like Facebook can continue through comments and updates over the course of weeks.

If, as several literacy researchers contend, spatial literacies are based on constantly changing and multiplying interpreted contexts, phones act as a mode of recontextualizing readings of school-based literacy practices (Leander & Sheehy, 2004; Hagood, 2004). This is a feature that may both frustrate a taking in of a spatial literacy topology and expedite student growth of these literacy skills. Ultimately these disruptions can be funneled into strategies to reshape classroom practices.

In addition to disrupting adult-created ways of being in schools through distributed communication and varied modes for textual production, this study engaged my typically low-performing students. For instance, though Katherine is usually a quiet student within the classroom, she contributed emails and text messages of her contributions to the class almost daily. Though some of these were received during the hours the class was held, she would also send emails in the evening of her work tied to class conversations.

During the third week of class, for instance, students were asked to reflect on the ways individuals outside of South Central may understand the geographical community. Katherine sent an email that begins:

> 5.19.11 homework; I think our community has a bad rep. Because we kinda make it look bad but unintentionally, & then we realize that people judge our community because Of us but in reality we can change this because we're not really bad as people we're just Human beings. I could't [*sic*] really get the pictures because idk [I don't know] what proves my statement

Though Katherine points to the shortcomings of her work, her reflection allowed for an opening dialogue the next day in class. Katherine granted permission to share her sentiments with the rest of the students and her homework became the lynchpin for an ongoing discussion about perceptions of South Central Los Angeles.

As a result, then, a quieter student like Katherine, who previously needed gentle prodding to participate, emerged as natural leader; submitting work, voicing ideas via text messages, and engaging in multimodal inquiry expanded the palate of engagement options available for students. Disrupting the traditional repertoires of in-school practice, mobile media devices act as a foundation of support for the entire class.

THE HAZARDS AND LIMITATIONS OF A
MOBILE MEDIA ENRICHED CLASSROOM

Though much of this chapter explored how mobile media devices can be added to a framework for a wireless critical pedagogy, what follows are narrative vignettes of limitations faced while researching mobile media use in the classroom. As the disruptive challenges of mobile media are the focus of many inconsistent school policies at present, being able to pinpoint the nature of these disruptions is necessary for articulating a path forward (Rojas, 2011). Three particular limitations are discussed:

Relying on youth expertise

Theft and out of school limitations

Mobile media as a source of distraction

By discussing these three aspects of the challenges faced in utilizing mobile media in the classroom, a goal is to present a balanced view of the positive and challenging aspects of mobile devices in the classroom. Doing so is an attempt to clarify how technological inequity in public schools impacts youth learning. Before delving into these limitations, it is important to note that the first limitation, "Relying on youth expertise," is fundamentally different from the other two. While the other limitations were aspects that led to a decrease in classroom engagement because of mobile devices, the reliance on youth expertise was a perceptive shift necessary for me as a teacher.

As stated, this project began with the anticipation that the teacher would control and serve as the authority of the mobile devices. Those assumptions were challenged by realization that youth knowledge far exceeded that of the teacher and the incorporation of these devices into classroom life thus shifted power. As a result, it was also necessary to shift practice to better match the framework for wireless critical pedagogy by redistributing classroom power and embracing indigenous youth knowledge.

WRESTING ADULT AUTHORITY VIA YOUTH EXPERTISE

Like computers today, iPods require users to set a password to deter unwanted users from accessing and deleting content. Additionally, like computers, users load their iPods with applications that customize each iPod based on their users' viewing, listening, playing, and productive dispositions. Prior to handing these out, we created accounts for each using the teacher's computer and installed several applications on the devices we anticipated using in the classroom. All devices required the teacher's administrative password to install additional applications, music, and other media content on the devices.

It was clear that this action severely limited the kinds of social practices that these devices richly enable. As a teacher, however, the principal concern was the learning taking place in the classroom; therefore, the attempt was made to cordon the ways the devices could be used. However, we also deliberately installed ways for students to communicate socially with each other, including text messaging applications and the popular Facebook application.

In conversations with students, we acknowledged that they were likely to use their own mobile media devices to install applications and "be social." The stated intentions were to apply these devices as tools for shaping pedagogy and learning. Students were also reminded that this was an experiment we were conducting together, so their thoughts on learning with mobile devices would be important for the class.

This acknowledgment also brings up one of the major limitations of this study. By *adding* an additional, teacher-provided device that students would use, this research design collapses the natural familiarity of a mobile device and makes it an impersonal imposition. It would be much more natural for students to use their own mobile media devices during the activity; the devices would be familiar to the students from a technical proficiency standpoint and also ascribed with personal value.

Additionally, the students were also informed that if they opted to create a password on their iPods to limit others' use of the devices, they needed to share the password with the teacher as well, to make the addition of information relevant to the class possible. Again, this imposition of adult, teacher authority is a break from the way the devices act as "personal, portable, pedestrian" (Ito, 2006).

The initial intent was to control the ways students used mobile media in classroom contexts. However, within a day of handing out the iPods, it became obvious that the teacher underestimated the ability of the students to overcome his digital mandate. This negotiation of the *meaning* of school-issued mobile devices (Philip & Garcia, 2013) is being wrinkled out as more schools and districts move to 1:1 device initiatives.

A day after handing out the iPods, students came into class transfixed by games, music, and customized backgrounds on their iPods. Within this twenty-four-hour period, students had quickly figured out how to install applications on the iPods, including the popular game Angry Birds, pirated music, and—on a few devices—a program that acted as a local police scanner. In trying to bring devices into the classroom for academic purpose, a significant oversight was in not intentionally allowing for students to shift mobile devices toward a social use.

STUDENT PERSONALIZATION AND OWNERSHIP OF MOBILE DEVICES

Student transgression of the imposed—and password protected—decision to limit what material was available on the iPods mirrors the way students also transgress adult authority in terms of mobile use in classrooms. Prior, students would frequently hide phones and iPods beneath their desks or in their backpacks when using them during class. However, after handing out iPods, students flaunted the latest additions and modifications they made to the iPods on loan to them in the class. For instance, during the second week of the class, Ras shared the background image he had installed on his iPod (see figure 3.2).

The fact that Ras demonstrated his new background while also sharing the pages of games and applications suggests that he saw the iPod not solely as an educational tool, but also as a tool for entertainment and identity construction. During my thirty-minute advisory class, Ras would sometimes allow other students to use the iPod he was borrowing for other students to play games.

Though Ras would then sit at his desk sometimes turning the pages of a book or talking with a classmate, he seemed content that his device was being used. Through borrowing and using his device, peers accepted Ras as a content curator, and accepted the decisions he made when installing specific content on his device.

Figure 3.2.   Ras's Modified Background

The content youth curate on their mobile devices does not simply reflect personal tastes but may also cater to peers for acceptance, socialization, and affiliation. Ras's screen not only demonstrates a preference for a colorful backdrop for his device and predilection for gaming, it signals his *familiarity* with mobile device use. By looking at his screen, peers can glean that Ras is capable at quickly and—based on the titles of many of the displayed apps—freely adding content to his phone.

Ras's iPod image highlights an important theme within the collected data. Students personalized their devices in significantly varied ways. Through an examination of student use of the iPods in the weeks following the course, it was apparent that nearly every iPod in the class had been personalized. By altering screen backgrounds, putting iPods in glitter cases, and prominently using bright green ear buds instead of the standard white ear buds provided with the devices, students altered their devices in ways that deviated from their initial appearance.

Though some students, like Dede, did not add additional programs, the iPod was still customized with images that were imbued with personal meaning and value. Dede's iPod background image, showing a stock image of a rose, personalizes her device. Even as a device that wasn't her primary tool for communication, Dede's iPod is personalized in a way that signals to classmates aspects of her identity she publicly enacts.

Students took personal ownership over the way their mobile media devices appeared and the content included on them. By ceding authority over mobile media use in my classroom, even involuntarily in this instance, student identity practices and student voice became more prominent within the classroom.

Though not all students were so eager to share their iPod modifications with their teacher as Ras was, the students comfortably displayed and shared their content choices with each other in the classroom community. As students shuffled in before class, they would exchange tips on where to download specific images, the songs they were listening to, or how to beat levels of certain games; social talk about student iPods helped seep participation into the class.

At play here are two considerations for teachers. First, by stifling student use of mobile media, many teachers are also, in effect, cutting students off from the social networks within their communities and from outside resources made available on Internet-enabled devices. Second, stifling student use of mobile media also stifles the ways students express and behave within a classroom setting.

As students "act out" when texting or utilizing mobile devices, these actions are largely efforts to display forms of identity that are made up by interactions with mobile devices—their own and others that they communicate with. By demonstrating something as innocuous as a digital flower on the screen of an iPod, students imbue the space around them with their personalities.

STUDENTS AS EXPERTS

Research related to this study (Garcia, 2012) found that student expertise with phones is prevalent and assumed within peer and family networks. In looking at the data, when using iPods within my classroom, this expertise became a necessary component of the classroom community.

A week after handing out the iPods, we added a PDF and set of audio files to each student's device for the classroom curriculum. During silent reading, students plugged their iPods into the teacher's laptop computer. However, an error message appeared on the computer, preventing the transfer of the files. After floundering frustratingly with the computer and iPod, Dante called out:

> "I can fix it," he said without looking up from his iPod, on which he was clearly typing something.
>
> "It's not accepting my computer or recognizing it, I guess," I said, frustrated.
>
> "Lemme see," Dante said, rising from his seat and walking to the computer.
>
> Taking over the space in front of my computer, Dante asked me which files I needed transferred and quickly showed me how to properly transfer the files with which I was struggling.

Even though technologically literate, the teacher ultimately relied on Dante's expertise. Within our community of practice, Dante's expertise shifted how students in the class understood power. Dante continued to sit quietly in class, eyes often glued to his own device, and whenever another technical difficulty emerged with regard to the iPods, Dante would be solicited for his assistance. In brokering dialogue around mobile devices, Dante became used to answering questions, engaging in dialogue, and participating directly in classroom conversations.

When focusing on academic content, the teacher often assumed the role as classroom expert to begin classroom work. However, frequently, when troubleshooting the school's wireless network and iPods—as illustrated previously—or investigating historical inequalities within our school, student expertise guided the classroom work.

THEFT AND OUT-OF-SCHOOL LIMITATIONS

Though mobile devices continue to be presented as a major component to today's educational reform, stereotypical narratives about urban youth still play a factor in universal roll out. The anecdote of Holden's stolen iPod that begins this chapter was not extraordinary in terms of the challenges my students faced with mobile media within their campus and school community. Further, narratives of recent attempts to implement iPads in urban schools in Los Angeles warned of theft and student "hacking" of the devices (Blume, 2013).

Holden's iPod was not the only device in the class that was stolen. A week later, Jay came into class visibly upset. As the bell rang and the students took their seats, Jay asked if we could talk outside. He explained that his locker was broken into during P.E., his backpack was stolen, and his iPod was taken, along with his backpack.

Reported theft continued throughout the quarter. By the last day, when collecting iPods from students, the iPods that returned in functional condition had significantly dwindled. Of the seventeen iPods that were originally handed out to students, seven were returned in functional condition, two were cracked, one displayed a frozen screen and was not usable, six were reported stolen, and one student was withdrawn from the school and numbers to reach him were not functioning.

As my initial study posited the positive opportunities of using these devices in the classroom, the lack of devices returned was significantly worrisome. However, as a researcher, the data suggests the rich ways in which mobile devices provided in classrooms may be folded into more direct ownership of campus and community members. As students were taken at their word that the six iPods were stolen, there is obviously the possibility that some students continued to possess and own the devices lent to them beyond the dates of this study.

ENTERTAINMENT PORTALS AND SOURCES OF DISTRACTION

The final limitation is the not-so-silent elephant in the mobile media debate room. While it would be ideal to present a report of a distraction-free classroom—iPods functioning solely to guide students toward continually engaged, focused learning experiences—there were plenty of instances when they impeded academic learning and focus in the classroom, based on my perspective. An additional learning space, it could be argued, expanded in the discourse offered by iPods similar to Gutierrez, Rymes, and Larson's description of a "third space" (1995).

Every attempt was made to note these incidents while also teaching the class. Noted were times when students were focused on activities not tied directly to the classroom activities, times when students were verbally asked to stop using devices, and moments when students were tangentially talking about things unrelated to classroom material. The research process also included a daily review of the audio recordings of these classes while writing fieldnotes in order to ensure the capture of as much accurate data as possible about these instances of distraction.

Were there moments of frustration at the lack of focus in the classroom? Of course. In the daily fieldnotes during the seven weeks that students were given iPods were coded 138 instances of mobile media—either the issued iPods or students' personal phones—as sources of distraction, averaging almost four instances of disruption per day.

Students were distracted based on three general categories: "socializing and communicating," "listening to music," and "gaming." Also coded were the times when the teacher intervened and addressed the in-class distractions and the times he chose not to address them. The majority of student mobile use in the class was for social purposes (82 of the 138 coded instances). Additionally, teacher efforts to stifle these distractions by intervening generally had mixed results. Approximately 38 percent of the time students would continue to use their mobile devices despite being asked to stop.

Though these data are specific to one particular classroom, they suggest that classroom practice, in attempting to reign in mobile device use solely for academic purposes, finds resistance in the student interpretation of school time as fluidly social and academic. These patterns reflect both blind spots within my own practice as a teacher, and persistent areas of mobile use throughout the classroom time.

CONCLUSION: MOBILE IS SOCIAL, SOCIAL *CAN* BE CRITICAL

Oftentimes, discussions of twenty-first-century skills and tools describe uses of technology like social media, mobile media, and digital networks of communication. While the research in this chapter points to the value of all of these components in a powerful pedagogical approach to learning, they artificially divide learning practices. To be clear, mobile media *is* social media. Not only are mobile devices used regularly for youth to check their Facebook pages and communicate on the social network, the mobile device also functions as a primarily social tool.

As noted in the descriptions of how these devices differentiate and socialize for and within student learning environments, this social function of mobile media can be leveraged for a liberatory pedagogy when sharing power among students and teachers. To disregard the social application of mobile media is to denigrate the way these potential learning tools are embraced by youth and to naturally include these organizational networks within the framework of educational research.

Critical use of mobile media means specifically bringing in youth expertise of mobile media and, in turn, bringing in the devices as sites of social capital; these are not tools for educators to appropriate, but sources for powerful lessons in critical media literacy (Philip & Garcia, 2013; Garcia, Seglem, & Share, 2013). While this chapter details some of the challenges experienced with mobile media devices, similar challenges are largely occurring within our schools, while furthering the fissure of power between teachers and students in schools.

Without collectively working toward a responsible, humane use of mobile media in schools, our in-school mobile media practice will perpetually run out of sync from the real-world experiences for which we are preparing youth daily. That adults regularly text, email, and socialize with others while at work without worry of rebuke illustrates the ways acceptable participatory media use is cleaved at this particular school site.

A wireless critical pedagogy pushes for an empowered identity for young people in relation to their mobile devices; through continual and responsible use of these devices within classrooms, students can enter universities, job settings, and the public sphere with an orientation toward purposeful use of mobile media.

As we reinvent a critical pedagogy in an era of mobile media and media production, a democratization of in-class learning experiences becomes a greater possibility. Mobile media signals the opportunity to further ally teachers, our students, parents, and community partners in redefining an English education that liberates as well as educates.

NOTE

1. An iPod Touch, as a portable media device like many smart phones today, can play music and videos, run applications, access the Internet, and create still photographs and video. With a glass touchscreen, the device is used through touching and swiping various items displayed on the screen.

REFERENCES

Blume, H. (October 16, 2013). L.A. students breach school iPads' security. *Los Angeles Times.* Retrieved from http://articles.latimes.com/2013/sep/24/local/la-me-lausd-ipads-20130925.

California Department of Education (2010). California Basic Educational Data Systems.

Davidson, C. (2011). *Now you see it: How the brain science of attention will transform the way we live, learn and work.* New York, N.Y.: Viking.

Collins, A., & Halverson, R. (2009). *Rethinking education in the age of technology: The digital revolution and schooling in America.* New York, N.Y.: Teachers College Press.

Freire, P. (1970). *Pedagogy of the oppressed.* New York, N.Y.: Continuum.

Frey, N., & Fisher, D. (2008). Doing the right thing with technology. *English Journal, 97* (6), 38–42.

Garcia, A. (2008). Rethinking MySpace: Using social networking tools to connect with students. *Rethinking Schools, 22* (4), 27–29.

Garcia, A. (June 10, 2011). Rethinking the "New" in "New Media." *DMLcentral.* Retrieved from http://dmlcentral.net/blog.

Garcia, A. (2012). *Good reception: Utilizing mobile media and games to develop critical inner-city agents of social change.* Unpublished doctoral dissertation, University of California, Los Angeles.

Garcia, A. (Ed.). (2014). *Teaching in the connected learning classroom.* Irvine, Calif.: Digital Media and Learning Research Hub.

Garcia, A., Seglem, R., & Share, J. (2013). Transforming teaching and learning through critical media literacy pedagogy. *Learning Landscapes, 6* (2), 109–23.

Gee, J. P. (2004). *Situated language and learning: A critique of traditional schooling.* New York, N.Y.: Routledge.

Gee, J. P. (2011). *Language and learning in the digital age.* New York, N.Y.: Routledge.

Gutierrez, K., Rymes, B., & Larson, J. (1995). Script, counterscript, and underlife in the classroom: James Brown vs. Board of Education. *Harvard Education Review, 65* (3), 445–72.

Hagood, M. C. (2004). A rhizomatic cartography of adolescents, popular culture, and constructions of self. In K. M. Leander & M. Sheehy (Eds.), *Spatializing literacy research and practice* (pp. 143–60). New York, N.Y.: Peter Lang.

Ito, M. (2006). *Personal, portable, pedestrian: Mobile phones in Japanese life.* Cambridge, Mass.: MIT Press.

Ito, M. et al. (2009). *Hanging out, messing around, and geeking out: Kids living and learning with new media.* Cambridge, Mass.: MIT Press.

Ito, M., Gutiérrez, K., Livingstone, S., Penuel, B., Rhodes, J., Salen, K., Schor, J., Sefton-Green, J., & Watkins, S. C. (2013). *Connected learning: An agenda for research and design.* Irvine, Calif.: Digital Media and Learning Research Hub.

Jenkins, H. (2008). *Convergence culture: Where old and new media collide.* New York, N.Y.: New York University Press.

Jenkins, H., Clinton, K., Purushotma, R., Robison, A. J., & Weigel, M. (2009). *Confronting the challenges of participatory culture: Media education for the 21st century.* MacArthur Foundation. Cambridge, Mass.: The MIT Press.

Leander, K. M., & Sheehy, M. (Eds.). (2004). *Spatializing literacy research and practice.* New York, N.Y.: Peter Lang.

Lenhart, A. (2009). *Teens and mobile phones over the past five years: Pew Internet looks back.* Pew Internet & American Life Project.

Lenhart, A., Purcell, K., Smith, A., & Zickuhr, K. (2010). *Social media & mobile Internet use among teens and young adults.* Pew Internet and American Life Project.

Ling, R., & Horst, H. (2011). Mobile communication in the global south. *New Media Society, 13* (3), 363–74.

Middaugh, E., Conner, J., Donahue, D., Garcia, A., Kahne, J., Kirshner, B., & Levine, P. (2012). *Service & activism in the digital age: Supporting youth engagement in public life.* DML Central Working Papers. Retrieved from http:civicsurvey.org.

Morrell, E. (2008). *Critical literacy and urban youth: Pedagogies of access, dissent, and liberation.* New York, N.Y.: Routledge.

Morrell, E., & Garcia, A. (Eds.). (2013). City youth and the pedagogy of participatory media [Special issue]. *Learning, Media and Technology, 38* (2), 123–27.

Philip, T. M., & Garcia, A. (2013). The importance of still teaching the iGeneration: New technologies and the centrality of pedagogy. *Harvard Educational Review, 83* (2), 300–319.

Rojas, R. (2011). California school districts have inconsistent cellphone policies, ACLU report finds. *Los Angeles Times.* Retrieved from http://www.latimes.com/news/local/education.

Thomas, D., & Brown, J. S. (2011). A new culture of learning: Cultivating the imagination for a world of constant change. CreateSpace.

UCLA IDEA (2010). *California Educational Opportunity Report.* UC Regents.

Chapter Four

Toward a Literacy Continuum

Culturally Relevant Teaching Sustains

Latrise P. Johnson and Maisha T. Winn

Scholars are beginning to chart the literacy narratives of African American male youth in order to present a more complete picture of their literate lives—one that is contrary to those that suggest that all black boys can fit into monolithic categories or that there are prescriptions for fixing the poor black boys in "crisis" (Tatum, 2006). There are countless data suggesting that African American male youth are failing according to every literary measure available.

However, emerging scholarship complicates relationships between literacy and black male existence, thus presenting a more nuanced portrait of the importance of literacy participation in the lives of young black men (Johnson, 2012; Kirkland, 2013). For this chapter, the authors consider the literate lives of three African American male youth—Jeremy, Donavin, and Caesar (pseudonyms)—and examine how their literacy learning and educational experiences at a high school in the urban southeast influenced their literate identities.

Their narratives serve as guides as the authors address two essential questions about what it means to be an English educator in the twenty-first century: In what ways can literacy teaching and learning contribute to the making of literate identities of these young black men? What can we learn from these youth that will prepare all youth for meaningful literacy participation beyond high school English classrooms?

Jeremy, Donavin, and Caesar provide critical analyses of their schooling experiences, recognize their personal role in their literacy learning, and offer insight to teacher practice from a retrospective position. They do not explicitly have to overcome conditions (that is, gang activity, discipline, extreme

49

poverty) most commonly used to describe the lives of black male youth. However, they do identify with a certain set of circumstances that are exclusive to the black male.

In schools, black males are met with low expectations; literacy curricula do not include texts, practices, and ideologies that many black male youth identify with; and they are most likely to be affected by rules and policies that question their actions, character, and identity. It is important to consider the lives of young men like Jeremy, Donavin, and Caesar because even though none are directly faced with issues of violence, poverty, or school failure, there is something to be learned about the diverse experiences of black males all over this country in order to inform literacy teaching and learning.

An acknowledgment of the multiple experiences of black male youth has the potential to support teachers and teacher educators in rethinking literacy teaching. To be sure, Kirkland (2013) calls for a "profit perspective" when discussing the literate lives of black male youth.

Literacy scholars have a responsibility to share a broader range of black male narratives that adds depth and breadth to black male discourse that has essentialized the lives of black male youth as violent, resistant, and deficient. "Damage-centered" research is dangerous (Tuck, 2009) and scholars must seriously consider the stories of resilience that emerge from youth that largely go untold.

Such an approach, one that challenges normalized views of young black men, is needed to speak to how teachers can be better prepared to work with young black males in their classrooms without 1) making assumptions about the literate lives of young black males that are rooted in deficit thinking; 2) assuming that all black male youth connect with identities that are ascribed to them (for example, hyper-masculinity, hip hop culture); (3) and by acknowledging one's own responsibility in preparing young black males for meaningful literacy experiences that extend beyond the classroom.

THE FRUITS OF LABOR: WITNESSING PAST AND PRESENT CONNECTIONS OF THE ENGLISH CLASSROOM

Jeremy, Donavin, and Caesar were students at Ellis High School (pseudonym) and part of a small learning community (SLC) in which Latrise was one of two founding English teachers and Maisha was a literacy coach. These young men were freshmen when both Latrise and Maisha met them. Latrise left the SLC after their sophomore year, while Maisha continued to coach through graduation. Jeremy, Donavin, and Caesar continued to submit their papers to Latrise as if she were still their teacher, seeking feedback, suggestions for revision, and affirmation of their literate identities.

It was not uncommon for Jeremy to visit Latrise's house when he was home from college. She was his ninth- and tenth-grade English teacher and for the past few years they have been neighbors. His family had lived in the West End neighborhood for as long as he could remember. It was by chance that Latrise moved into the house four doors down from his. On this particular day, Jeremy was not just dropping by to catch up like usual; he actually wanted help on a research paper he was writing for his English 101 class. He sat down at her computer, pulled up his draft, and removed books and other materials from his backpack.

Jeremy had chosen to write a paper about female image and Barbie dolls, which Latrise found to be quite interesting because she initially felt that it had very little to do with his life or what she had come to know as his interests, talents, or hobbies. Jeremy explained to Latrise that, "I have written so much about me and what I know, especially in your class, I can write about anything." Jeremy's claim struck her because Latrise, his former English teacher, was witnessing the fruits of her (and his other teachers') labor. Jeremy had become a competent writer who actually enjoyed writing.

It's hard to believe that he is almost twenty-one. She remembers Jeremy as being a good kid in high school who stood out as a "cool nerd" of sorts. He was interested in technology and had a video camera in his hands whenever possible. He grew up with both parents in the home—an occurrence that most would consider rare in black families throughout the nation. He made slightly above-average grades and now brags about being able to "make As on papers" that he writes the night before their due date.

Donavin was like the Barack Obama of Ellis High School. He held the office of class president from ninth through twelfth grade because everyone agreed that he was the best for the job. He carried himself like a president. He had a smile and an authoritative presence that commanded respect. Also savvy in his dealings with adults, he could talk and smile his way out of assignments and out of attending class.

Donavin was now a junior at Morehouse College, the only all-male historically black college in the United States. The youngest boy, with three older brothers and one younger sister, he is the only boy to finish high school and attend college. Hearing him describe his family life reveals that he is tenacious and resilient. "My mother tells me that I think I am better than the rest of them because I graduated high school and because I'm in college. You would think she would be proud of me," Donavin describes himself as sort of an outsider in his family.

Almost six years ago, Jeremy, Donavin, and Caesar sat in Latrise's ninth-grade English class among a majority of other black boys and only a handful of girls. They were the first class of Ellis High School, one of four small schools that now make up the once large and failing comprehensive high school in one of the city's most infamous neighborhoods. It was their freshman year and Latrise's first year as a high school teacher.

She was more nervous than they were because as she looked around the classroom, she noticed that eleven of sixteen students were African American males. She thought, "What am I going to do with all these boys?" Latrise was experiencing something few teachers ever get a chance to; she was witnessing how her choices as their literacy teacher had impacted the lives of these young men.

In the following sections, through the literate lives of these three young men, we learn from their experiences in high school and college classrooms: What does it mean to be an English educator in the twenty-first century? Although the answers to this question are understood through the lens of young black men, we understand that it is *their* opinions, critiques, and analysis of the problem with black boys that are missing from the narrative. From their literacy narratives, we emphasize the following:

- English educators need to be "practitioners of the craft" (Fisher, 2007).
- English educators need to practice "culturally sustaining" pedagogy (Paris, 2011).
- English educators need to support students in building literate identities.
- English educators need to use a "sociocritical" lens when considering student needs (Gutierrez, 2008).

"BUT THE STATE DON'T KNOW WHAT'S GOING ON IN THE CLASSROOM": ENGLISH EDUCATORS AS "PRACTITIONERS OF THE CRAFT"

In her ethnography of a collaborative of youth poets and their teachers in the Bronx, New York, as well as in her ethnohistory of writing, Fisher (2007, 2009) explores what it means for students in English language arts classrooms when their teachers are writers, readers, and share their work with their students. Fisher argues that English educators must be "practitioners of the craft": literacy teachers who model literate behaviors and build and sustain relationships with students that, in turn, foster more literate practices.

In other words, teachers should be readers and share those books with their students, write for and about their students, share/exchange their writing with students, and, when relevant, read their work publicly with students. Here Latrise was actively participating in sustaining relationships with students around writing, reading, and discussion she had built years before.

In one instance, when Donavin and Jeremy sat down to talk to Latrise about their experiences, Donavin was excited to print a six-year-old essay entitled "Three things my teacher should know about me" from his email, dated August 24, 2005. He described that he liked the topic because "I didn't have to worry about trying to figure out what to say. Can't no body talk about me like I can talk about me."

He also remembered that Latrise had first modeled the assignment for them by describing three things her students should know about her—a detail she had forgotten. "[Ms. Johnson] always wrote with us and shared her stuff like she was a student."

"Remember the poetry unit, bruh?" Jeremy interjected as he recalled another literacy experience from his ninth-grade year. "We had that poetry night and parents came and we read our poems. Teachers didn't really do stuff like that after you left."

In order to bring closure to a month-long poetry unit, Latrise and her students planned a poetry night during which she and her students shared poetry with family and people in the community. "See, students, not just the teacher, were invested in what was happening in the classroom," Donavin described mutual investment from teachers and students as a tenet for meaningful literacy experience.

Jeremy and Donavin began to recall instances in which they were not as engaged in other literacy classrooms. Donavin and Jeremy had the following exchange about their senior English class:

Donavin: It was British Lit. People were asleep in class. [The teacher's] voice was so monotone. Her assignments were just always so . . . [long pause]. She was just talking at kids and writing on the board. And then the writing assignments were boring.

Jeremy: She used to just give us writing assignments that were required by the state. She wasn't interested in it, we weren't. But the state don't know what's going on in the classroom.

Donavin: A lot of times [the teacher] didn't really make it relevant. It was never interesting to me. I was not engaged in what was going on. And she wasn't either. It was apparent that she didn't care. She was Teach for America and would always talk about what she was going to do once her two years were over. She wasn't invested. So, I didn't care. (December 30, 2011)

Several things are notable here. Donavin and Jeremy offered critique of their literacy experiences and felt connected to those in which teachers participated and seemed invested. They also described teachers in other subject areas who were invested in their learning.

For example, Jeremy described Mr. Map, the video production teacher, as being able to connect "what we wanted to do" with the curriculum. According to Jeremy, "We had to write newscasts, interview people, and record ourselves speaking on camera. It was fun, but Mr. Map made sure we did it right." Conversely, teachers who did not actively engage material with students could not get students to invest in their literacy learning as successfully.

With increased accountability to "cover" state standards in order to prepare students for standardized testing, and because of an influx of unprepared or divested individuals allowed to teach in urban classrooms, there seems to be a culture of teaching in which students are no longer the center (Haymes, 1995; Lipman, 2004). The young men described their most meaningful literacy experiences to include ones in which the teachers and students were equally engaged in material and participating in literacy learning together.

Donavin concludes, "After your class, we never got to write about ourselves anymore." What he and the other students in Latrise's class witnessed was quality teaching and quality texts, both of which mattered in "shape[ing] the lives of African American adolescent males and mov[ing] them beyond the limitations that impede their literacy development" (Tatum, 2009).

What Donavin describes as missing from much of his educational experience was the connection to human and textual literacy models that were apparent in the teaching and learning that took place in Latrise's and Mr. Map's classrooms.

"THAT'S THE KIND OF STUFF THAT STICK WITH YOU": ENGLISH EDUCATORS AND "CULTURALLY SUSTAINING" PEDAGOGY

Revisiting Ladson-Billing's groundbreaking work calling for culturally relevant pedagogy, Paris (2011) challenges education researchers and educators to revisit the salient characteristics of Ladson-Billing's definitions that have been taken for granted. Paris asserts that a "culturally sustaining" pedagogy is committed to preserving the languages of multiethnic youth in practice rather than just in theory.

When Donavin began to recite the first few lines of Paul Lawrence Dunbar's "We wear the mask," Latrise was astonished. He added, "I will never forget reading that poem in your class. It's not that we had to remember it. It was just relevant towards me." Donavin described his connection to McKay's poem and how it has remained meaningful to his life after five years. He also describes the relevance (of lack) of other literacy experiences in his life. As a volunteer at Carver, Donavin was still very much involved with the school.

He described how one of the literacy teachers there solicited his help to try to get students to read more. He recalled:

Ms. Reed told me that they were trying to get students to read more. She said they were starting with the book *Dracula*. I was like *Dracula*? I hate to use this phrase, but Dracula is a book white people love to read. It's something they're interested in. So I was like why don't you start them off with something like *The Miseducation of the Negro* because what Carter G. Woodson was saying then, is still relevant now. Start there, get them thinking about themselves and their lives, and maybe you can ease in to stuff like *Dracula*. Now it will be hard to go to books like that but at least they will have a foundation.

He continues to describe how his love for books came from being able to start with books that he felt were relevant to his life. He says that books like "*13 Ways of Looking at a Black Man* and *Signifying Monkey,* and *Things Fall Apart* prepared me to read and really analyze other kinds of books." Donavin considers the development of his literacy engagement.

For him, literacy development begins with a connection to text and recognizes that, in order to extend the literacy trajectory of black boys, teachers should begin with relevant texts (Tatum, 2009; Winn & Johnson, 2011). The urgent need to build and sustain the literate lives of students of color begins with texts, practices, and pedagogies that support and sustain their cultural competence, while offering academic rigor and access to dominant literacies (Paris, 2011).

"I STARTED TO SEE A DIFFERENT WORLD": ENGLISH EDUCATORS NEED TO SUPPORT STUDENTS IN BUILDING LITERATE IDENTITIES

In our work with teachers in small learning communities (SLCs) in the urban southeast, we have focused on what it means to support teachers as they support their students in building a literate identity. A finding from Maisha's ongoing work with youth poets in the Bronx that continued to haunt her long after was an interview with student poet Amanda when she discussed doing "the school's work" as opposed to writing about issues that mattered most to her and people in her world (Fisher, 2007).

Similarly, in Latrise's work with adolescent black boys in a middle school in the urban southeast, qualitative interviews with boys in one school revealed that much of the work they did felt inauthentic, irrelevant, and an attempt by the teacher to keep them busy, as opposed to engaging them in a robust learning opportunity. We argue that English educators must move beyond asking youth to do "the school's work" and invite students to join permissive spaces where they can do their own work with the understanding that they will be reading, writing, and thinking for a variety of purposes beyond the classroom walls.

We know this can be achieved through supporting youth to exercise agency via their literate identities. There are many young people who are engaging in reading, writing, speaking, and "doing" the word (Peterson, 1995) unbeknownst to the school; they are waiting for an invitation to exchange, engage, and, thus learn from each other as well as their teacher.

There has not been a classroom, youth detention center, or after-school space in which we have not met young people who were already engaged in writing, including poems, plays, songs, and, in some cases, memoirs at the tender age of sixteen (Winn, 2011).

There is a mindset that indigenous, black, and Latina/o youth are always in need of academic intervention in literacy teaching and learning environments. English education must move into a "restorative" framework; that is, teachers (with the support of teacher educators) must work hard to eradicate their own monolithic ideas of who youth are and who they can be and use the powerful tools of the English classroom—literature, memoir, poetry, writing, performing writing, etc.—to keep young people engaged and in the room, at the table, in the "circle" (Winn, 2013).

A "Restorative English Education" pedagogy, then, is one that is committed to learning about students' (and their families') histories in order to begin to build relationships. This pedagogy also involves making curricular choices that include inquiry-driven questions about race, class, gender, identity, and justice using a variety of texts.

"IT'S NOT JUST THE TEACHER TELLING YOU INFORMATION": ENGLISH EDUCATORS AND A "SOCIOCRITICAL" LENS WHEN CONSIDERING STUDENT NEEDS

Young people enter our classrooms with knowledge, histories, stories, and lived experiences that are robust and ready to be tapped into to build literate identities. We are compelled by Gutierrez's use of a "sociocritical" lens while considering language and literacies as "civil rights" (Gutierrez, 2008). Through this lens, English educators pay close attention to young peoples' "historicized selves" in order to think about possible lives. A sociocritical lens would also invite a dialectical relationship between personal and academic literacies and literate practices.

The National Council of Teachers of English (NCTE) argues that literacy is "inextricably linked with particular histories, life possibilities, and social trajectories of groups and individuals." This notion of linking literacy learning and "civil rights" (Greene, 2008) must be taken seriously in an unprecedented age of mass incarceration in the United States, when youth are experiencing more "urban pedagogies" and less opportunities for learning (Duncan, 2000).

TOWARD A LITERACY CONTINUUM:
RECOMMENDATIONS FOR EDUCATORS

Ultimately we understand that English educators cannot do all the work. Our young people need many resources, yet we believe what Martin Luther King, Jr., expressed in his text *Where Do We Go from Here: Chaos or Community?* when he argued, "the job of the school is to teach so well that family background is no longer an issue" (King, 1968). We know our medium as English educators is transformative—words, language, poetry, prose, reading, and writing for a variety of purposes—has the ability to inspire and incite a new generation of literate and engaged citizens.

Stories of the young men here represent the possibilities of literacy learning that is engaging and personal. However, just as researchers and literacy scholars call for literacy learning that encompasses transformative views, social justice, sustainability, and relevance, the purposes of literacy engagement and learning must reach beyond individuals as we prepare students for high-stakes testing, global competition, and academic achievement.

A literacy continuum that recognizes that the purposes for literacy engagement are fluid can be used to remind educators that literacy participation and involvement can be more or less personal and academic, culturally relevant and culturally distant, as well as communal and global.

The ways in which these young people talk about their participation in literacy activities provide information for how teachers can be practitioners of the craft in which they create literacy opportunities that prepare young people for academic success, as well as connect to their personal lives. Teachers must also recognize the power of culturally sustaining pedagogy that preserves students' identities while balancing culturally distant curricula that are mandated by states.

For example, teachers should consider pairing culturally relevant texts with culturally distant texts, in order to teach English language arts concepts. Also, teachers who use culturally relevant and sustaining pedagogy to inform their practice should do so not as an accommodation, but should consider it as a pedagogical stance and consistent practice to engage before, during, and after instruction (Johnson & Gonzales, 2014). In addition, building literate identities is important to help students see how literacy participation is important to their lives outside of classrooms.

REFERENCES

Duncan, G. A. (2000). Urban pedagogies and the celling of adolescents of color. *Social Justice*, *27* (3), 29–42.

Fisher, M. T. (2007). *Writing in rhythm: Spoken word poetry in urban classrooms*. New York, N.Y.: Teachers College Press.

Fisher, M. T. (2009). *Black literate lives: Historical and contemporary perspectives*. New York, N.Y.: Routledge, Critical Social Thought Series.

Greene, S. (Ed) (2008). *Literacy as a civil right: Reclaiming social justice in literacy teaching and learning*. New York, N.Y.: Peter Lang.

Gutierrez, K. (2008). Language and literacies as civil rights. In S. Greene (Ed.), *Literacy as a civil right: Reclaiming social justice in literacy teaching and learning* (pp. 169–84). New York, N.Y.: Peter Lang Publishers.

Haymes, S. (1995). *Race, culture, and the city: A pedagogy for Black urban struggle*. Albany, N.Y.: State University of New York Press.

Johnson, L. P. (2012). *Shaping literate identities: African American male youth, literacy, and middle school*. Unpublished Dissertation, Emory University, Atlanta, Georgia.

Johnson, L. P., & Gonzales, J. (2014). The culturally relevant practices and management of an ELA teacher: A tale of two classes. *Journal of Balanced Reading Instruction, 2* (1), 18–24.

Kirkland, D. E. (2013). *A search past silence: The literacy of young Black men*. New York, N.Y.: Teachers College Press.

King, M. L. (1968). *Where do we go from here: Chaos or community?* Boston, Mass.: Beacon Press.

Lipman, P. (2004). *High stakes education: Inequality, globalization, and urban school reform*. New York, N.Y.: Routledge.

Paris, D. (2011, November). "The consciousness of the verbal artist": Understanding vernacular literacies in digital and embodied spaces. Paper presented at the annual meeting of the National Council of Teachers of English, Chicago, Illinois.

Peterson, C.L. (1995). *"Doers of the word": African-American women speakers & writers in the North (1830–1880)*. New York: Oxford University Press.

Tatum, A. W. (2006). Engaging African American males in reading. *Educational Leadership, 63* (5), 44–49.

Tatum, A. (2009). *Reading for their life: (Re)Building the textual lineages of African-American adolescent males*. Portsmouth, N.H.: Heinemann.

Tuck, E. (2009). Suspending damage: A letter to communities. *Harvard Educational Review, 79* (3), 409–28.

Winn, M. T. (2011). *Girl Time: Literacy, justice, and the school-to-prison pipeline*. New York, N.Y.: Teachers College Press.

Winn, M. T. (2013). Toward a restorative english education. *Research in the Teaching of English, 48* (1), 126–35.

Winn, M. T., & Johnson, L. P. (2011). *Writing instruction in culturally relevant classrooms*. Urbana, Ill.: National Council of Teachers of English.

Chapter Five

Black and Latina/o Youth Communicative Repertoires in Urban English Language Arts Classrooms

Danny C. Martinez

During his years as a middle and high school English language arts (ELA) and English as a second language (ESL) teacher in both San Francisco and Los Angeles, the author found himself listening carefully to the languages spoken by the students, all of whom were black and Latina/o youth. Careful attention was paid to their utterances as they spoke to one another in and out of the classroom. The range of languages spoken by these black and Latina/o youth proved fascinating. These youth were expert code switchers and style shifters who used language in creative and meaningful ways. [1]

The most interesting and surprising moments were those occasions when he *heard* the voices of youth in these schools before actually *seeing* them. In these moments it was easy to make assumptions about the race of a student simply based on how they *sounded*. Often one would *hear* what appeared to be a black youth approaching, and would learn that these seemingly black voices belonged to Latina/o youth.

Years later, as a researcher this author found himself halfway into a year-long ethnographic study documenting the sociolinguistic landscape (Paris, 2011) of black and Latina/o youth in urban ELA classrooms when Chanel, a black immigrant youth from Belize, had the experience captured below in a fieldnote. The fieldnote below shares the moment when Chanel heard the voices of three Latina youth that she believed *sounded* like "black people."

> The tardy bell rang and several youth continued walking into Mr. Esperanza's class making their way to empty seats. Chanel (a black female youth) sat in a pod of desks situated in the middle-rear section of the class. When in her seat,

she began chatting with Jorge (a Latino youth) while organizing papers in her folder. Mr. Esperanza was about to begin speaking when several loud voices from outside of the class were heard through a door that was left ajar. Chanel looked toward the door and said loudly, "that sounds like black people." Immediately after, three Latina students walked into the classroom. Chanel looked at the girls entering, then at me, raised her eyebrows and shrugged her shoulders. She immediately returned to her conversation with Jorge. (Fieldnote, February 9, 2011)

Here Chanel participated in what Alim (2009; see also Alim & Smitherman, 2012) has called "race-ing language," that is, making decisions about an individual's race based on how they "sound." Throughout this study at Willow High School (pseudonym), Latina and Latino youth were often heard speaking a range of languages, and with regularity these youth drew on their ability to speak and/or approximate forms of black Language to communicate with their peers, in addition to shifting into a range of English(es) (Kirkland, 2010) that were communicatively acceptable among peers.

While Chanel guessed that the voices she heard were those of black people, she was not surprised when her Latina peers walked through the doors. Chanel's reaction captured for me the dynamic ways that black and Latina/o youth used language despite the circulation of standard language ideologies (Milroy, 2001) rampant in their schooling experiences.

Given this, the goals of this chapter are twofold: 1) to showcase the linguistic dexterity (Paris, 2009) of black and Latina/o youth communicative repertoires (Rymes, 2010), and 2) to highlight how these youth use language to make and communicate meaning to others. The chapter concludes by suggesting ways that educators can begin the work of leveraging the communicative repertoires of non-dominant youth as means to engage in powerful English language arts pedagogies in our schools.

The sociocultural reality of many urban schools is that black and Latina/o youth attend these schools with one another more than any other racial/ethnic group (Paris, 2011). Additionally, some studies have revealed how in these black and brown spaces, black language is often elevated within youth cultural practices (Alim, 2004; Paris, 2009, 2011). This does not hold true, however, in official classroom spaces, like the ELA classroom context in this study. Instead, students' non-dominant language practices continue to be indicators of their low academic achievement by their teachers.

While it became evident that these youth displayed expansive communicative repertoires, they were not leveraged or treated as a resource for learning in their ELA classrooms. However, non-dominant language practices do not stop at the classroom door, therefore it is important for ELA instructors to begin thinking about new ways of understanding the linguistic realities of the youth in their classrooms, specifically non-dominant youth whose languages have historically been deemed flawed.

SOCIOCULTURAL LANGUAGE RESEARCH

Given the cultural and linguistic interactions between black and Latina/o youth in U.S. schools, it should come as no surprise that their language practices have influenced one another. However, the ways in which these youth have socialized one another's language practices are not considered beneficial to their own academic development because schools privilege dominant language practices over all others (Alim, 2005; Dyson & Smitherman, 2009; Kirkland, 2010). This is especially true in the ELA context in which teachers may feel pressure to monitor and model academic language practices (Beach, Thein, & Webb, 2012).

While sociocultural scholars have called on practitioners and researchers to build on the home and community language and literacy practices of non-dominant students, few studies have documented the regularities across the language practices of black and Latina/o youth as these youth interact with one another in school and community contexts (for exceptions see Paris, 2009, 2011; and Zentella, 1997).

LANGUAGE RESEARCH IN MULTIETHNIC CONTEXTS

To examine the nature of one ethnic group appropriating and uttering the language typically associated with another group, we turn toward the work on *language crossing* in sociolinguistic and linguistic anthropological scholarship. Rampton (1995) introduced the notion of *language crossing* to describe how diverse youth in London "crossed" into languages associated with an ethnicity other than their own as a means to align themselves with that group, or take on a "new ethnicity" within peer interactions. It was common for Rampton's white youth participants to "cross" into the language of their non-dominant group's peers.

For example, white London youth shifted into a style of Punjabi British English to index a specific identity for themselves or to align themselves with their Punjabi peers. Similarly, in Bucholtz's (1999) study of white youth in a northern California high school, her close analysis of one white male youth, Brand One, demonstrated how he crossed into black language practices to communicate his alignment with black youth culture and physical prowess locally associated with black youth.

Work on language crossing helped to expose the necessity of examining the phenomenon of one group taking up the language of another racial/ethnic group. However, most studies on language crossing focus on white youth "crossing" or taking up the language of a non-dominant group.

Noteworthy studies of non-dominant groups taking up the language of another racial or ethnic group have also emerged in sociocultural language research, including how black youth shift into standard American English (Alim, 2005) and how Asian (Chun, 2001; Reyes, 2005) and Puerto Rican (Zentella, 1997) youth speak the language associated with black youth. Paris's (2009; 2011) study of black, Latina/o, and Pacific Islander youth in a northern California school highlights specifically how in multiethnic spaces like Sun Vista High School, black language emerged as the lingua franca of the context.

Paris describes how these youth "shared" black language in ways that were ratified by black peers. Black language in Paris's multiethnic context was viewed by youth as a way to connect across their varied racial and ethnic differences.

Several scholars have called for additional research that examines black language use across ethnic groups (Paris, 2009; Reyes, 2010; Zentella, 1997), particularly with black and Latina/o youth because "demographic shifts coupled with the continued residential segregation of poor communities of color have increased the numbers of black and brown students who share the same communities and classrooms" (Paris, 2009, p. 430).

While language researchers have paid some attention to the role of language in multiethnic spaces of language contact, this area of research is still underexplored in its relationship to the pedagogical needs of non-dominant groups in the English language arts content area and beyond.

ELA teachers must also contend with the notion that national- or state-level standards do not treat non-dominant language practices as a resource for learning in schools. Therefore, while we often celebrate a student's acquisition of "foreign" or "world" languages, there is reluctance to celebrate language practices that are intimately connected to a group of people who have historically experienced the most severe inequalities in our society. Given the history of non-dominant English(es) in the United States, today's English educators must work to provide generative and robust ways of leveraging the linguistic skills of black and Latina/o youth as a resource for learning.

Several sociocultural literacy scholars *have* explored ways to leverage the marginalized language practices of non-dominant children and youth. For example, researchers working with black (for example, Ball, 1992; Dyson & Smitherman, 2009; Godley, Carpenter, & Werner, 2007; Lee, 2007) and Latina/o (for example, Bunch, 2006; Díaz & Flores, 2001; Gutierrez et al., 1999; Martinez, Orellana, Pacheco, & Carbone, 2008; Orellana & Reynolds, 2008) children and youth have documented that the expansive learning opportunities garnered with the varied language and literacy practices of these groups are treated as a resource for learning in ELA instruction.

Other scholars have examined ways of providing culturally and linguistically responsive teaching and learning for non-dominant youth in ways that privilege and leverage home and community practices (Duncan-Andrade & Morrell, 2008; Jocson, 2008; Morrell, 2008; Winn, 2007).

METHODS

This study took place at Willow High School (WHS), a comprehensive public school located in the Tajuata (pseudonym) neighborhood of southern California during the 2010–2011 academic year. Before introducing Willow High School and the participants, it is important to briefly describe Tajuata because the cultural historical past of this neighborhood resonated with the varied cultural and linguistic practices reported in this chapter.

Tajuata was and is still considered a black community, and for several decades, this was the case because black residents were the majority. The author's mother was raised in Tajuata and remembers being one of few Mexican families in the 1950s. Within the last twenty years demographic shifts in Tajuata encouraged a Latina/o majority, a phenomenon that has occurred and is occurring across many historically black communities (Pastor, De Lara, & Scoggins, 2011).

Tajuata's demographic shift led to media headlines about black and brown conflict: from local conflicts between neighbors to gang violence between black and brown gangs, political struggles for power in civic leadership positions, and misallocated resources for the needs of two distinct communities in the neighborhood and within schools (Davis, 1992; Sears, 2000). Despite these master narratives, the children and youth of Tajuata continued to attend schools with one another, and despite the dwindling black population, the varied cultural and linguistic practices of black youth continue to hold value across the local practices of this community.

Additionally, while many view Willow High School as a site rife with educational failure, racial conflict, and depressed resources, black and Latina/o families continued to send their children to WHS, hopeful that academic success and upward mobility were possible for their children (Noguera, 2003).

When this study took place, 1,577 students were enrolled at WHS, and of this population 19.7 percent were reported as black, and 79.6 percent reported as Latina/o (CDE, 2011). One hundred percent of students at WHS were considered economically disadvantaged according to free and reduced lunch measures. The large population of black and Latina/o students considered economically disadvantaged mirrors the larger Tajuata demographic in which unemployment rates are consistently higher than state and national averages and over 40 percent of families live below national poverty levels (Rogers, Bertrand, Freelon, & Fanelli, 2011).

The shift in student population over the years increased the number of Latina/o immigrants that required English Language Learner (ELL) services. During this study, 35.9 percent of students at WHS were designated ELLs. WHS also had its share of students considered long-term English Learners, youth who are designated English Learners for more than five years (Callahan, 2005).

In addition to the various English Learner designations, several teachers agreed that many of their students were "Standard English Learners" (LeMoine & Hollie, 2007), a category used in the district (unofficially) to distinguish those students who were learners of dominant ways of speaking English. While schools across the country rely on language designations for their students, these labels are often oversimplistic and deficit in orientation (Gutiérrez & Orellana, 2006; Orellana & Gutiérrez, 2006).

At WHS, tenth-grade English courses were the first time students formerly enrolled in the English Leaner program came in contact with the larger school population in an ELA setting. The English 10 course was a space in which diverse black and Latina/o youth at WHS would interact in interesting ways. For example, former ESL students were less likely to receive support from bilingual instructors or paraprofessionals and had to rely on their peers for language support.

Additionally, for many former ESL students, it was likely the first time they were enrolled in a course other than physical education with their black peers. For this reason, the study focused on three sophomore-level English courses to capture fruitful communicative interactions. Specifically, Mr. Esperanza, a senior English teacher, offered access to his twelfth-grade ELA because he believed the student population mirrored the larger school population. Overall, four ELA courses were observed, three of which mirrored the school-wide population, and one, an Honors English 10 course that did not have any black youth enrolled, although the official roster indicated otherwise.

Three teachers participated across these four ELA classes: Ms. Luz, a Latina tenth-grade English teacher with seven years of experience; Ms. Lyn, a white English teacher with six years of teaching experience; and Mr. Esperanza, a white senior English teacher with nine years of teaching experience. WHS operated on a "4x4" block schedule in which students completed one entire academic course within one semester.

Therefore the study captures a total of four complete ELA courses over one academic year, two courses with Ms. Luz, one with Ms. Lyn, and the other with Mr. Esperanza, two courses each semester. Each semester lasted fifteen weeks, and I observed approximately two to three classes per week. This chapter focuses on interactions that occurred only in Ms. Luz's classes.

METHODS FOR COLLECTING DATA

The methodology draws on ethnographic research tools inspired by methods from the ethnography of communication tradition (Hymes, 1964), as well as the sociocultural tradition of language and literacy research (Heath & Street, 2008), which views language as a premier tool that mediates culture, learning, and development (Cole, 1996; Hull & Schultz, 2001) while placing an emphasis on lengthy ethnographic observations of a community and its sociocultural practices (Cole, 1996; Duranti, 1997).

The study utilizes both observation and participant observation, writing fieldnotes, and fleshing these out soon after (Emerson, Fretz, & Shaw, 1995). All classroom interactions, small group discussions had by youth participants, and semi-structured interviews with youth participants and their teachers are audio recorded using the Livescribe Echo Pen, a tool that allowed me to simultaneously take notes and audio record surrounding interactions.

Beyond the classroom observations made throughout the year, data were also collected via "hanging out" during nutrition and lunch periods, school-wide assemblies, pep rallies, school-wide celebrations, and weekend college workshop activities. All these data were analyzed to understand the features of black and Latina/o communicative interactions, with close attention to the linguistic features available to black and Latina/o youth.

TOWARD AN UNDERSTANDING OF LINGUISTIC REPERTOIRES FOR ENGLISH EDUCATION

In classrooms, the range of utterances produced by students are many, and with one teacher facilitating the learning of up to forty students in today's public school classrooms, it is impossible to listen, document, and analyze what each communicative act can mean without the support to engage in teacher inquiry via classroom discourse analysis (Rymes, 2009). What follows are examples from everyday classroom interactions in which youth deployed a range of languages to communicate meaning in their ELA classroom.

Building on one twenty-three-second interaction that took place in Ms. Luz's fall semester tenth-grade English classroom, it is possible to examine the communicative repertoires of black and Latino youth to highlight 1) the linguistic dexterity of these youth and 2) how the communicative practices of these youth are continually monitored and positioned in relation to dominant varieties of English.

The first analysis will highlight the agility of Lorenzo, a Latino youth who is attempting to enter an ongoing conversation. From where he was seated, Lorenzo did not have a complete view of what was projected onto the wall by his teacher, and we enter where he is trying his best to ask Ms. Luz to move the image upward. While this analysis is not directly related to ELA content instruction, Lorenzo's agile linguistic moves provide an example of what youth *can* do with language.

Next, attention will shift to the interactions of Troy and Dave, two black male youth, within the same transcript. The analysis examines how black language practices are monitored in ways that stump genuine youth participation in literary analysis, critique, and overall meaning making in a discussion about Shakespeare's *Julius Caesar*.

The analysis that follows is steeped in a commitment to view our students' non-dominant language practices as a resource for learning rather than an indication of their lack of academic potential. It is a call for teachers and researchers to listen very carefully to the ways in which non-dominant youth *make meaning* via the languages available to them (Martínez, Durán, & Hikida, 2013). As our public schools become increasingly diverse, multiethnic groups will be in contact with one another more than ever. In these spaces, we must begin changing what counts as language for learning.

LINGUISTIC DEXTERITY IN EVERYDAY CLASSROOM TALK

Paris (2011) defines linguistic dexterity as "the ability to use a range of language practices in a multiethnic and multilingual society" (p. 15). The notion of linguistic dexterity is useful to describe how youth at WHS deployed a range of languages to communicate meaning across racial and ethnic boundaries. These youth flexibly shifted registers, code switched into hybrid features of these languages, and ultimately they were creative with language.

While this might not seem extraordinary, since monolingual speakers of any language tend to shift depending on their audience and context, it *is* extraordinary given that the non-dominant language practices of these youth are never granted the prestige over dominant language practices, particularly in schools. Ball, Skerrett, and Martínez (2011) note that too often, youth who are speakers of non-dominant languages are often glossed over as monolingual, while others argue that some youth are treated as not having enough language (Orellana, Lee, & Martínez, 2011). Lorenzo provides us with an opportunity to imagine him speaking in his tenth-grade English classroom, vying for the attention of his teacher, Ms. Luz.

Lorenzo

During the final weeks of the first semester, Ms. Luz provided her students with study notes to help them on their final exam. On this day, she wanted students to understand the role characters from *Julius Caesar* had in Caesar's assassination. On a transparency film, she had a list of characters, and students were asked to determine whether these characters were "pro" or "anti" Caesar, explained as "for or against" Caesar. Ms. Luz placed her notes, written on a transparency film, onto a noisy overhead projector whose image shone onto a screen hanging from the front wall of the room.

Lorenzo was seated in the last row of the classroom on this day and he did not have a clear view of the projected notes. Attempting to get a full view, he squirmed in his chair, stretched his neck, and eventually stood up, stretching his arms down to his notebook where he tried to take copious notes. Lorenzo, seemingly frustrated with his limited view, asked Ms. Luz to move the transparency up so that he could see.

In the following, Lorenzo engaged in an interaction with Ms. Luz and his classmate Troy to communicate his desire to get a better view of the notes. Here we will focus only on Lorenzo's utterances within this interaction. We will return to Troy and David later in this chapter.

Transcript 1.0 Pick it up Miss Luz I can't see[2]

01	Ms. Luz:	Now let's go back to Portia. ((to class))
02		Portia's tricky. [Okay?
03	Troy:	[Where she- where she from ((to Ms. Luz))
04	**Lorenzo**:	*Con permiso.* ((to Ms. Luz)) (with your permission)
05		Can you push it up [miss?
06	Ms. Luz:	[she's Brutus' **wife?** ((to S1 and class))
07	Troy:	She a **pro**
08	**Lorenzo**:	(2.0 sec) pa-**rr**iba:: ((to Ms. Luz))
09	Dave:	Yeah but she was- she was
10	Troy:	She don't even know wassup
11	**Lorenzo**:	[Hey miss: ((to Ms. Luz))
12	Ms. Luz:	[She doesn't know what's going on
13		but [she's worried about her father right? ((to class))
14	Troy:	[((stands up blocking more of Lorenzo's view))
15	**Lorenzo**:	[Stoopid **move** yo' bald head ma::n ((to black peer))
16	Ms. Luz:	So [**maybe** she would be neutral?
17	**Lorenzo**:	[Ms. Luz. (1.0 sec)
18		move yo (xx) man:: (to S1)
19		(1.5) pick it up miss-Luz ((to Ms. Luz))
20		**I can't see**::
21	Ms. Luz:	hold on ((adjust image projection))

Taken together, this twenty-three-second interaction may not seem re-markable. A quick gloss over Lorenzo's utterances only makes visible that he can shift between English and Spanish, a notable skill that many Latina/o youth have available to them at WHS, and well documented in other studies (Gutierrez, Baquedano-Lopez, & Tejeda, 1999; Martínez, 2010; Orellana, 2009; Valdés, 1996).

Yet a more thorough examination of this interaction highlights the lin-guistic tools available to Lorenzo as he deployed a range of languages and styles of these languages extending beyond narrow conceptions of English and Spanish. Lorenzo's attempts to bring a legitimate concern into the offi-cial space of the classroom in lines 04–05, 08, 11, and 20 were up against larger discursive practices already in progress. It was evidently difficult for Lorenzo to make his way into the official classroom space.

In line 04 Lorenzo attempted to interject, uttering *to* Ms. Luz "Con permi-so. Can you push it up miss?" (line 04–05). In these lines, Lorenzo uttered what researchers call an intersentential code switch, in which a speaker in-itiates an utterance in one language and ends in another. Here he also begins with the honorific "con permiso" (with your permission) demonstrating his awareness that he is disrupting an interaction in progress, perhaps choosing to soften his interruption with these words.

Immediately after, however, Lorenzo code switched into English when he uttered, "can you push it up," asking Ms. Luz to raise the bulb of the projec-tor to provide him with a better view. His use of "can you" supports the notion that Lorenzo was still trying to use terms that index respect and acknowledgment of his interruption. However, Ms. Luz did not fulfill Loren-zo's request, perhaps not hearing him at all. The overlap between his final word "miss" in line 05 and the beginning of her next utterance in line 06 indicates this where she responded to Troy's question.

Lorenzo then shifted in line 08 to a variety of Spanish that some might argue demonstrates features of Chicano Spanish (Anzaldúa, 1999; Garcia, 1979), but may well be a prominent feature used by a range of Spanish speakers who clip the end of "para" and the beginning of "arriba" to utter "parriba," particularly in everyday conversations. There was no uptake of Lorenzo's request, instead Troy and David entered the official space in lines 09 and 10.

Again, in line 11, Lorenzo entered with "Hey miss:" this time using a common pronoun "miss" used for teachers by some Latina/o students at WHS. "Miss" was often used for "La Maestra" or "La Miss" an endearing term that has made its way into usage among Latina/o children and youth for their teachers.[3]

The informal use of "Hey," however, to get Ms. Luz's attention is inter-esting given his previous use of the honorific "con permiso," suggesting that he may have slowly become less tolerant and more frustrated with his situation. Despite his attempt, there is yet another overlap in Lorenzo and Ms. Luz's utterances, and his request was dismissed as she began her next utterance in line 12 in response to Troy and Dave's comments.

At this point Lorenzo was frustrated and his body movement changed erratically as he attempted to better his view. Instead of directing his attention to Ms. Luz in the utterances that followed, he directed them toward Troy in his seat located in front of the projector, obstructing Lorenzo's view even further. In line 15, Lorenzo exclaimed "Stoopid **move** yo' bald head ma::n" shifting styles to use a language he and his peers regularly identified as "urban" or "ghetto" language.

Here I argue that Lorenzo shifted into black language features. It is interesting to consider whether Lorenzo might be using black language because he is interacting with his black peer, which begs the question: How would Lorenzo respond to a Latino peer? Given other observations of Lorenzo speaking to his peers, I'd argue that he might have responded in a similar tone, in addition to shifting into black language.

The conversation among Ms. Luz, Troy, and Dave continued despite Lorenzo's utterances that became louder. In lines 17 and 18 Lorenzo tried again to grasp Ms. Luz's attention, yet this attempt was dejected by another overlap. Here he uttered, "Ms. Luz" but still did not succeed. This interaction comes to a close beginning on line 18 when Lorenzo stood up from his chair, seeming exasperated, yet intent on getting what he needed.

Troy once again moved in a way that blocked Lorenzo's entire view, causing him to style shift in line 18 "move yo (xx) man::" to voice his annoyance. He shifted styles once more in line 19–20 as he spoke to Ms. Luz, uttering "pick it up miss-Luz I **can't see**::" in lines 19–20, this time uttering bald directive to Ms. Luz, who responded with "hold on." Finally acknowledging Lorenzo, she moved the bulb to manipulate the image being projected.

Each of the linguistic moves made by Lorenzo are detailed here, which include code switching and style shifting to communicate with each individual in this sequence. Lorenzo may not have been consciously aware of his linguistic moves (Rymes, 2010); however, we gather how Lorenzo *can* draw from a range of languages. Counting each language is *not* the point here; however, the analysis highlights *how* Lorenzo communicated in this setting. His language was not uniform throughout this interaction, and even in his shifting the way he used language changed with his interlocutors as his frustration levels rose.

Lorenzo provides us with a glimpse of the communicative repertoires available to him. In considering the language abilities of bilingual Latina/o youth, research tends only to consider English and Spanish varieties as evidence of bilingualism and fails to consider the *variance* in the language practices of Latinas/os, neglecting the *hybrid* language varieties and the influence and socialization of black languages. In much of the research or talk about bilingualism, there is little attention given to the social and cultural significance of Latina/o children and youth having black language available to them (for exceptions, see Alim, 2005; Paris, 2009, 2011; Zentella, 1997).

Therefore, the larger argument is that a view of language through the metaphor of the repertoire can widen what counts as language in schools in order to expand what we make available for meaning making among non-dominant groups as a resource for learning. If we expand what counts as language in our classrooms, Lorenzo and the countless other speakers of non-dominant languages can be treated as agile in their linguistic abilities, capable of using many linguistic tools to make meaning and to use as a resource for further academic or standard language development.

Lorenzo's statement above was one of many communicative interactions in which youth shifted into and out of a range of languages as their interlocutors changed. In Lorenzo's interaction above, he shifted languages and varieties of those languages in speaking to his teacher, Ms. Luz, beginning in Spanish and ending in English. Like Lorenzo, many Latina/o youth shifted into forms of black language when they spoke to black and Latina/o peers.

While Lorenzo's interaction with Tony was very brief, he uttered "move yo' head man," indexing his awareness of a specific language that he and Tony had in common, similar to the youth in Paris's (2011) study who used black language as a unifying language "across their differences." Lorenzo's utterances also serve to challenge the prevalent idea that non-dominant youth who are speakers of marginalized and stigmatized languages are inherently monolingual (Ball, Skerrett, & Martínez, 2011) and unable to use standard varieties of English.

Instead, in this moment-to-moment classroom interaction, Lorenzo shifted into a variety of English that is more typical of Standard English. Lorenzo's interactions, and those of many of his peers that consistently shifted as they communicated with peers in their settings, went unnoticed in the everyday hustle and bustle of classroom interactions. Lorenzo and many of his peers drew from a range of languages to communicate meaning, and often these linguistic utterances were inclusive of standard varieties of English.

"CORRECTING" THE SOUNDS OF BLACK LANGUAGE

In this section, we shift our attention to the interaction between Troy and David, both black male students, and Ms. Luz. She has sanctioned Troy and David as speakers in the official classroom space. This sequence began when

Ms. Luz and her students completed the entire list of characters that were either "pro" or "anti" Caesar and returned to discuss Portia's involvement in the assassination.

Since Portia's role was more complex than other characters, Ms. Luz decided to leave discussion about Portia to the end of the activity. It is during this interaction that Troy and David asked clarifying questions and commented on Ms. Luz's statements and questions. Here it is the black language features of Troy and David that undergo a process of being "corrected," via Ms. Luz's teacher-student repair event. The following sequence began as Ms. Luz diverted her student's attention back to a discussion about Portia.

Transcript 2.0

01	Ms. Luz:	Now lets go back to Portia.= ((to class))
02		Portia's tricky. Okay?
03	Troy:	Where she- where Ø she from ((to Ms. Luz))
04	Lorenzo:	Con permiso. ((to Ms. Luz))
05		Can you push it up [miss?
06	Ms. Luz:	[she's Brutus' *wife* ((to Troy))

In line 03, Troy asked Ms. Luz a clarifying question "Where she- where Ø she from," attempting to understand or remember Portia, the character, and where "she is from" in relation to *Julius Caesar*. Throughout the observations and audio recordings, there were several moments in which youth could have been "corrected" based on their deviation from standard or academic varieties of English. However, not every possible correction or repair[4] (Razfar, 2005) was taken up.

For example, in lines 01–06, Ms. Luz did not repair Troy's question, "Where she- where Ø she from?" which featured a zero copula, or the absence of "is" or "are," in dominant varieties of English, such as "where is she from?" Instead, Ms. Luz answered Troy's question in line 06 with "she's Brutus' wife" without bringing attention to his black language feature, a practice that did occur often across the observations.

Troy continued:

07	Troy:	she~Ø~a~**pro?**
08	Lorenzo:	(2.0 sec) pa-**rr**iba:: ((to Ms. Luz))
09	Dave:	yeah but she was- she was [(xxx)
10	Troy:	[she don't even know wassup
11	Lorenzo:	[Hey miss: ((to Ms. Luz))
12	Ms. Luz:	[She doesn't know what's going on

13   but [she's worried about her father right? ((to class))
14   Troy: [(((stands up blocking more of Lorenzo's view))

In line 07, after hearing that Portia was Brutus's wife, Troy declared, "she~Ø~a~**pro?**" to which Dave replied in line 09, "yeah but she was- she was (xxx)," attempting to explain that her marriage to Brutus did not immediately implicate her as a "pro" Caesar character. Again, Ms. Luz did not repair Troy's utterance, "she~Ø~a~**pro?**" which again featured a zero copula.

In line 10, Troy's utterance overlapped with Dave's final utterance. He calmly but rapidly and confidently stated, "she don't even know wassup." Here Troy's utterance featured the omission of the third-person singular present tense *s*, common in black language, when he stated, "she don't," as opposed to the dominant English inclusion of *-s* or *-es* as in "she doesn't" (Rickford & Rickford, 2000).

Troy also uttered the popular word "wassup," often attributed to black language or Hip Hop Nation language to stand in for "what is up" or "what is going on." The meaning behind Troy's utterance is clear, "Portia does not even know what is going on." Ms. Luz, however, revoiced[5] Troy's statement in lines 12–13, and stated, "She doesn't know what's going on."

Ms. Luz's revoicing of Troy's utterance brings attention to the *form* of his statement. In revoicing, she engaged in a type of repair that Jefferson (1987) calls an embedded correction, a form of "other repair" in which ongoing conversation does not stop to attend to the "correction." Instead, the repair is embedded in the natural flow of conversation, and in this case, within the revoicing practices controlled by Ms. Luz.

This type of participation framework, however, did not provide Troy the ability to agree and align himself (or not) with Ms. Luz's revoicing or "correction" of his phrase. Ms. Luz quickly moved into her next utterance "but she's worried about her father right?" with a rising intonation at the end of "right," which provided a space for Troy, David, and other students to either align with this statement or not. After this, neither Troy or Dave contributed any further to the topic, rather they nodded their heads along with other students in the class, displaying their alignment or agreement with Ms. Luz's final statement potentially accommodating to the expected ways of responding in classroom routines.

Both Troy and Dave, in this short interaction, are displaying their ability to engage in content-specific discussions about *Julius Caesar*, using their varied communicative repertoires to engage in the official classroom space being facilitated by Ms. Luz. However, when there is a moment in which the two can engage in debate about Portia given that Troy believes she is pro-Caesar and Dave announces that "she don't even know wassup." Ms. Luz's revoicing of Dave's comment ends any further interaction about the matter. The form of the message, which Ms. Luz deemed improper and in need of correction, got in the way of the function of Dave's message. One wonders, however, with respect to Troy and Dave, what could have come of their discussion? A healthy debate about Portia's role in Caesar's death seemed to be emerging before the interruption to correct the form of Dave's message.

This short interaction was one of many experiences in which black and Latina/o youth were corrected in the midst of meaning making. The utterances of these youth are prime examples of the ways in which ELA teachers and researchers must work to allow meaning making to flow without interruptions for the sake of "correcting" the non-dominant communicative practices of black and Latina/o youth.

MOVING BEYOND TRADITIONAL
ENGLISH LANGUAGE ARTS INSTRUCTION

Now let's turn to imagine what might be possible had these youth had their language practices valued and treated as a resource for learning in ELA classrooms. Now more than ever, we must think of creative ways for teachers to "listen" to what their students are doing with language, to examine what meaning can be garnered with free-flowing talk about a given topic. Currently, with the wide adoption of the Common Core State Standards (CCSS), we have an opportunity to rethink approaches to the teaching of ELA (Beach, Thein, & Webb, 2012).

In this context, Lorenzo and the countless other black and Latina/o youth at WHS and in similar schools across the country should have their language practices valued and respected. This statement, of course, is easier stated than done, since scholars—linguists, sociolinguists, linguistic anthropologists, and educational scholars in language and literacy—have been spreading this message for some time.

However, the hegemony of English in our schools circulates standard language ideologies that position dominant English practices over all others. It is for this reason that Lorenzo's agility and linguistic dexterity go unnoticed. It is also why Troy and Dave's "debate" never came to fruition, because it became more important to "correct" non-standard language practices.

In the observed ELA courses, there was an overall focus on providing youth with academic language development, a cause that may be just only when it is done without devaluing home and community languages. In too many ELA classrooms, providing academic language development means socializing students to and through English language skills that mirror white dominant ways with words.

The teachers in my study most often engaged in this development by providing students with worksheets and having discussions on how to strategically engage in exams. This was most evident in the English 10A/B courses in which the youth in these classes would take the California High School Exit Exam for the first time during the academic year.

The *artistry* of language was never present in any class discussions, nor was there any attempt to bring *language* into the forefront. The *language* of literature was left out of discussions; the *language* behind technical documents required of youth to understand was left untouched. Most important to this study, the *language* of the youth was rarely brought into the official space of the classroom.

There were several spaces of opportunity in which the youth were ready to bring their own experiences in their ELA classrooms, and most often these opportunities were being mediated via languages that youth found most appropriate to describe the betrayal, love, anger, and excitement expressed by narrators and characters from their books.

The moments that stand out the most were in Ms. Luz's class when students began making connections to the universal theme of betrayal in Shakespeare's *Julius Caesar*. While reading *Julius Caesar*, students connected with the language of anger expressed by Caesar, the language of conspiracy voiced by Brutus. However, too often, potential discussions were never realized.

The larger problem in English language arts instruction is the existence of a very narrow notion of what counts as language. The youth in this study were capable of engaging in an English language arts curriculum in ways in which their linguistic repertoires could be built on and their multimodal literacy skills developed. Morrell (2011) argues:

> The children now passing through our school doors will daily engage in literacy practices that would have been incomprehensible to us only a few years ago. With all of these changes, one of the few things remaining the same is secondary English instruction (Applebee, 1993), and that is not a good thing. (p. 158)

Morrell correctly asserts that English instruction has lagged in redefining what skills will be essential for non-dominant youth beyond the ELA classroom. The youth in this study are capable of shifting and switching depending on their interlocutors and the contexts in which they are speaking. This practice is one that needs to be considered in the educational lives of these youth.

Several other scholars have documented the linguistic dexterity of youth, such as Alim's (2004) study of style shifting among black youth in a northern California community; Paris's (2011) study of *language sharing* among black, Latina/o, and Pacific Islander youth in a northern California charter school; Zentella's (1997) study of Spanish-English code switching among Puerto Rican youth in New York City; R. Martínez's (2010) study of Latina/o *Spanglish* speakers in an East Los Angeles school; and Orellana's (2009) decade-long study of child language brokers in Los Angeles and Chicago. In these studies, non-dominant youth are highlighted, participating in sophisticated practices that, as each author argues, are not valued in schooling contexts, and overall public spaces.

NOTES

1. Code shifters.
2. Transcription conventions: brackets indicate overlapping speech; a period indicates falling contour; a question mark indicates rising intonation; colons indicate the sound preceding is noticeably lengthened; bolded words indicate loud speech; numbers in parentheses mark silences in seconds; translations appear in parentheses; and author notes appear in double parentheses.
3. "El mister" was also commonly used for male teachers, pronounced "el mizter."
4. An individual can engage in self-repair, correcting one's one speech, or in other repair, repairing the speech of an interlocutor.
5. Revoicing has been defined as "the reuttering of another person's speech through repetition, expansion, rephrasing, and reporting" (O'Connor & Michaels, 1993).

REFERENCES

Alim, H. S. (2004). *You know my steez: An ethnographic and sociolinguistic study of styleshifting in a Black American speech community.* Durham, N.C.: Duke University Press for the American Dialect Society.

Alim, H. S. (2005). Hearing what's not said and missing what is: Black language in white public space. In S. F. Kiesling & C. Bratt Paulston (Eds.), *Intercultural discourse and communication* (pp. 180–97). Malden, Mass: Blackwell Publishing.

Alim, H. S. (2009, February 27). *Race-ing language, languaging race.* Paper presented at the Center for Language Interaction and Culture, University of California, Los Angeles.

Alim, H. S., & Smitherman, G. (2012). *Articulate while Black: Barack Obama, language, and race in the U.S.* New York, N.Y.: Oxford University Press.

Anzaldúa, G. (1999). *Borderlands: La frontera* (2nd ed.). San Francisco, Calif.: Aunt Lute Books.

Ball, A. (1992). Cultural preference and the expository writing of African-American adolescents. *Written Communication, 9* (4), 501–32.

Ball, A. F., Skerrett, A., & Martínez, R. A. (2011). Research on diverse students in culturally and linguistically complex language arts classrooms. In D. Lapp & D. Fisher (Eds.), *Handbook of research on teaching the English language arts* (pp. 22–28). New York, N.Y.: Routledge.

Beach, R., Thein, A. H., & Webb, A. (2012). *Teaching to exceed the English language arts common core state standards: A literacy practices approach for 6-12 classrooms.* New York, N.Y.: Routledge.

Bucholtz, M. (1999). You da man: Narrating the racial other in the production of white masculinity. *Journal of Sociolinguistics, 3* (4), 443–60.

Bunch, G. C. (2006). "Academic English" in the 7th grade: Broadening the lens, expanding access. *Journal of English for Academic Purposes, 5* (4), 284–301.

Callahan, R. M. (2005). Tracking and high school English learners: Limiting opportunity to learn. *American Educational Research Journal, 42* (2), 305–28.

CDE. (2011). *Enrollment by ethnicity for 2010–11: School enrollment by ethnicity.* In C. D. o. Education (Ed.). California Department of Education: California Department of Education.

Chun, E. (2001). The construction of white, black and Korean American identities through African American vernacular English. *Journal of Linguistic Anthropology, 11* (1), 52–64.

Cole, M. (1996). *Cultural psychology: A once and future discipline.* Cambridge, Mass.: Belknap Press of Harvard University Press.

Davis, M. (1992). L.A. Inferno. *Socialist Review, 22* (1), 57–81.

Díaz, E., & Flores, B. (2001). Teacher as sociocultural, sociohistorical mediator: Teaching to the potential. In M. de la Luz Reyes & J. J. Halcón (Eds.), *The best for our children: Critical perspectives on literacy for Latino students* (pp. 29–47). New York, N.Y.: Teachers College Press.

Duncan-Andrade, J. M. R., & Morrell, E. (2008). *The art of critical pedagogy: Possibilities for moving from theory to practice in urban schools.* New York, N.Y.: Peter Lang.

Duranti, A. (1997). *Linguistic anthropology.* Cambridge, U.K.: Cambridge University Press.

Dyson, A. H., & Smitherman, G. (2009). The right (write) start: African American language and the discourse of sounding right. *Teachers College Press, 111* (4), 973–98.

Emerson, R. M., Fretz, R. I., & Shaw, L. L. (1995). *Writing ethnographic fieldnotes.* Chicago, Ill.: University of Chicago Press.

Garcia, M. (1979). Pa(ra) usage in United States Spanish. *Language and Linguistics, 62* (1), 106–14.

Godley, A. J., Carpenter, B. D., & Werner, C. A. (2007). "I'll speak in proper slang": Language ideologies in a daily editing activity. *Reading Research Quarterly, 42* (1), 100–131.

Gutiérrez, K. D., Baquedano-López, P., & Tejeda, C. (1999). Rethinking diversity: Hybridity and hybrid language practices in the third space. *Mind, Culture, and Activity, 6*(4), 286–303.

Gutiérrez, K. D., & Orellana, M. F. (2006). The problem of English Learners: Constructing genres of difference. *Research in the Teaching of English, 40* (4), 502–7.

Heath, S. B., & Street, B. V. (2008). *On ethnography: Approaches to language and literacy research.* New York, N.Y.: Teachers College Press: NCRLL/National Conference on Research in Language and Literacy.

Hull, G. A., & Schultz, K. (2001). Literacy and learning out of school: A review of theory and research. *Review of Educational Research, 71* (4), 575–611.

Hymes, D. (1964). Toward ethnographies of communication. *American Anthropologist, 66* (6), 1–34.

Jefferson, G. (1987). On exposed and embedded correction in conversation. In G. Button & J. R. E. Lee (Eds.), *Talk and social organization* (pp. 86–100). Clevedon: Multilingual Matters.

Jocson, K. M. (2008). *Youth poets: Empowering literacies in and out of schools.* New York, N.Y.: Peter Lang.

Kirkland, D. E. (2010). English(es) in urban contexts: Politics, pluralism, and possibilities. *English Education, 42* (3), 293–306.

Lee, C. D. (2007). *Culture, literacy, & learning: Taking bloom in the midst of the whirlwind.* New York, N.Y.: Teachers College Press.

LeMoine, N., & Hollie, S. (2007). Developing academic English for Standard English learners. In H. S. Alim & J. Baugh (Eds.), *Talkin Black talk: Language, education, and social change* (pp. 43–55). New York, N.Y.: Teachers College Press.

Martínez, R. A. (2010). Spanglish as literacy tool: Toward an understanding of the potential role of Spanish-English code-switching in the development in academic literacy. *Research in the Teaching of English, 45* (2), 124–49.

Martínez, R. A., Durán, L., & Hikida, M. (2013, April). "They are *bilingüe*, but I am *trilingüe*: Listening to trilingual students in dual language classrooms." Paper presented at the Annual Meetings of the American Educational Research Association, San Francisco, California.

Martínez, R. A., Orellana, M. F., Pacheco, M., & Carbone, P. (2008). Found in translation: Connecting translating experiences to academic writing. *Language Arts, 85* (6), 421–31.

Milroy, L. (2001). Britain and the United States: Two nations divided by the same language (and different language ideologies). *Journal of Linguistic Anthropology, 10* (1), 56–89.

Morrell, E. (2008). *Critical literacy and urban youth: Pedagogies of access, dissent, and liberation.* New York, N.Y.: Routledge.

Morrell, E. (2011). Critical approaches to media in urban English Language Arts teacher development. *Action in Teacher Education, 33* (2), 157–71.

Noguera, P. (2003). *City schools and the American dream: Reclaiming the promise of public education.* New York, N.Y.: Teachers College Press.

O'Connor, M. C., & Michaels, S. (1993). Aligning academic task and participation status through revoicing: Analysis of a classroom discourse strategy. *Anthropology & Education Quarterly, 24* (4), 318–35.

Orellana, M. F. (2009). *Translating childhoods: Immigrant youth, language, and culture.* New Brunswick, N.J.: Rutgers University Press.

Orellana, M. F., & Gutiérrez, K. D. (2006). What's the problem? Constructing different genres for the study of English Learners. *Research in the Teaching of English, 41* (1), 118–23.

Orellana, M. F., & Reynolds, J. (2008). Cultural modeling: Leveraging bilingual skills for school paraphrasing tasks. *Reading Research Quarterly, 43* (1), 48–65.

Orellana, M. F., Lee, C., & Martínez, D. C. (2011). More than just a hammer: Building linguistic toolkits. *Issues in Applied Linguistics, 18* (2), 1–7.

Paris, D. (2009). "They're in my culture, they speak the same way": African American language in multiethnic high schools. *Harvard Educational Review, 79* (3), 428–47.

Paris, D. (2011). *Language across difference: Ethnicity, communication, and youth identities in changing urban schools.* Cambridge, U.K.: Cambridge University Press.

Pastor, M., De Lara, J., & Scoggins, J. (2011). *All together now? African Americans, immigrants and the future of California.* Los Angeles, Calif.: Center for the Study of Immigrant Integration.

Rampton, B. (1995). Language crossing and the problematisation of ethnicity and socialisation. *Pragmatics, 5* (4), 485–513.

Razfar, A. (2005). Language ideologies in practice: Repair and classroom discourse. *Linguistics and Education, 16* (4), 404–24.

Reyes, A. (2005). Appropriation of African American slang by Asian American youth. *Journal of Sociolinguistics, 9* (4), 509–32.

Reyes, A. (2010). Language and ethnicity. In N. H. Hornberger & S. L. McKay (Eds.), *Sociolinguistics and education.* Buffalo, N.Y.: Multilingual Matters.

Rickford, J. R., & Rickford, R. J. (2000). *Spoken soul: The story of Black English.* New York, N.Y.: Wiley.

Rogers, J., Bertrand, M., Freelon, R., & Fanelli, S. (2011). *Free fall: Educational opportunities in 2011.* Los Angeles, Calif.: UCLA/IDEA, UC/ACCORD.

Rymes, B. (2009). *Classroom discourse analysis: A tool for critical reflection.* Cresskill, N.J.: Hampton Press.

Rymes, B. (2010). Classroom discourse analysis: A focus on communicative repertoires. In N. H. Hornberger & S. L. McKay (Eds.), *Sociolinguistics and language education* (pp. 528–46). Bristol, U.K.: Multilingual Matters.

Sears, D. O. (2000). Urban rioting in Los Angeles: A comparison of 1965 with 1992. In P. Kivisto & G. Rundblad (Eds.), *Multiculturalism in the United States: Current issues, contemporary voices* (pp. 81–95). Thousand Oaks, Calif.: Pine Forge Press.

Valdés, G. (1996). *Con respeto: Bridging the distances between culturally diverse families and schools: An ethnographic portrait.* New York, N.Y.: Teachers College Press.

Winn, M. (2007). *Writing in rhythm: Spoken word poetry in urban classrooms.* New York, N.Y.: Teachers College Press.

Zentella, A. C. (1997). *Growing up bilingual: Puerto Rican children in New York.* Malden, Mass.: Blackwell Publishers.

2

Teacher Education

Chapter Six

Service Learning in Third Spaces

Transforming Preservice English Teachers

Lisa Scherff[1]

> I am glad that I am taking this class during the summer because I will be able
> to work with the TAEP program. I want kids to be excited, ∴ . . I want the next
> few weeks to flow well, but I also want the experiences to be able to handle
> trials that may come up. I think it will definitely be a learning curve, but it will
> be great preparation, . . . I think the fact that we will be working with the high
> schoolers both on a small group, larger group, and whole class arrangement
> will be really beneficial to both us as future teachers as well as the students.
> —Amy

Amy's reflection (all names pseudonyms), written the week before she and
fifteen fellow preservice teachers began "teaching" high school students their
required summer reading novels, gets to the heart of two interrelated concepts integral to this chapter. First is the concept of third, or hybrid, spaces in
education, those new spaces that can emerge when students and teachers
come together, bringing their varied D/discourses and challenging the status
quo (for example, Barton, Tan, & Rivet, 2008; Gutierrez, Rymes, & Larson,
1995; Moje et al., 2004). A second concept is service learning—mutually
beneficial activity between service providers and recipients.

In this chapter the author argues that if we want preservice English teachers to become critical, culturally responsive teachers, then we need to provide
them with field experiences in which they have opportunities to do this. Far
too many times university supervisors visit interns' classrooms only to see
them teach pre-outlined grammar and research paper lessons that their cooperating teacher does not want to do. Or preservice teachers attempting to
include critical literacy in their lessons face resistance from their more traditional mentor teachers (Morrell et al., 2012).

To elucidate her argument, the author presents information from two years (2009 and 2010) of a summer program she created that brings high school students and preservice teachers together, through service learning, to read and discuss young adult literature and other texts. Such a pedagogical space can promote collaborative inquiry and open up spaces for more dialogic talk. This chapter contends that service learning initiatives in teacher education can provide teaching and learning experiences that are equally and mutually beneficial for K–12 students and preservice literacy teachers.

Readers are taken through the process of setting up such a program, providing suggestions from what worked and what did not in the program. Then, through excerpts from literature discussions between and among the students and preservice teachers, the author shows how incorporating service learning into literacy courses can provide pedagogical experiences that encourage preservice teachers to think about teaching their students, and themselves, in new and expanded ways.

THIRD SPACE/HYBRIDITY THEORY

The concept of a third space is based on hybridity theory and has been used to describe both physical and emotional spaces (Bhabba, 1990, 1994; Soja, 1996), and recognizes the numerous cultural and discursive practices that people draw from to make sense of themselves and the world (Bhabba, 1990, 1994). When people come together, bringing diverse forms of knowledge and ways of talking, such differences can work together to yield new learning, forms of discourse, and student identities (Moje et al., 2004; Barton, Tan, & Rivet, 2008).

Moje et al. (2004) and Barton, Tan, & Rivet (2008) summarize three perspectives on hybrid/third space. First, such spaces can be viewed as a scaffold between academic and out-of-school (for example, marginalized) knowledge. Second, third spaces can be seen in terms of how people can cross between different discourse communities. Third, third spaces can be described as places where differing beliefs, cultures, knowledge, and ways of talking come together to create both new academic and out-of-school knowledge.

The experience of preservice English teachers is comparable to K–12 students. Just like the students they will teach, preservice teachers come to teacher preparation programs with their own set of beliefs about teaching and learning based on their past experiences, culture, and community (Darling-Hammond, 2006). These beliefs can be at odds in/with teacher preparation programs in which they learn how to teach and the classrooms in which they find themselves placed as part of their clinical experiences—spaces where they are writing official lesson plans and being observed and evaluated by university supervisors.

Zeichner (2010) claims that a persistent dilemma in teacher education has been the disconnect between campus-based teacher education courses and what candidates experience in the field—a disconnect that is tied to first and second spaces. Third (or hybrid) spaces, Zeichner (2010) claimed, are a solution and comprise, "an equal and more dialectical relationship between academic and practitioner knowledge in support of student teacher learning" (p. 92).

In relation to the summer program described in this chapter, Gutierrez et al.'s (1999) view on third spaces is significant: they are less about a "space in which new types of knowledges are generated and more a scaffold used to move students through zones of proximal development toward better honed academic or school knowledges" (as cited in Moje et al., 2004, p. 43). Viewed this way, such third spaces also provide preservice teachers with scaffolds to move them through zones of proximal development toward sharpened methods of teaching.

SERVICE LEARNING

Of particular relevance to third space theory is service learning. Although outwardly similar to what preservice teachers experience during their internships, service learning is a different enterprise. In traditional field experiences, the primary beneficiary is the preservice teacher who learns to hone his or her craft; in contrast, service learning seeks to create equal partnerships between the servicer and the serviced so that groups benefit equally.

Some researchers advocate for service learning as a way for preservice teachers to become more culturally aware; it creates the potential for preservice teachers to develop a better understanding of their local community's culture and context (Boyle-Baise, 2005; Murell, 2001), including its assets and needs. For preservice teachers whose backgrounds differ from their students', service learning compels them to "critique assumptions they bring to the encounter and to respect the different virtues and assets" of the students with whom they work (Jay, 2008, p. 257).

In their study of preservice English education students, Hallman and Burdick (2011) found that incorporating service learning created a pedagogical third space, disrupted the notion of teacher as authority figure, and promoted respect for students' out-of-school literacies. Jay (2008) adds that service learning can bring issues surrounding race, multiculturalism, and social justice to the forefront. Thus, service learning can be a method for preservice teachers to learn and practice critical teaching practices, transform existing practices, scrutinize power differentials and social inequities, and take social action (for example, Bruce & Brown, 2010).

SETTING UP THE SUMMER SERVICE LEARNING PROGRAM

Based off summer programming that originated at Johns Hopkins University, with support from the author's department, college, and the Center for Ethics & Social Responsibility at the University of Alabama, the author created the Tuscaloosa Academic Enrichment Program (TAEP) in 2007 with two equally important goals in mind: 1) to provide academic and cultural enrichment for students placed at risk in order to reduce their summer learning loss, and 2) to give preservice teachers an opportunity to learn to teach outside of the traditional field placement (with its checklists, evaluation forms, and already-established structures).

Since the first year of the program—in which preservice teachers alternated time working with adolescents using varied young adult (YA) novels—the program became more organized. From 2008 to 2010, the high school students were bussed to campus and the program was held in the College of Education. Outside sources of funding were secured to provide breakfast and lunch, and the author worked with local high school teachers to identify quality YA novels to assign for summer reading.

Creating a summer reading program like this one is not hard, nor is it expensive; it just takes collaboration and coordination between/among stakeholders. Here are some points to consider when planning a summer (or any other) service learning initiative.

Location

After the first year, the author felt it was imperative that the program be held on the university campus. The students needed to be away from their high school, where they had spent the past nine months. The university would be a "new" place where they could try on new identities. Working with her department chair, the author reserved classrooms that would be used for the duration of the program.

The university also offers countless places to visit and activities to engage in—libraries, science labs, art galleries, recreation facilities, dance studios, etc. By working with colleagues across campus, the author set up a range of free things for the students to do. Moreover, with a campus bus system, everyone was able to get across campus quickly and easily in the summer heat.

Funding

It is not very expensive to run a summer program (the author's program ran each summer for less than $10,000). However, one of the greatest barriers to holding the program on the university campus was transportation for the high school students because they most often could not get family members to bring them. In addition, the city bus system was not accessible to most students.

Thus, the biggest expense was transportation. A school district bus was chartered, which required hiring a bus driver, paying him or her by the hour, and paying for gas (this can cost between $3,500 and $7,000, depending on the length of the program and the routes the bus has to take). One summer the program ran concurrent with the school system's Title 1 program, and buses were shared with elementary students, which cut down the cost.

To fund the program, the author worked with various non-profit groups who were interested in youth development. Because of their non-profit status, funding from sources (such as Dollar General) could be awarded that the university could not have applied for. Collaborating with the school district was also beneficial. At times it secured state or federal funding for summer initiatives, and the program could piggyback off them (for example, the breakfasts and lunches were part of a nutrition program). In addition, the university's service learning office provided the administrative support necessary to schedule everything.

When she moved to another university, with the support of her dean, the author was able to tap into an endowment fund that focuses on literacy education efforts. By working with the college endowment office, additional sources of funding were also identified.

Scheduling

One of the reasons why the program was successful, both for the students and the preservice teachers, is because the service learning (that is, teaching) was scheduled within the course meeting time. Preservice teachers' free time is very limited. With a full-time course load and the demands of their field experience hours, it is hard to ask them (and for them to schedule) to complete additional service learning hours. Moreover, many students work, which also cuts down on their availability.

The YA literature class met Monday through Thursday from 8:30 a.m. to 11:00 a.m., so that the author had one week to work with the teachers before the students came for the program. Once the program started, the teachers rotated between class days (MW) and teaching days (TR). This worked well because the teaching (service learning) was embedded within the course and, more importantly, this schedule provided the preservice teachers with time to learn the material and also plan, teach, and debrief together.

Table 6.1 presents an example of the 2009 course schedule. While the students were having breakfast in one room, the YA class was able to plan in another. On days that the YA class met, the high school students were taking part in other campus-based activities—critical thinking instruction, math instruction, creative writing, dance lessons, etc. (figure 6.1 shows how the 2012 schedule was modified based on a course that met four days per week).

Teaching

As the schedule from 2009 shows, during the first week of the course, the author worked with the preservice teachers as they read and discussed *Sold* and *Copper Sun* (the students' required summer reading) and several other young adult novels. Integral was incorporating critical literacy and literary theories in our discussion of the novels; the teachers were given time to come up with discussion questions that centered on both so that they could use this type of talk and language with the students. [2]

The goals of the program (to learn and have fun at the same time) were also discussed. The author told the teachers that they were in charge of instruction, and it was critical that they understood that their work with the summer program was not like another required field experience. The author was there, rotating between classrooms, to assist, mentor, and answer questions, but it was up to them to plan and teach. This would be an opportunity for them to hone their craft without formal grades and evaluations of their teaching.

Each year, the preservice teachers decided how they wanted to group themselves. In 2009, for example, they divided themselves into two groups, with eleven teaching *Sold* to seventeen ninth-graders and five teaching *Copper Sun* to seven tenth-graders in order to keep the teacher-to-student ratio low. In 2010, the teachers divided into three groups; four taught *Black and White* to seven tenth-graders, nine taught *Ties That Bind* to fourteen ninth-graders, and three taught *Keesha's House* to the whole group (based on past summers, we wanted a novel to bring the two groups of students together, so *Keesha's House* was chosen, even though it was not required summer reading). [3]

"Research" and Service Learning

Over the years of this program, a few colleagues asked about how "service" can count toward tenure and promotion. Without a doubt, this type of summer service learning program (and service learning initiatives that others lead) can lead to formal research and scholarly publications. [4]

Table 6.1.   2009 YA Literature Course Schedule

Date	Topic	Readings/Assignment(s)
6/1	Course introduction; meeting readers where they are; reading influences; what is YA literature?; textual lineages; working with TAEP	*Sold; Copper Sun*
6/2	Four resource model; critical literacy; planning for TAEP ("hooking" students; building background knowledge; during reading strategies)	*Sold; Copper Sun*
6/3	Literary theories (reader response, feminist, Marxist, black feminist, cultural studies); planning for TAEP (ways to respond to reading)	*Sold; Copper Sun*
6/4	Classic and YA connections; planning for TAEP	*Mr. Pip; Little Brother*
6/8	Planning for TAEP	Reflection #1
6/9	TAEP (9–10:15); debrief	Materials and lessons for TAEP (TBD)
6/10	Plan and debrief	
6/11	TAEP (9–10:15); debrief	
6/15	Discuss and respond to novels using 4R, Critical Literacy, and applicable theories	*Monster; Looking for JJ;* Reflection #2
6/16	TAEP (9–10:15); debrief	
6/17	Discuss and respond to novels using 4R, Critical Literacy, and applicable theories	*Ten Mile Island*
6/18	TAEP (9–10:15); debrief	*Black and White*
6/22	Discuss and respond to novels using 4R, Critical Literacy, and applicable theories	*Evolution, Me, and Other Freaks of Nature;* Reflection #3; YA Interview
6/23	TAEP (9–10:15); debrief	*Before I Die*
6/24	Discuss and respond to novels using 4R, Critical Literacy, and applicable theories	*What I Saw and How I Lied or The Disreputable History of Frankie Landau-Banks*
6/25	TAEP (9–10:15); debrief	*The Absolutely True Diary of a Part-Time Indian*
6/29	Discuss and respond to novels using 4R, Critical Literacy, and applicable theories	*I Am the Messenger; The Hunger Games;* Reflection #4
6/30	Discuss and respond to novels using 4R, Critical Literacy, and applicable theories	*Laika or Pride of Baghdad;* Individual Project—Rough Draft
7/1	Final Exam and Project (draft) Presentations	Final Exam and Project (draft)

Monday	Tuesday	Wednesday	Thursday
		6 8:30-9:00 breakfast, welcome, and program overview 9:00-9:30 Introductions and get to know you activity in groups 9:30-9:40 break 9:40-10:20 baseline assessments 10:20 leave Stone for University Center B for campus tour 10:30-12:00 campus tour and snack	7 8:30-9:00 breakfast and independent reading 9:00-9:30 reading instruction 9:30-9:40 break 9:40-10:20 break out groups 10:20 leave COE for Bobby Bowden statue for stadium tour 10:30-12:00 stadium, athletic facilities tour, and snack
11 8:30-9:00 breakfast and independent reading 9:00-9:30 reading instruction 9:30-9:40 break 9:40-10:20 break out groups 10:20 leave COE for ISSM (at track) 10:30-12:00 campus activity and snack	12 8:30-9:00 breakfast and independent reading 9:00-9:30 reading instruction 9:30-9:40 break 9:40-10:20 break out groups 10:20 leave COE for physics building (108 Richards Bldg) 10:30-12:00 stars video, solar observation, and snack	13 8:30-9:00 breakfast and independent reading 9:00-9:30 reading instruction 9:30-9:40 break 9:40-10:10 break out groups 10:10 leave COE for music school 10:25-12:00 visit jazz recital and choral performance and snack 12:00 BESS THE BOOK BUS!!!	14 8:30-9:00 breakfast and independent reading 9:00-9:30 reading instruction 9:30-9:40 break 9:40-10:20 break out groups 10:20 Break 10:30-12:00 CROP activity and snack
18 8:30-9:00 breakfast and independent reading 9:00-9:30 reading instruction 9:30-9:40 break 9:40-10:20 break out groups 10:20 leave COE for College of Medicine 10:30-12:00 College of Medicine tour and information session	19 8:30-9:00 breakfast and independent reading 9:00-9:30 reading instruction 9:30-9:40 break 9:40-10:20 break out groups 10:30-12:00 Campus Tour	20 8:30-9:00 breakfast and independent reading 9:00-9:30 reading instruction 9:30-9:40 break 9:40-10:20 break out groups 10:30-12:00 Thank you notes	21 8:30-9:00 breakfast and independent reading 9:00-9:30 reading instruction 9:30-10:00 post assessments 10:00-12:00 awards & lunch with family/friends/mentors (Stone Bldg)

Figure 6.1.   TAEP June 2012 Calendar

In order to further and improve the program, and continue scholarly efforts, numerous forms of data were collected. The preservice teachers used video and audio recorders to record all planning, teaching, and debriefing sessions. Graduate research assistants aided in the typing of transcripts to analyze. The planning and debriefing sessions were recorded in order to capture how the teachers negotiated, discussed, and reflected on their teaching. Teaching sessions were recorded to study how instruction was carried out, including looking at teacher-to-student talk and teacher-to-teacher talk.

The students and preservice teachers completed program evaluation surveys, and all artifacts (for example, handouts, student-created documents) were collected and/or photocopied. Weekly written reflections from the pre-service teachers, as well as a final project/portfolio regarding their experience, were additional data.

HOW THE SERVICE LEARNING
EXPERIENCE TRANSFORMED TEACHERS

How did participating in the summer program, and service learning, positively impact the preservice teachers? In the sections that follow—through excerpts from the preservice teachers' reflections—one can see that the impact of service learning and the pedagogical third space afforded by the summer program served as change agents for the preservice teachers.

In particular, transformations in the teachers' beliefs and pedagogy are shown through the three perspectives of third spaces as summarized in the research (Barton, Tan, & Rivet, 2008; Moje et al., 2004): bridges between academic and out-of-school knowledge, places where boundary crossing occurs, and spaces where more equal dialectical relationships build new knowledge.

A Bridge between In- and Out-of-School Discourses

Barton, Tan, & Rivet (2008) note, "What one is able to do in a setting is dialectically related to what one can access and activate in that setting, and that includes an understanding of content or of rules for participation. It also includes the individuals who are present as well as the physical environment" (p. 75). Holding the summer reading program at the university provided a new setting—physically, pedagogically, and discursively—for everyone.

The teachers, dressed casually, offered a new model of "teacher" for the students. Being able to work collaboratively changed the rules for participation. This, in turn, positively impacted both groups. At first, the preservice teachers were concerned about students completing the summer reading, often using their own experiences as a reference. However, the preservice teachers soon found that setting can make a difference. Kim reflected,

> The students . . . actually said that they felt compelled to read this novel because it was in a laid back setting and because they did not feel they were being forced to read anything. The students commented that because in school they feel forced to read, they often do not do the assignments. This is something that I need to keep in mind when I become a teacher. I don't think it will be a bad idea to teach my students a novel in much the same way we did to the students in the TAEP program.

In-school literacy practices, according to Spooner and Yancey (1996), are tied to "identity formation" and can serve to limit and define students' identies. Moreover, school-based literacy is inherently tied to the broader political discourses that shape schooling (as cited in Yagelski, 2000). The preservice teachers found that the discourses in the summer created a very different identity for the students than the one they took on during the academic year. For example, after playing a relay question game in which the students beat "the teachers" on their knowledge of the book, Courtney wrote,

> The highlight of the day was when a student said that school would be easier and that she would remember more information, if fun games like the one we played, were played in an actual school/classroom setting. They actually said that they liked the reading class the best and were now enjoying reading. The students said that the program made them feel like it was their choice to read. They did not feel forced into doing work, which made them want to do work.

Jennifer echoed Courtney's comments, stating, "The students got to ask the teachers the questions. I think they liked that, because we let them be the leaders for once. I could tell that they rarely ever get opportunities like that in school."

Boundary Crossing

In the same way that third spaces provide data on in-school learning and processes for students (Barton, Tan, & Rivet, 2008), they also shed light on learning how to teach and how to dialogue with students rather than at students. Part of this stems from their own experience as students; part of it comes from a fear of students or things getting out of control. In traditional classrooms, explicit and implicit boundaries are oftentimes marked—teachers are in control at the front of the room dispensing knowledge. In some classrooms, masking tape marks a no-contact zone around the teacher's desk.

But the space offered by the summer program created possibilities for fluidity in the teachers where they could be teacher/mentor/advisor at the same time. Sam reflected on this:

> Adam and I took the guys and Jess and Brenda took the girls. I'm not sure what Jess and Brenda did, but Adam and I let the guys choose a character they wanted each of us to be. The two boys we had already read the book, so we got to have an interesting conversation. Adam pretended to be Marcus' mother and I pretended to be Coach Casey. The questions the guys asked were really good. At one point, I forgot I was pretending to be Coach Casey and answered a question as myself, when I realized it, I let the boys know, and answered it as Coach Casey. It was a slip, but it's okay because it let the boys know a little bit more about me. I think they probably appreciated that. I wasn't just some college kid talking to them about a book; I was someone sharing with them. That was pretty cool.

A collaborative space like TAEP also creates a third space for preservice teachers in terms of room to experiment. Missing are formal assessments. Also missing are formal student teacher evaluations—another set of boundaries in teacher education programs—with checklists and rubrics. In an era of increased standardization and accountability, this autonomy is critical in order for novice teachers to resist hegemonic teaching practices. "Third spaces become more like the contexts in which real practitioners engage with problems and create knowledge to overcome the weakest features of traditional schooling, like recitation and rote learning" (Wilhelm, 2010, p. 57).

A Space to Move between Different Discourse Communities

The most important aspect of the third space is that it has the potential to promote positive change for all who are involved. In order for this to happen, teachers need to re-envision what the classroom and classroom discourse looks and sounds like. Teachers are key to constructing spaces where students can have access to and take part in a wide range of discourse and discourse communities.

The goals for the summer program were that students would have the opportunity to read and discuss their required summer reading in a relaxed setting. Equally important was that the teachers could use the space to help them grow as educators, learning how to not perform the dominant, traditional teacher discourse. In such third spaces "teachers' structural and pedagogical choices allow them to share authority with their students . . . and where students can feel what they have to contribute matters and is of value" (Barton, Tan, & Rivet, 2008, p. 98).

However, that is not to say there were no doubts about a teaching experience markedly different from the typical field placement. Katie reflected, "At first, I was skeptical when our two groups were not given any . . . limitations or instructions on how to teach . . . but were told rather that this was a chance to try anything we wanted." Other teachers had their assumptions about the take-for-granted discourse(s) regarding students challenged. Ricci, an adult returning to school to earn her English education degree, commented,

> What has been a surprise is that once I was able to look beyond my own selfish concerns, there are some kids who seem to want to be there. I'm not sure exactly what I was expecting, but I think it was something in the vicinity of a lot of kids sighing and groaning over reading and talking about a book. Perhaps I was just preparing for the worst. However, that first day there was one girl in my group, Mira, who was engaged, answering questions, *asking* questions, and genuinely interested in what was going on. This is the same one who told you she went home and looked up feet binding herself on her computer because she wanted to learn more. What has bonked me over the head is that

this isn't really about me teaching, it's about them reading and learning. I'm embarrassed to say I underestimated these students.

Jennifer summed up well how taking part in different discourse communities was critical for the teachers and the students.

We can all tell how much the students are enjoying this experience. Sometimes I wonder if the kids are having more fun or the teachers. I have had the best experience doing this. I feel like my students that I am working with are getting comfortable with me and can talk to me as a mentor. We have legitimate discussions of the issues in the book and relate the issues to the lives we lead.

FINAL THOUGHTS

Given the rather monolithic nature of the teaching force and the growing diversity of students, it is imperative that we identify and create opportunities for preservice teachers to confront and overcome assumptions, learn about themselves as teachers and human beings, and hone their pedagogical skills. This means moving both beyond and reimagining traditional field placements and student teaching assignments. Data suggest that the summer offers a wide range of possibilities for accomplishing this.

First, the experience of teaching in a third space impacted the preservice teachers' deficit thinking about the students. Because the students in the summer program came from a school that was often assumed to be and/or called "the worst" by many in the community, some preservice teachers' initial reactions about teaching "those kids" seemed informed by these characterizations. However, by the end of the first teaching session, those feelings quickly changed.

Teaching in a third space also changed the teachers' beliefs about how to teach. Most had been used to "doing school" (that is, sitting in rows, working quietly and alone). However, by working with adolescents in a new kind of space and setting, they realized that teaching could be "flexible," becoming "more inclusive and . . . more just" (Kirkland, 2009, p. 12). Benson (2010) claims that constructing a third space alters classroom dynamics, "positioning students and teachers as colearners and coteachers" (p. 562).

This has major implications for the students not only in our English education program, but also other programs. Most of us live and work in communities in which there are "struggling" schools or schools (and their students) that are perpetually labeled as "bad." Through service learning preservice teachers learn to "critique assumptions they bring to the encounter and to respect the different virtues and assets" of students (Jay, 2008, p. 257). This will make them better teachers of the students with whom they will work during their formal field experiences and, hopefully, later as classroom teachers.

Jessica's final reflection gets to the heart of the change that is possible. She went from being fearful and nervous to confident. More importantly, she now wanted to continue to work with students from Steel Town:

> I feel like I've learned so much, and I just hope the students have learned half as much from me as I've learned from them. I can't wait to get them to fill out the anticipation guide again so that we can see if their attitudes have shifted in the ways we thought they might have after reading the book with us. I believe in the power of this book in particular to change the way they see the world, and I hope we've done it justice in our treatment of it so that the kids will really get something out of it. I find myself hoping I'll do some of my hours at Steel Town HS so that I can see how some of the kids are doing as they adjust to high school. I knew I would care about my students, but I don't think I really anticipated how much of my thoughts would be taken up by them. I can only imagine how much more attached I'll get when I have a full semester or year to spend with them. Now I really understand why my high school teachers are so excited to hear from me and see me when I go back for visits. I'm looking forward to future visits from my high school kids one of these days!

Seen in this way, a collaborative space that brings together teenage students and preservice teachers during the summer where assessment, evaluation, standardization, and a mandated curriculum are absent creates a third space for learning, a space that also offers opportunities for preservice teachers and students to take on new roles and identities and (re)frame their thinking about literacy instruction.

NOTES

1. The material for this chapter was collected while the author was on faculty at the University of Alabama, and this chapter was written while she was a faculty member at Florida State University.

2. The novels were the high school students' required summer readings, and they would have a 50- to 100-question test when they returned to school in the fall. Moreover, this test would be their first grade of the year. Although preparing students to do well on this test was on their minds, the author told the preservice teachers that reading the novel, having authentic discussions, and using literary theory(ies) and critical literacy were more important goals.

3. Working with one high school makes the summer program run more easily. Although the author does not like to leave other schools out, without the staff and funding it is too hard to work with several schools. In addition, each high school has its own summer reading list. Thus, working with several schools would prohibit the low teacher-to-student ratio that the program has. The author made a conscious effort to collaborate with high schools that are in the most need.

4. There are several peer-reviewed journals that focus on service learning. In addition, at the time of writing, Valerie Kinloch hosted a service learning conference at Ohio State University. The author and her students have also presented their work at conferences and in journals.

REFERENCES

Barton, A. C., Tan, E., & Rivet, A. (2008). Creating hybrid spaces for engaging school science among urban middle school girls. *American Educational Research Journal, 45* (1), 68–103.

Benson, S. (2010). "I don't know if that'd be English or not": Third space theory and literacy instruction. *Journal of Adolescent & Adult Literacy, 53* (7), 555–63.

Bhabba, H. (1990). The third space. In J. Rutherford (Ed.), *Identity, community, culture and difference* (pp. 207–21). London: Lawrence and Wishart.

Bhabba, H. K. (1994). *The location of culture.* New York, N.Y.: Routledge.

Boyle-Baise, M. (2005). Preparing community-oriented teachers: Reflections from a multicultural service-learning project. *Journal of Teacher Education, 56* (5), 446–58.

Bruce, J., & Brown, S. (2010). Conceptualising service-learning in global times. *Critical Literacy: Theories and Practices, 4* (1), 6–14.

Darling-Hammond, L. (2006). *Powerful teacher education: Lessons from exemplary programs.* San Francisco, Calif.: Jossey-Bass.

Draper, S. (2008). *Copper sun.* New York, N.Y.: Atheneum.

Frost, H. (2003). *Keesha's house.* New York, N.Y.: Farrar, Straus and Giroux.

Gutierrez, K. D., Baquedano-Lopez, P., Alvarez, H., & Chiu, M. M. (1999). Building a culture of collaboration through hybrid language practices. *Theory Into Practice, 3* (8), 87–93.

Gutierrez, K., Rymes, B., & Larson, J. (1995). Script, counterscript, and underlife in the classroom: James Brown versus Brown v. Board of Education. *Harvard Educational Review, 65* (3), 445–71.

Hallman, H. L., & Burdick, M. N. (2011). Service learning and the preparation of English teachers. *English Education, 43* (4), 341–68.

Jay, G. (2008). Service learning, multiculturalism, and the pedagogies of difference. *Pedagogy: Critical Approaches to Teaching Literature, Language, Composition, and Culture, 8,* 255–81.

Kirkland, D. E. (2009). Researching and teaching English in the digital dimension. *Research in the Teaching of English, 44* (1), 8–22.

McCormick, P. (2006). *Sold.* New York, N.Y.: Hyperion.

Moje, E. B., Ciechanowki, K. M., Kramer, K., Ellis, L., Carrillo, R., & Collazo, T. (2004). Working toward third space in content area literacy: An examination of everyday funds of knowledge and Discourse. *Reading Research Quarterly, 39* (1), 38–70.

Morrell, E., Scherff, L., Miller, s., Groenke, S., & Laughter, J. (2012, April). Literacy in the 21st Century: Re-envisioning Teaching and Research. Symposium at the annual meeting of the American Educational Research Association (AERA), Vancouver, B.C., Canada.

Murell, P. (2001). *The community teacher: A new framework for effective urban teaching.* New York, N.Y.: Teachers College Press.

Namioka, L. (1999). *Ties that bind, ties that break.* New York, N.Y.: Delcaorte.

Soja, E. W. (1996). *Thirdspace: Journeys to Los Angeles and other real-and-imagined places.* Malden, Mass.: Blackwell.

Spooner, M., & Yancey, K. (1996). Postings on a genre of email. *College Composition and Communication, 47,* 252–78.

Volponi, P. (2006). *Black and white.* New York, N.Y.: Speak Books.

Wilhelm, J. D. (2010). Creating "third spaces": Promoting learning through dialogue. *Voices From the Middle, 18* (2), 55–58.

Yagelski, R. P. (2000). *Literacy matters.* New York, N.Y.: Teachers College Press.

Zeichner, K. (2010). Rethinking the connections between campus courses and field experiences in college- and university-based teacher education. *Journal of Teacher Education, 61* (1–2), 89–99.

Chapter Seven

English Teacher Education for Rural Social Spaces

Leslie S. Rush

As an English teacher educator coming to the University of Wyoming in 2002, fresh out of a doctoral program in literacy education, it became abundantly clear early both the privilege and burden of carrying a singular role in the state of Wyoming. The University of Wyoming is the only four-year institution of higher education in the Equality State, and it also offers the only English teacher certification program in the state. Because of this unique situation, the author is the only English teacher education faculty member in the state of Wyoming, although she is a colleague to many outstanding English faculty members and literacy education faculty members as well.

At the University of Wyoming, responsibilities for the sole English educator include: teaching English methods and young adult literature courses, supervising English student teachers, collecting data for and writing accreditation reports on the English education program, and advising English education majors, as well as teaching master's- and doctoral-level courses in literacy education. Other colleagues in the Department of Secondary Education are also the single teacher educators in their own disciplines: agriculture, art, mathematics, modern languages, science, social studies, and technical education.

This is—to say the least—a unique situation, but one that is perhaps perfectly suited to the rural nature of the state of Wyoming. Like many other rural areas, with low population density and long distances between towns, Wyoming is both a pleasure and a challenge to those who have come from outside the state to make it their home. One popular saying is *Wyoming is really just a small town, one with really long streets.*

In ten years of working with English education majors at the University of Wyoming, the truth of this saying has become very apparent. It is the nature of the rural setting—its population density, its communities, and its geography—that offers unique challenges and some interesting affordances.

This chapter provides a discussion of what *rural* means, and presents information about the state of Wyoming and the challenges its rural nature presents for English teacher education. It then offers some recommendations for English teacher educators in rural settings, always acknowledging that each rural setting presents its own constellation of the challenges and affordances of rural education.

WHAT DOES RURAL MEAN, ANYWAY?

The U.S. Census Bureau defines rural areas based on their low population or their distance from urban centers (U.S. Census Bureau, 2010b). Simply because they are not urban, they are rural. Other than population density, however, what does *rural* mean? The term *rural* is often used to indicate that something is lacking: the number of people, opportunities, quality education—all of these are considered by some to be deficit in rural areas. As Reid et al. (2010) describe it, however, this deficit perspective on rural settings does not come close to the potential complexity of rural social space:

> We argue . . . that rural social space is richly complex and contradictory—and that many rural communities are characterised by extremes of wealth, age, health, and capacity, as well as by racial and cultural diversity. They are not all the same, and they are not all difficult to staff or work in. Moving beyond the stereotypes symbolically evoked in descriptions of the rural "problem" in education is essential for sustaining and enhancing the diversity of rural communities. (p. 267)

Instead of operating on commonly held, deficit perspectives of rurality, Reid et al. define *rural* using a variety of measures: population density statistics as described by census takers; geographic descriptors, which make clear that rurality occurs in particular regions or places; and cultural descriptors, which address how rural people interact in communities.

Conceptualizing rurality as inclusive of a consideration of not only population numbers or density, but also encompassing geographic settings and cultural markers, makes a reconceptualization of the preparation of English teachers for rural settings possible. When we imagine what it means to prepare preservice English teachers in Wyoming—many of whom come from rural settings themselves—the notion of rural social space makes it possible to take into consideration the preservice teachers' backgrounds, their potential long-term professional considerations, and their awareness—or lack of awareness—of what rural teaching entails.

Other aspects of rurality that bear importance for this discussion are described in the literature around rural education. These include the notion of education for sustainability (White et al., 2011) and the role of rural literacies in ensuring sustainability through education for democratic citizenship in rural spaces (Donehower, Hogg, & Schell, 2007).

The idea of *sustainability* is one that is often used in terms of the ecology, to describe how systems can maintain diversity and productivity over time. Scholars who investigate rural education, however, think of sustainability in rural settings as a critical link among rural schools, rural school leadership, and community renewal. In this perspective on rural education, community sustainability is made possible by partnerships between schools and universities through ensuring an educated rural workforce (White et al., 2011).

In addition, the development of critical literacy for democratic citizenship is a crucial part of influencing community policies and practices (Donehower, Hogg, & Schell, 2007). By participating in the development of rural literacies as preservice and inservice teachers and as teacher educators, we are contributing to the development of a shared social space in which "a critical, public pedagogy interrogates constructions and representations of rural people and life" (Donehower, Hogg, & Schell, 2007, p. 9).

Thus, the interpretation of *rural* for this chapter considers not only the population density of Wyoming, but also ways in which preservice English teachers can be part of ensuring the sustainability, the critical literacy, and the ongoing economies of the communities in which they will work. This way of thinking about rurality eschews a deficit perspective and honors the ways of life and the history of these communities, while imagining a future for them that is both thoughtful and critical.

WYOMING AS A RURAL SOCIAL SPACE

This section presents information about the state of Wyoming, describing it as a rural social space in terms of its population and population density, diversity, and the impact of distance on our English teacher education program. In spite of the way in which Wyoming personifies the deficit perspective commonly held about rural settings, there are also some aspects of Wyoming that shed light on rurality, particularly in consideration of educational sustainability and critical literacy.

The 2010 U.S. Census describes urbanized areas (based on census tracts) as those with 50,000 or more people and urban clusters as those having between 2,500 and 50,000 people; rural areas are "all population, housing, and territory not included within an urban area" (2010b). In 2010, Wyoming's population density was the lowest of any state, with approximately 5.8 people on average per square mile (U.S. Census Bureau, 2010a). This means that it is probably true—as commonly stated by Wyomingites—that Wyoming has more antelope than people.

Wyoming spends approximately $15,000 per student annually on education (U.S. Department of Commerce, 2012), which means it ranks sixth in the nation on per capita education spending. However, the percentage of Wyoming's 2011 high school graduates who were prepared for college-level work is lower than the national average in composition, algebra, social science, and biology, according to the ACT (2011). The impact of this statistic, however, might be mitigated by an acknowledgment that the ACT is required for all high school juniors, unlike other states where only college-bound students take the ACT.

Relative to the rest of the United States, Wyoming ranks forty-fourth in cultural diversity (Beyond Diversity Resource Center, 2005). The percentage of individuals below the poverty level in Wyoming is 9.4 percent (U.S. Census Bureau, 2012), which means that the state ranks forty-fourth among others in the United States in percentage of population living in poverty.

It is apparent, from the information cited above, that Wyoming could be seen as a rural state, with the concomitant problems related to distance, lack of urban population centers, lack of diversity, and educational problems. Instead of viewing Wyoming's low population density as a deficit, however, this author troubles that deficit perspective by proposing that Wyoming is an ideal site for public education reform.

As noted, the state of Wyoming has a relatively low percentage of citizens living below the poverty line, and the state's investment in education per student is quite high. In keeping with the notion of the importance for rural education of educational sustainability (White et al., 2010), the small population makes it possible for us to work together to improve the education available to all children in the state with an ease that would not be present if the population were larger.

For example, the Wyoming School-University Partnership (WSUP) (www.uwyo.edu/wsup/index.html) was established to bring together instructors from K–12 schools, community colleges, and the university, with a specific focus on improving public education so that Wyoming communities will be improved. The focus of the WSUP on renewal among all school faculty and on the development of stronger communities makes it a perfect fit for an understanding of the work of rural educators for community development and for community sustainability.

This partnership has been quite active in bringing together community college and university professors with high school teachers in the life sciences, mathematics, English, social studies, and the modern and classical languages to focus on how to make the transition from high school to college less bumpy for Wyoming high school students.

Perhaps because of the relatively small number of individuals and institutions involved, this collaboration has brought about some much-needed awareness among high school and college instructors, as well as policy changes and instructional revisions. For example, the University of Wyoming's life science courses—with a long history of high student failure rates—were recently remodeled to include an inquiry focus, based in part on the collaborative work through WSUP that has taken place over the last few years.

Perhaps because the number of individuals and institutions involved is so small, a program such as that put in place by the Wyoming School-University Partnership has potential to effect change in a way that would not be so far reaching in a more densely populated state. As a result, there is great potential for improving the education of our rural workforce and for subsequently improving the communities in which those citizens live.

PREPARING PRESERVICE ENGLISH TEACHERS IN AND FOR RURAL SETTINGS

What does it mean to prepare preservice English teachers to teach in rural settings in the early part of the twenty-first century? This chapter next focuses on recommendations that are both practical and pedagogical in nature, drawn from personal experience as an English teacher educator in Wyoming and from relevant research on teacher education for rural settings.

Tie Instruction to the Rural Setting

Perhaps the most important recommendation is to help preservice English teachers gain a sense of the importance of culturally relevant pedagogy for rural settings. In order to do this, teacher educators must not only provide preservice teachers with tools for planning and carrying out English language arts instruction, but must also ensure that opportunities are provided for preservice teachers to get to know rural communities and rural people and to match their instructional texts and tools to the needs of those rural communities.

Imler (2009) suggests that preservice teachers must be given the tools to respond to the needs of all students and to connect pedagogy with students' families, ethnicities, native languages, and cultural norms. This means that preservice English teachers must be able to step outside their own traditions and see where disconnects are happening with their rural students.

Much like teachers in urban areas, rural preservice and inservice English teachers must be able to connect students to texts that will engage and interest them; to provide writing experiences that are authentic and compelling; and to give students opportunities to work together in creative ways to make meaning with both the texts they read and those they write.

Perhaps one way to ensure that instructional choices for English language arts classrooms in rural settings are more closely tied to students' rural backgrounds is to offer a place-based pedagogy (White, 2008). Such pedagogies foreground the local, allowing teachers to structure curriculum around what is known in the local surrounding.

One example of this work in Wyoming is Deb Bass's (2007) development of a Wyoming-based curriculum that focuses on the literature of the Rocky Mountain West. Using a combination of local fiction and non-fiction, Bass's curriculum encourages students to ask questions such as:

> Why did migrants come to mining towns?
> What motivated people to become sheepherders, cowboys, and ranchers?
> How can someone who is not from an area come to know (and write) about it?
> What gets lost between an insider's view and an outsider's view? (p. 14)

Bass's curriculum fuses literature study with outdoor experiences and journaling. Students read excerpts from three anthologies of western writers:

- *The Roadless Yaak: Reflections and Observations about One of Our Last Great Wild Places* (Bass, R., 2007)
- *The Landscape of Home: A Rocky Mountain Land Series Reader* (Lee, Calderazzo, & Campbell, 2006)
- *Deep West: A Literary Anthology* (Shay, Romtvedt, & Rounds, 2003)

Students also experience a range of outdoor settings for their literary study, including writing in their journals outside on the school campus, field trips to community green spaces, and chaperoned camping trips. By connecting local literature with local places, Bass suggests that students will engage more deeply in questions about the human condition that literature is uniquely framed to address.

White (2008) suggests that "as teachers come to know, and know about, a particular rural place, and come to understand its relationships to, and with other places, they are developing knowledge, sensitivities, awareness, skills, attitudes, and abilities that will allow them to feel more at home and more powerful in a rural setting" (p. 6). The kind of place-based English curricula that Deb Bass (2007) and White (2008) advocate has potential to not only engage students in understanding their localities with a deeper sense of the culture and literature tied to them, but also to engage students in the kind of critical literacies that are needed for the continued development of critical citizenry in rural spaces.

Recognize the Importance of Connections and Relationships

In order to be prepared to teach English in a rural setting, preservice teachers need to understand the importance of connections and relationships within rural communities. According to Burton and Johnson (2010),

> To teach effectively in a rural community, preservice and novice teachers must not only see themselves as individuals who want to teach in rural communities but also be given opportunities for building relationships with the surrounding community in addition to connecting with students in the classroom. In this way, preservice and novice teachers develop a consciousness of the significance of place and community for their teaching. (p. 377)

Building relationships with rural communities can happen in a variety of ways, including service learning experiences (Burton & Johnson, 2010), university-school partnerships (Pennefather, 2008), and other types of exchanges. Much as researchers in multicultural teacher education have encouraged preservice teachers to become students of the communities in which they will teach (Cochran-Smith, Davis, & Fries, 2004), evidence exists that inquiry into local/rural communities can bear fruit for teacher preparation programs (Wenger & Dinsmore, 2005).

This inquiry work into the student teaching community can certainly be made complicated by the distances sometimes involved in travel between the university community and that of the rural student teaching placement. However, inroads into this connection aspect can be made by requiring preservice English teachers in the methods class to collect information about the school, the community, and the students in their prospective student teaching classrooms.

The author asks students to take at least one day from their methods semester coursework to visit the community and the classroom in which they will be student teaching. Occasionally such a visit is not possible because of the distances involved between the university town and the student teaching classroom, which can range from twenty minutes to six hours of travel time. In these cases, students are encouraged to make these connections through a variety of distance technologies, including Skype, compressed video, and—at the very least—email.

Preservice English teachers in our teacher education program are encouraged to develop a clear understanding of not only the classrooms and schools in which they will be working, but also the community in which the school is located. Some options that they are given, in order to gain this clearer understanding, include an interview with a student or teacher, an exploration of the history of a community issue through analysis of newspaper articles and interviews with community members, or other projects that illustrate community norms and events.

During their student teaching experiences, English student teachers are required to submit lesson plans and to indicate how they used the information they gathered about the community—as well as the academic knowledge and prior experiences of their students—to choose texts and instructional techniques.

Encourage Both Collegiality and Independence

Rural teachers may find themselves in settings in which their opportunities for collegiality and collaboration are limited. English student teachers in our programs have been placed in K–12 schools where their mentor teacher is the only English teacher in the school, not to mention the county. Such rural teachers may have six different course preps, as they are teaching grades 7 through 12.

English teachers in rural settings often take on reading instruction as well, whether or not they are prepared for such work. They may be required or encouraged to take on responsibility for a plethora of extracurricular activities, including theater, school newspapers, and yearbook editing. Leadership may come early to the careers of English teachers in rural settings: they may be on the district curriculum development team or state committees for standards review.

On the other hand, some teachers in Wyoming are employed in larger towns or school districts, where they are part of teams of teachers who work together—in core subjects or in departments—on school and district data analysis, on curriculum development, and on school improvement plans.

In both of these cases, rural English teachers need to recognize the importance of both collegiality and independence. Rarely do rural English teachers manage to shut their doors and teach without being involved in the work of education in a larger setting. However, they also need to be prepared to work independently, because they may need to occupy a position of leadership early in their careers, without much mentoring or support.

As an English teacher educator who prepares beginning teachers for the realities of both small rural settings, where they must operate independently, and larger towns, where collegiality and collaboration is possible, it is necessary to prepare students to be capable in both settings. This requires engaging preservice English teachers in group work and independent work, as well as developing preservice English teachers' awareness of the need to develop competence in both settings.

To prepare preservice English teachers in the methods courses for both the need to work collegially and to be independent, multiple opportunities are provided for them to work in teams, while also having independent responsibility for their work. For example, in the writing methods course, preservice teachers participate in writing feedback groups in which they give and receive feedback on their personal writing and on their planning for writing instruction.

Although the participation in the writing feedback groups is part of the responsibility for the course, preservice English teachers ultimately take responsibility individually for the personal writing and for the instructional planning that they create in the course. Similarly, preservice English teachers who are moving into student teaching work collaboratively with their mentor teachers to plan units of instruction, but the preservice English teacher is ultimately responsible for the materials, assessments, and for the instruction itself.

This combination of group and individual responsibility is perhaps common in English teacher education programs; however, students are also asked to reflect on the skills and abilities they are developing through these projects, not only in pedagogical content knowledge, but also in the types of skills that will be needed in a variety of rural settings. In clarifying for students how these variations of collaborative and individual work relate to their potential experiences as first-year teachers in rural schools, students are given the opportunity to reflect on their strengths and weaknesses and to plan for how they might build on their strengths and remediate their weaknesses.

Enact Rural Literacies

One final recommendation is to help preservice English teachers see the significance of rural social space, the importance of sustainability within that space, and their role as educators for critical literacy and a democratic participation in that space. Rural English language arts teachers must become aware of the particular needs related to sustainability and to literacy as a practice of democratic citizenship in order to best meet the needs of rural communities.

As Reid et al. (2010) describe:

> The experience of rural life and teaching that is available to an eco-socially aware teacher—one with an ingrained (that is, learned) sense of rural places and people, their history and complexity, their problems and their potential, the activities and industry that exist in them and the particular issues of sustainability with which they are dealing—will be richer and more satisfying than that available to a teacher who does not have this awareness. These aspects of rural social space are all forms of knowledge on which teachers can capitalise. Our responsibility, as teacher educators and teacher education researchers, is to be effective as a force for rural-regional sustainability by providing preservice teachers with access to the professional and pedagogic capital that can successfully underwrite their investment in rural social space. (p. 268)

Many of the preservice English teachers are from Wyoming and thus have a sense of what *rural* means in their own experiences; what they often lack is an awareness of their role as an English teacher in furthering the sustainability of the rural communities in which they will work, and perhaps most importantly, their role as an English teacher in furthering a democratic population as part of that move toward sustainability. This is perhaps the most difficult of my recommendations to enact, because it is invariably political in nature.

Providing preservice English teachers in Wyoming with the pedagogical and professional capital described by Reid et al. (2010) involves working on an ongoing basis to bring preservice teachers' attention to the political movements—and moments—in the state that impact educators and students. In addition to providing preservice teachers with pedagogical theory, research, and tools, it is also important to help them to bring a critical eye to assessment regimes, funding sources, research projects, and how education is portrayed in state media.

Similar to the "current event" assignment that is popular in many junior high and high school social studies classes, assignments require preservice teachers to bring in newspaper articles, blogs, tweets, and other media sources related to education in Wyoming. We spend a few minutes during each class session attending to these sources and then stepping back to debrief about their potential sources and impacts, evaluating the perspective from which these sources come and the potential impact of those perspectives on schools, rural communities, and the people in those communities. It is my hope that this work serves to ground preservice English teachers with an understanding of the importance of their role as facilitators of democracy in process.

CONCLUSION

For those of us who live in and teach in rural settings, the "small town with really long streets" means that we have the opportunity and the responsibility to establish and maintain connections with teachers and school district personnel that play a vital role in the ongoing success and sustainability of our programs. Hopefully this chapter will spark renewed research, practice, and discussion of rural literacies and rural English teacher education.

REFERENCES

ACT. (2011). *ACT profile report—state: Graduating class 2011 Wyoming.* Retrieved from http://www.act.org/newsroom/data/2011/pdf/profile/Wyoming.pdf.

Bass, D. (2007). *Finding yourself in Wyoming: Place-based literature in the secondary classroom.* Laramie, Wyo.: University of Wyoming.

Bass, R. (Ed.) (2007). *The roadless Yaak: Reflections and observations about one of our last great wild places*. Guilford, Conn.: Lyons Press.

Beyond Diversity Resource Center. (2005). Mapping diversity in the United States. Retrieved from http://www.rightcode.net/development/beyonddiversity/article.html?id=1142537950 54397.

Burton, M., & Johnson, A. (2010). "Where else would we teach?" Portraits of two teachers in the rural south. *Journal of Teacher Education, 61*, 376–86.

Cochran-Smith, M., Davis, D., & Fries, K. (2004). Multicultural teacher education: Research, practice, and policy. In J. A. Banks & C. A. M. Banks (Eds.), *Handbook of research on multicultural education* (2nd ed., pp. 931–75). San Francisco, Calif.: Jossey-Bass.

Donehower, K., Hogg, C., & Schell, E. (2007). *Rural literacies*. Carbondale, Ill.: Southern Illinois University Press.

Imler, S. (2009). Becoming culturally responsive: A need for preservice teacher candidates. *Teacher Education & Practice, 22*, 351–67.

Lee, J., Calderazzo, J., & Campbell, S. (Eds.). (2006). *The landscape of home: A Rocky Mountain land series reader*. Boulder, Colo,: Johnson Books.

Pennefather, J. (2008). "Rural" schools and universities: The use of partnerships as a teaching strategy in enhancing a positive response to rurality. *Perspectives in Education, 26* (2), 81–94.

Reid, J., Green, B., Cooper, M., Hastings, W., & Lock, G. (2010). Regenerating rural social space? Teacher education for rural-regional sustainability. *Australian Journal of Education, 54*, 262–76.

Shay, M., Romtvedt, D., & Rounds, L. (Eds.). (2003). *Deep west: A literary anthology*. Cheyenne, Wyo.: Pronghorn Press.

U.S. Census Bureau. (2010a). *Resident population data*. Retrieved from http://2010.census.gov/2010census/data/apportionment-dens-text.php.

U.S. Census Bureau. (2010b). 2010 census urban and rural classification and urban area criteria. Retrieved from http://www.census.gov/geo/www/ua/2010urbanruralclass.html.

U.S. Census Bureau. (2012). *Statistical abstract of the United States: 2012*. Retrieved from http://www.census.gov/compendia/statab/2012/tables/12s0709.pdf.

U.S. Department of Commerce. (2012). *Public education finances: 2012*. Retrieved from http://www2.census.gov/govs/school/10f33pub.pdf.

Wenger, K., & Dinsmore, J. (2005). Preparing rural preservice teachers for diversity. *Journal of Research in Rural Education, 20* (10), 1–15.

White, S. (2008). Placing teachers? Sustaining rural schooling through place-consciousness in teacher education. *Journal of Research in Rural Education, 23* (7), 1–11.

White, S., Lock, G., Hastings, W., Cooper, M., Reid, J., & Green, B. (2011). Investing in sustainable and resilient rural social space: Lessons for teacher education. *Education in Rural Australia, 21* (1), 67–78.

Chapter Eight

Learning from Equity Audits

*Powerful Social Justice in English Education
for the Twenty-First Century*

sj Miller

This chapter prompts the field of English education to consider what preservice teachers can learn from using equity audits in their field placements to assess the absence and/or inclusion of social justice. This discussion also highlights what preservice teachers can come to understand and embody, or how their dispositions can be cultivated by equity audit findings. One key question guides this chapter: How can assignments with socially just foci cultivate critical preservice English teachers for *social justice* in the twenty-first century?

SOCIAL JUSTICE AND SOCIAL INJUSTICE

Miller and Kirkland (2010) provide a working definition of *social justice*, which suggests that when conducting or enacting social justice work and in order for it to be sustained, reflection, change, and participation are essential.

> Each student in our classrooms is entitled to the same opportunities of academic achievement regardless of background or acquired privilege. . . . Educators must teach about injustice and discrimination in all forms with regard to: race, ethnicity, language, gender, gender expression, age, appearance, ability, disability (author added), national origin, spiritual belief, weight (height and/or size), sexual orientation, socioeconomic circumstance, environment, ecology, culture, and the treatment of animals. (pp. xx–xxi)

Social justice cannot be examined without understanding social injustice. Social injustice is marked by how a student experiences pain or a microaggression, which is "the everyday verbal, nonverbal, and environmental slights, snubs or insults, whether intentional or unintentional, that communicate hostility, derogatory, or negative messages to target persons based solely upon their marginalized group membership" (Sue, 2010, p. 3) and that are typically categorized by social, emotional, physical, or psychological violations.

Social justice and injustice are situated in particular local histories as well as within the inhabitants who dwell in a locale. These remnants leave (in)visible scars, or what I refer to as a geo-history, that are woven into educational geographies that cannot be separated from their social precursors and are deeply entrenched in cultural and ideological policies. Since social justice and injustice are geographically co-produced by its inhabitants, sustained by policy and behavior, and even co-opted into discourses, understanding and embodying social justice can have endless possibilities.

Bringing social justice work into English classrooms and schools at large can disrupt and interrupt practices that reproduce social, cultural, moral, economic, gendered, intellectual, and physical injustices. By teaching preservice English students how to unpack the history of a place, they can become spatially agentive, or able to enact change in a place.

An equity audit assignment can teach them how to shift social justice work into "spatial praxis" (Soja, 2010, p. 169), or learning from and then moving embodied knowledge from one space to another. Combined, these two significant and powerful learning experiences can cultivate a social justice consciousness.

English education, as an activist branch in education, has a great responsibility to not only prepare preservice teachers for the classroom, but also to provide them with an ethic of care (Noddings, 1992) that demonstrates a genuine attention to the well-being of their students and how they experience the schooling process, which is often fraught with social injustices. Adopting a disposition for social justice can interrupt how unchallenged geo-histories reproduce and sustain ideologies that reinforce inequitable schooling practices, yet also how to reimagine and re-embody dominant narratives.

METHODS FOR CULTIVATING SOCIAL JUSTICE DISPOSITIONS

There are four developmental stages that help to organize the varying levels of awareness students bring to coursework in English education with regard to social justice (Miller, 2010): critical reflection; acceptance; respect; and affirmation, solidarity, and critique. It is highly likely that students come to coursework and programs at varying levels in this developmental model, as well as experience a continuum of understanding related to social justice.

This model accounts for these differences and suggests that educators assess student understanding and experience related to social justice in order to scaffold activities and assignments that are developmentally, socially, and politically relevant to their learning experiences. Therefore, the model works best when approached as nonlinear because people are likely to move back and forth between stages.

Related to these overarching stages is a performative model called the "6 re-s," which consists of reflection, reconsideration, refusal, reconceptualization, rejuvenation, and reengagement (Miller & Kirkland, 2010). Drawing on this process, preservice teachers develop skills whereby they move from a potentially destabilizing moment into a restabilizing stance and articulate a response to the best of their abilities. Such movement is a strategy to preserve and enhance social justice and other kinds of teaching in the classroom.

For this model to be beneficial to students, instructors and their students select activities based on student need(s) and where to begin the work. In fact, the developmental identity model for social justice can be individualized based on a student's awareness of social justice. As we work within this model, the curriculum we teach and how we construct our lessons will support and facilitate the cognitive, emotional, and corporeal growth of our students.

THE CONTEXT: PREPARING PRESERVICE ENGLISH TEACHERS FOR THE TWENTY-FIRST CENTURY

This brief discussion about cultivating social justice dispositions comes out of a larger two-year study that examines how preservice English teachers come to understand their dispositions for socio-spatial justice and their role as agents for social change.

The study is organized around three layers that move from the university classroom into secondary practice: 1) teaching preservice English teachers about socio-spatial justice and injustice; 2) preservice English teachers conducting research about geo-histories and equities/inequities in a school; and 3) preservice English teachers making meaning of their dispositions for socio-spatial justice.

Each of these layers provide windows for seeing how our field can play with how spatiality, social justice, and student experience can inform how to edit or revise particular dominant narratives that have shaped and informed, and that even "represent" student identities.

This research also has several specific aims. First it seeks to understand the initial, emerging, and exiting inner filters, inclinations, and contexts that impact the understanding and embodiment related to social justice that pre-service students bring to a master of arts in teaching English (MATE). Next it aims to build on initial inclinations and filters as a way to scaffold learning about social justice within a developmental framework, while exploring what a disposition toward socio-spatial justice means to the individual.

Lastly, a purposeful aim of this study is to try to avoid indoctrination. Social justice, in that light, although foundational to each student's projects, was supported through their own interpretations, with only minimal research-er input that entailed clarifying questions about what a social justice/injustice was and how it was experienced in relation to reading and topics in the course Critical Pedagogy in English Education, as well as what they ob-served or experienced in out-of-classroom contexts.

Critical Reflection: *Tapping In*

As mentioned previously, assessing where students are in their awareness of social justice can benefit all stakeholders. Because students bring with them layered histories of past schooling experience related to social justice and injustice, readings, questions, discussions, assessments, and activities would be designed based around the initial assessment to support students in explor-ing their past experiences and how their current beliefs related to schooling were informed by their prior experiences.

A goal of these critical reflective histories was to help them understand and observe the ways in which schooling practices shape, inform, and cast their identities as people and later, as teachers, while simultaneously provid-ing a space for them to make sense on their own about the importance of taking a stand for social justice in their schools and in the teaching profession writ large.

Prior to asking students to take on a major assignment for the class, the first third of the semester was dedicated to self-reflection on issues related to social justice and injustice in school. In order to assess their inner filters regarding their trajectories around social justice, students were asked to de-fine social justice and injustice related to schools.

They were also asked to reflect and describe any time in their pre-K through university experience in which they recalled a teacher or professor make a stand for a social justice or enact an injustice in the classroom, the hallway, the lunchroom, or in the larger school or community.

From here, they were asked to consider a time when they experienced a social justice or injustice enacted on them in school, on a peer, on a group of students, on a teacher or any other school personnel, or through a policy or lack of a policy. Students also participated in The Level Playing Field activ-ity that is designed to help students reflect on how their sense of privilege (related to ethnicity, sexual orientation, social class, ability, age, gender, national origin, language) or lack thereof manifests in the classroom.

As students moved their bodies away from a center line by responding to questions, they visually and spatially observed how different/alike they are from their peers. Students also participated in a whole-group analysis of who has power and privilege institutionally over others in which they were able to spatially see how certain groups in society make and sustain decisions that often disempower and deny access for those who have less power and cultural capital.

Through participation in class activities, personal reflections, readings, and lots of dialogue, students began to develop a burgeoning awareness about the role that social injustice and justice play in school.

Acceptance: Preservice English Teachers Conducting Research — Moving toward Respect

Based on what I learned from student reflections about their inner filters and inclinations, by scrutinizing their writing and comparing it to the frameworks for this study, the activities and major assignments that were scaffolded using the "6 re-s" were done either individually or collaboratively, which was gently encouraged by researcher input. During each class, students participated in a social justice-related activity (Miller & Kirkland, 2010).

The purpose of these activities could be to experience and embody in first space (real or actual space) how their inner filters and inclinations bump up in various contexts when asked a potentially sensitive question while teaching. When doing these specific activities initially, students were shown how the "6-re-s" model worked through the model of fourth space (Miller, forthcoming), or how they might enact that as a critical pause time when asked a question they needed time to respond to.

They each drew for themselves in second space (imagined space) what their own fourth space looked like and thought about how they might respond when a student, colleague, administrator, parent, or community member challenged them on a topic related to social justice. As a class, we performed in third space (lived space where the real and imagined come together) these experiences and tried on various scenarios so that we could become more comfortable with potentially destabilizing situations.

For the two major assignments in class, students were asked to draw from their critical reflections and "6 re-s" activities that would span the rest of the semester. The first assignment was a three-part equity audit (see Groenke, 2010; Skrla et al., 2004), and the second was a geo-history investigation. For the first part of the equity audit, students were to do an autobiographical narrative in which they reflected in more depth on several questions relating to social justice and injustice in school.

Some of these questions included:

- What labels were attached to the classes you took? (Honors, college prep, AP, regular, etc.) What did you understand these labels to mean? Why did you take these courses?
- Were advanced (AP) courses offered at your school? In what subjects?
- Did you ever take vocational classes (home economics, automotive, cosmetology, etc.)? Why or why not?
- Were there groups of students in your school that you never saw in your classes? Who? Why do you think this was?
- Did you ever have classes where you were the minority (in race/ethnicity, gender)? Or were other students in your classes similar to you? How so?
- Did you have non-white teachers? In what subjects? Was the school faculty predominantly white?
- Did you get free or reduced-price school lunch? If not, did you buy your lunch every day or bring your lunch to school?
- Was bullying a problem at your school? Who got bullied? Was anything ever done about it?
- What extracurricular clubs/groups existed at your school? What activities were valued at your school?
- Who were the popular kids at your school? How did you know they were popular? What did their popularity afford them?
- Did teachers/administrators treat some students/classes differently than others? How so?
- Who were "good" teachers at your school? How did you know? What is your definition of a "good" teacher?

For the second part of the equity audit, students conducted an equity audit at a school site of their choice (adapted from Groenke, 2010). Depending on prior assessments, they were encouraged to tackle this task alone or in teams of three and locate someone in the field who is either doing an internship or student teaching in the undergraduate English education or MATE program.

Because there was quite a lot of work to be completed (see Table 8.1), students were encouraged to divvy up the categories. Students presented (PowerPoint, Prezi, or Excel chart) their findings, as well as any new insights gained and possibilities the team had for considering individual or collaborative action research projects.

The third part of the equity audit was to complete a final reflection (again, either individually or collaboratively) for which they were asked to respond to the following questions:

- Was it hard to get the data? Why?
- What did you have to do to get the data?

Table 8.1. Assignment 2: Equity Audit

General Data
Report fraction and percentage of each as applicable
*Number of students in your district:
Number of students in your school:
Number of staff in your school (certified and noncertified):
How many teachers in your school teach outside of their content/expertise area?
How many teachers in your school hold: a) bachelor's degrees; b) master's degrees; c) doctoral degree?
How many teachers in your school have been teaching: a) 1–5 years; b) 6–15 years; c) 16–20 years; d) more than 20 years?
What is the teacher mobility/attrition rate at your school?
Who teaches advanced classes at your school? Long-time teachers or beginning teachers? Who teaches lower-track classes? Who teaches seniors? Freshmen?
Number of students who transferred or moved into the school the last academic year (disaggregate by race, disability, gender, ELL, and free/reduced-price lunch):
Students who transferred out of the school in the last academic year (disaggregate using above info):
Fraction and percentage of staff in your school who are associated with student services (for example, special education, counselors, nurses, bilingual specialists, reading specialists, literacy coaches, etc.):

Status of Labeling at Your School
Report total number (fraction) and percentage (*all)

1. Students labeled "gifted" in your school:
2. Students labeled "at-risk" in your school:
3. Students labeled with a disability in your school:
4. Students labeled ESL, ELL, or bilingual in your school:
5. Students with any other kind of label in your school (include the label):
6. Graduation tracks at your school (for example, "basic," "advanced," "honors," "college prep," "AP")

Discipline Data

1. *Students who were suspended in the past year (disaggregate by gender, race, disability, free/reduced-price lunch, ELL; divide into in-school and out-of-school suspensions):
2. Students who were expelled in the past year (disaggregate using above info):
3. Students who were placed in alternative school setting (disaggregate using above info):
4. Low attendance and/or truancy (disaggregate by race, free/reduced-price lunch, ELL, disability, and gender):
5. Other relevant discipline data:

General Achievement Data

1. Eighth-grade achievement (disaggregate by race, free/reduced-price lunch, ELL, disability, gender):
2. Tenth-grade achievement (disaggregate using above info):
3. *Graduation rate (disaggregate using above info):
4. Graduated with an advanced/academic diploma (disaggregate using above info):
5. *Drop-out rate (disaggregate using above info):
6. Participation in ACT, SAT, AP courses/exams (disaggregate using above info):
7. Test results of ACT, SAT, AP exams (disaggregate using above info):

Social Class Data

1. *Students receiving free/reduced-price lunches in your school:
2. Students receiving free/reduced-price lunches in other schools in your district at the same level:
3. *Students identified for special education in your school:
4. *Of the number of students identified for special education, what fraction and what percentage receive free/reduced-price lunches?
5. How does the response to item 4 compare to item 1? The answers should be similar. If, for example, 60 percent of students identified for special education also qualify for free/reduced-price lunches, and your school has 20 percent of students receiving free/reduced-price lunches, students who receive free/reduced-price lunches are overrepresented in special education. Further, this means that, in this setting, if a student is from a lower socioeconomic class family, he or she is three times more likely to be labeled for special education than other students. What social class myths support these data?
6. Students labeled as "gifted" in your setting who receive free/reduced-price lunches. Compare with item 1.
7. Students identified as "at-risk" who receive free/reduced-price lunches. Compare with item 1.
8. *Reflect*: What do these social class data mean to you? What curriculum, programs, resources, etc., are available at your school for students of lower social classes? What ideas do you have for remedying weaknesses that exist in these programs?

Race and Ethnicity Data and Analysis

1. *Students of color in your school: How does this compare with other schools in your district?
2. Students of color in the total district:
3. *Of the number of students labeled for special education, what fraction and percentage are students of color?
4. How does this number and percentage compare with those in item 1?
5. How many students of color are labeled "at-risk"?
6. How many students of color are labeled "gifted"?
7. *Total certified and uncertified staff who are people of color in your school. Compare with response to item 1.
8. *Total staff who are people of color in your school:
9. People of color serving on the school board:
10. Report two pieces of academic achievement data (reading and math) as they relate to this area of diversity:
11. *Reflect :* Discuss the problems with the phrase, "I don't even see the person's color," and "But we do not have, or have very few, students of color in our school/district, so race isn't an issue here."

English Language Learners (ELL) and Bilingual Data

1. *How many English Language Learners are in your school and what languages do they speak? How does this compare to other schools in your district?
2. How many English Language Learners in the total district?
3. How many ELL students are labeled for special education?
4. How many ELL students are labeled "at-risk"?
5. How many are labeled "gifted"?
6. *What is the ELL service delivery model at your school? Are ELL students receiving quality instruction with certified teachers, or are they being "warehoused"?
7. *What is the total number of certified bilingual staff at your school?
8. Bilingual people on school board:
9. Report two pieces of academic achievement data (reading and math) as they relate to this area of diversity:

(Dis)Ability Data

1. Number of students labeled with (dis)abilities in your school:
2. How does this number compare with district total?
3. *Number of special education referrals a year:
4. Report two pieces of academic achievement data (reading and math) as they relate to (dis)ability:

Gender Data

1. *Females on the teaching staff at your school:
2. *Females teaching science/math classes:
3. *Females teaching English:
4. Females teaching history:
5. *Females teaching at the highest level of math:
6. *Females teaching AP courses:
7. *Out-of-school suspensions/expulsions by gender:
8. Females/males on administrative team:
9. Females on school board:
10. Report two pieces of academic achievement data (reading and math) as they relate to this area of diversity:

Sexual Orientation and Gender Identity

1. *Does your district have any active policies that address sexual orientation and gender identity?
2. How and to what extent does your district's curriculum provide instruction related to sexual orientation and gender identity?
3. *Does your school have a Gay/Straight Alliance? If not, why not?
4. Assess your school's library/media holdings related to sexual orientation and gender identity.
5. To what extent has professional development addressed sexual orientation and gender identity?
6. *To what extent are students teased or called names because of their gender identity or sexual orientation at your school? How do you know?
7. *Does your school have a gender-specific dress code?

Modified from Skrla, Scheurich, Garcia, & Nolly (2004) and Frattura & Capper (2007).
*=required

- Did any of the data surprise you? What? Why?
- Did you expect any of the data? Explain.
- What questions do you have about the data?
- What does the data reflect in terms of areas where equity-minded work is needed?
- How can/will you address this need in your action research?
- You will need to make sense of the data and analyze it in some cases, which you can do in your team. Some of this work can be done individually and some collectively, and you can turn in one paper for the entire group.

Students shared these findings with the rest of the class and engaged each other with some of their concerns about teaching in schools that lacked a social justice consciousness.

Simultaneous to the completion of the equity audit, students began their geo-history investigation. For the assignment students could draw from any of the findings in their equity audits and expand on it as a unit of investigation for their geo-history investigation.

Based on class discussions up to this point, as well as becoming more aware of broader social injustices that impact equitable schooling practices, students were asked to identify a topic of social injustice in the community where they were raised, where they currently live, or in the neighboring city to the university, and examine the injustice based on the following criteria:

1. **Describe the context of the location.** In your description, provide a sense of the geographic place of the injustice through explication of its economic, historical, and political history.
2. **Describe the inhabitants.** By approximating percentages, describe the mix of ethnicities, social classes, religions, typical family make-up, immigrants, persons with disabilities, English as a first language speakers, and the gay/lesbian/bi/transgender population.
3. **Describe the schools.** How many public versus private schools and universities are there? Be exact. Check the department of education website for this, and then cite it.
4. **Explicate the social injustice.** In detail, describe the social injustice, where the injustice came from, how it impacts the population of people in the environment and if law sanctions it.
5. **More specifically answer:**

    *   What is the dominant narrative about the social injustice?
    *   Is the casting of the geo-history's social injustice linear? In other words, was a policy enacted that created an injustice? Was there a social injustice first? What caused the change?
    *   What and who is left out, and how does that position the status quo or the population that is served?
    *   What are the general consequences of the injustice in the local community?
    *   Consider the accuracy of the geo-history (that is, who narrates it, who is left out, whose voices are included/excluded).
    *   *How has the geo-history generated dichotomies of inclusion/exclusion, normal/abnormal, superiority/inferiority, and desirability/undesirability?*
    *   What can your research now tell us about shifting an evolving geo-history? How can it be recast? What was learned? What can we as English educators learn from this?

6. **Describe how the social injustice impacts a school.** To the best of your ability, explain how you see the social injustice and the answers to the above questions manifesting in a school of your choice. For this section, interview two to three teachers (or an administrator) at the school and investigate its impact on the school environment. **Please prepare a note**

for the teacher that invites him or her to be interviewed and explain the reason for the interview. You should meet the teacher at a time and location that is convenient to the teacher. **Five to six** questions should be prepared *in advance,* and they could range from a) ***How does this social injustice impact your school? Consider how the geo-history has generated dichotomies of inclusion/exclusion, normal/abnormal, superiority/inferiority, and desirability/undesirability;*** b) How does this injustice impact your classroom?; c) What agency do you have in impacting change, and what do you foresee being able to do? You can either take notes or use an audio recorder, but you will need to transcribe your interviews. This can also be done via email or Skype. Your findings from these interviews should be woven back into your paper as appropriate.

7. **Suggest possible solutions or resolve.** Based on your findings, consider solutions or suggestions for change that might be applied in the school or larger community. How can recasting this geo-history facilitate an awareness around social justice? Also brainstorm a lesson that you could use in a secondary language arts classroom that draws attention to the social injustice. Your brainstorm should include a rationale and then briefly discuss how you would teach the lesson. Synthesize the answers found in part 5 as well as provide your own suggestions.

8. **Type a thank you letter to the teachers** (or administrator) and send it along with part 6 in this assignment (including the lesson idea), synthesizing ideas for change.

9. **References:** Minimum of three.

Write-up

Your write-up should be no longer than six pages (excluding the sources), and encompass all parts of 1 through 7, double-spaced, 10–12pt. font, either MLA or APA. Use sources as relevant to the research on the social injustice (citing its historical or political genesis), etc. Minimum sources: three.

Please also submit (these are not included in the write-up, but are appendices):

Appendix A: The letter to the teachers.

Appendix B: The transcription of the interviews, or notes from the interviews, with coding notes.

Appendix C: The copy of the thank you letter sent to the teachers or the administrator.

Both of these major assignments combined ask students to look at a dominant social injustice narrative that sustains itself in dominant culture and to think critically about the messages that are disseminated: Where does this narrative come from? How does it get perpetuated? What and who is left out of this narrative? How does the narrative position the status quo of the population being discussed?

Students are then asked to think through the consequences of that injustice, consider the accuracy of the geo-history (that is, who narrates it, who is left out, whose voices are included/excluded), question the casting of the geo-history's social injustice as linear (that is, was a policy enacted that created an injustice? Was there a social injustice first? What caused subsequent events?), and how the social injustice has positioned people, groups, ideas, and ideologies into various dichotomies of inclusion/exclusion, normal/abnormal, superiority/inferiority, and desirability/undesirability.

MOVING SOCIAL JUSTICE DISPOSITIONS INTO THE FUTURE

The impact of these assignments on preservice English teachers has the potential to offer the field of English education suggestions for threading social justice throughout our programs and for cultivating social justice dispositions. For instance, preservice English teachers, when afforded the opportunity to examine injustices in their own pasts and how it impacts their inner filters and inclinations when initially making sense of social justice and injustice, can be empowered to enact social justice in the schooling environments in which they teach and will teach.

Second, the design of assignments and measuring how it impacts preservice teacher growth, while simultaneously challenging students to consider how injustice impacts dichotomous social pairings, gains momentum for how to create more fair and equitable schooling experiences. The changes that occur within a teacher's inner filter and how that impacts inclinations can impact not only their school communities, but also their local communities, which then has potential to broaden in scope to the national community at large.

The emerging social justice consciousness that these preservice teachers can embody has the potential to sustain and spatialize those efforts through personal and communal agency, while simultaneously attempting to impact policy. Further, by tapping into the trichotomy of past/present/future and supporting students to think ahead about how to use past experiences in the future as a unifying framework that enabled them to gain agency, it can help them shift a situation and enact and try to sustain change.

Lastly, as more studies are conducted that continue to look at the performances and enactment of critical social justice work stemming from the practices and assignments in coursework, our standards for teacher assessment and dispositions can also shift. Such work can have far-reaching implications for policy and change.

However, in order for the spatiality of social justice change to be sustained, it would benefit our profession to embed social justice discourse into policies and into practice that can help to cement it into evolving geo-histories. As such, a social justice consciousness in the twenty-first century will have powerful momentum and movement in the contexts it inhabits now and into the future.

REFERENCES

Frattura, E., & Capper, C. (2007). *Leading for social justice: Transforming schools for all learners.* Thousand Oaks, Calif.: Corwin Press.

Groenke, S. (2010). Seeing, inquiring, witnessing: Using the equity audit in practitioner inquiry to rethink inequity in public schools. *English Education, 43* (1), 83–96.

Miller, s. (2010). Scaffolding and embedding social justice into English education. In s. Miller & D. Kirkland (Eds.), *Change matters: Critical essays on moving social justice research from theory to policy* (pp. 61–67). New York, N.Y.: Peter Lang.

Miller, s. (forthcoming). Spatializing social justice research in (English) education. In C. Compton-Lilly and Erica Halverson (Eds.), *Time and Space in Literacy Research.* New York, N.Y.: Routledge.

Miller, s., & Kirkland, D. (Eds.). (2010). *Change matters: Critical essays on moving social justice research from theory to policy.* New York, N.Y.: Peter Lang.

Noddings, N. (1992). *The challenge to care in our schools*: *An alternative approach to education.* New York, N.Y.: Teachers College Press.

Skrla, L., Scheurich, J. J., Garcia, J., & Nolly, G. (2004). Equity audits: A practical leadership tool for developing equitable and excellent schools. *Educational Administration Quarterly, 40* (1), 133–61.

Soja, E. (2010). *Seeking spatial justice.* Minneapolis, Minn.: University of Minnesota Press.

Sue, D. W. (Ed.). (2010). *Microaggressions and marginality: Manifestation, dynamics, and impact.* Hoboken, N.J.: Wiley.

3

Scholarship and Advocacy

Chapter Nine

Critical Engagement through Digital Media Production

A Nexus of Practice

Cynthia Lewis and Lauren Causey

Persistent disparities in educational opportunities and high school retention underscore an urgent need to understand settings that promote high school success and school engagement for youth who have been underserved, under-resourced, and marginalized in our educational system. This chapter focuses on such a project in one English class that was part of the Digital Media Studies (DigMe) program, a school-university partnership co-directed by the first author. EHS High School (EHS) (all names are pseudonyms) was situated within an urban district that has one of the largest achievement gaps in the country.

DigMe is a school-within-a-school program focused on rigorous interdisciplinary studies and critical literacy through the use and production of digital media in two subject areas: English and social studies. Given new forms of texts in digital times, students need to build "semiotic repertoires" (Comber, 2012, p. xi) for interpreting, analyzing, and producing myriad signs and symbols. The curriculum for DigMe was organized around project-based, cross-disciplinary instruction.

At the time of this study (2009–2010), the school had not met standards for Adequate Yearly Progress for two years. Eighty-six percent of its students qualified for free and reduced-price lunch, 91 percent were students of color (primarily African American, Latina/o, and Somali), and 42 percent were English Language Learners. This chapter presents research on critical engagement in learning through uses of digital media in the DigMe program. This is important for the field of English education because of the clear—and at times deeply personal—links students can make between classroom lives and their broader sociopolitical contexts using technology as a mediating tool.

FROM CRITICAL LITERACY TO CRITICAL ENGAGEMENT

We define "critical engagement" as building on the goals of critical literacy while also positing the need to go beyond rationalized approaches to critical literacy that leave selves untouched to focus on engagement, struggle, emotion, and aesthetics (Lewis & Tierney, 2011; Wohlwend & Lewis, 2011). From this perspective, we analyze students' uses of digital tools as mediating goal-driven activity, collaboration, audience uptake, and construction of agency (Carrington & Robinson, 2009; Hill & Vasudevan, 2008; Morrell, 2008) in terms of both critical distance *and* immersion.

Such activity in local spheres is always navigated across different scales (for example, local, institutional, and global scales). This dialectical relationship between the global and local, referred to as *glocalization* (Kraidy, 1999), is central to the analysis of classroom practices.

Over a decade ago, Peters and Lankshear (1996) focused on the intersection of critical literacy and technology with an early analysis of the ways that digital texts reposition readers and writers, sometimes opening new spaces for criticality and reframing. These features include: interactivity, which disrupts reader-writer distinctions; multimodality, which reconfigures the relationship between word, image, and sound; emerging discourses, which interrupt the privileging of academic discourse; and easy dissemination, which deconstructs the hegemony of publishing, making the way for more participatory authorship.

All of these features create opportunities for adopting a critical stance that, according to Peters and Lankshear, involve a combination of distance (for making critical evaluations) and closeness (for in-depth knowledge).

Few theorists in the intervening years have focused on the intersection of critical literacy and technology (see Fabos, 2008, for an exception) and few have offered alternatives to rationalized approaches to critical literacy in which we deconstruct lived language in ways that leave selves untouched. Misson and Morgan (2006) noted that dimensions of engagement, emotion, and aesthetics are generally absent from accounts of critical literacy and Janks (2002) provided an early critique of analytic approaches to critical literacy.

This chapter views critical literacy in terms of critical distance *and* immersion, a process that is analytic and playful, resistant and emotional. It argues that the goals and dimensions of critical literacy remain important but require expansive redefinition to keep up with work in digital and embodied literacies.

DIGITAL TECHNOLOGIES AND ENGAGEMENT

Burbules (2004) asserts that virtual spaces are particularly conducive to engagement in that they potentially promote the interest, involvement, imagination, and interaction that result in immersion. New practices related to digital media provide for a new set of tools that can transform typical classroom culture by engaging students in participatory learning, offering new forms of classroom interaction, and restructuring how communities are formed within the classroom.

Bringing digital media into the classroom capitalizes and builds on the features of engaged learning among adolescents in non-formal, out-of-school contexts, including an emphasis on collaboration, media production, and identity representation (Jacobs, 2009; Lankshear & Knobel, 2006; Lewis & Fabos, 2005). While early research and program development with digital technologies has been disproportionately oriented to privileged, white, and middle-class students, an increasing amount of research has begun to focus on racially, ethnically, and linguistically diverse students who are underserved by schooling.

Some of this work used new multimedia genres, such as digital storytelling, to engage working-class and minority youth in meaningful learning (Hill & Vasudevan, 2008; Hull & Katz, 2006; Rogers & Schofield, 2005; Rogers, Winters, & LaMonde, 2010). However, the opportunities for meaningful learning documented in these studies occurred in out-of-school contexts. This chapter focuses on youth producing digital media in the classroom in the hopes of understanding more about how students' engagement in digital media can be leveraged for learning within disciplines.

CRITICAL SOCIOCULTURAL THEORY, ACTIVITY THEORY, AND NEXUS OF PRACTICE

Our overarching theoretical framework is critical sociocultural theory (Lewis, Enciso, & Moje, 2007), which foregrounds agency, identity, and power relations as central to sociocultural theory. In order to highlight these elements, we draw on two related theoretical frameworks: Activity Theory (AT) and Nexus of Practice theory.

AT views human activity as object oriented and mediated by symbolic and concrete tools that have particular social, cultural, and historical uses within systems of activity (Engeström, 1999; Kaptelinin & Nardi, 2006; Sannino, Daniel, & Gutierrez, 2009). These tools mediate individual and social cognition and interaction within goal- or outcome-driven activity systems that include elements such as community norms, rules, and division of labor. Within an AT framework, students are purposeful actors creating meaning with tools to meet goals within a socially and culturally meaningful system.

Nexus of Practice theory also focuses on signs/tools that mediate situated as well as distal action (Scollon, 2001). These two levels—situated and distal—*are not distinct from one another* but linked as a nexus of practice. Situated action involves social actors whose identities are shaped moment to moment (for example, Holland et al.'s "identities in practice," 1998), mediated by discourse, objects, and space. However, this local scene is also linked to and constituted in more distal histories of participation (over time and across spaces), as well as to institutional conditions, social structures, and global flows.

Nexus of Practice theory is especially important to this study because it helps to understand students' responses to the activity system of their individual classroom—in this case, eleventh- and twelfth-grade media studies— as linked to the way their school is positioned within their community and within the larger discourses of urban education and neoliberal notions of school choice.

RESEARCH SITE AND METHODS

The focus in this chapter is on students' critical engagement in an eleventh- and twelfth-grade class on media analysis and production as part of the DigMe program. Ms. Vasich, the course instructor, was a white, middle-class teacher in her first year of teaching at the time of the study. She taught courses in media studies/production and documentary filmmaking for eleventh- and twelfth-grade students that were required English courses rather than electives.

DigMe classes such as these decentered literature study as the principal focus of disciplinary literacy in upper-grade English classes. Instead, students in DigMe learned to "read" (interpret, analyze, critique) signs and symbols across modes and genres. Ms. Vasich's graduate and undergraduate degree programs provided her with a strong digital media background (production, analysis, and pedagogy).

She developed a highly interactive curriculum that involved students in the production of knowledge as well as the analysis of texts of all kinds. Her media studies class, the focus of this paper, tackled complex issues of interest to students within the context of a deep respect for students' perspectives, which Ms. Vasich consistently demonstrated.

Media production must be at the center of any critical media curriculum (Fabos, 2008; Kellner, 2004), and such was the case in Ms. Vasich's class. Each unit progressed through first providing students with multiple texts in multiple media modes and genres related to the unit theme. Initially the entire class would critically analyze these texts (media and print) through dialogic discussion (Nystrand et al., 2003) before students practiced more independent analysis individually or in small groups.

Each unit culminated in a project that involved digital media production such as digital photography, audio diaries, films, propaganda spoofs, and so forth. These "products" were shared with various audiences at school community functions (for example, at Mosaic, an annual celebration of the school's diversity) and online. Major units of study and associated projects are included in table 9.1.

Data sources for the research included surveys (task-specific surveys administered after the major project that culminated each unit), focus group and individual interviews, fieldnotes taken during weekly classroom visits, audio and video recordings of classroom discussions and activities, and artifacts (such as assignments, students' digital and print projects and homework, digital media created outside of school that students chose to share with researchers, and school/district documents).

Throughout the chapter, examples are drawn from two focus group interviews of ten students in the class and from four student interviews. These students are Chevy (twelfth grade, African American female), Cody (twelfth grade, white male), Perla (eleventh grade, Latina female), and Serena (twelfth grade, African American female).

Analysis examined the links between engagement, identity, and learning. In keeping with the theoretical framework and research questions, we viewed

Table 9.1. Major Units of Study

Units of Study	Major Projects
Media Representations and Process of Analysis	Media ethnographies Spoof propaganda poster
Consuming Food/Consuming Culture	Photojournalism project: photography portfolio related to food consumption, distribution, and/or waste Reflective paper
Corporatization in a Globalized World	Corporate Watch Wiki Project: Each student group developed a wiki site using research and multiple forms of digital media to investigate the ethics of a chosen corporation and ways that the corporation has addressed ethical breeches

the class as an activity system, which means that we were interested in the complex and dynamic elements of human action in context. Analysis involved an iterative process that employed constant comparative approaches within the theoretical and methodological traditions of activity and nexus theory. We first coded all data sources related to components of activity and then recoded according to the five salient patterns developed in the first iteration and delineated here (textbox 9.1).

Critical Engagement in Learning through Digital Media

- *Social Justice and Social Action:* Agency to comment on injustice and effect change.
- *Production:* Opportunity to produce media rather than merely analyze.
- *Circulation:* Circulation of ideas (informal circulation in class, Internet circulation, school, community); transnational circulation of identities and ideas.
- *Identity Representation:* Connections to race, ethnicity, gender, and youth culture.
- *Counter-Narratives*: Opportunity to transform narratives about urban schools.

All components of the activity system shaped the patterns that emerged as salient. For example, because students' identity affiliations were engaged through classroom discourse and often central to class projects, students knew it was acceptable (and even desirable) to offer critical perspectives from their identity standpoints. In addition, these patterns were dependent, as well, on an equal emphasis on production as well as analysis. In fact, the process of speaking/writing back to texts and systems makes it difficult to separate text production from text consumption.

Following is a discussion of all salient patterns within the context of analyzing the class activity system. This analysis includes an important interpretation of the way that the low status of the school shaped some of the activity components. The focus then shifts to "social justice and social action," which also connected to opportunities for students to relate class work to their identities. Finally, the chapter concludes by returning to the issue of institutional status in a neoliberal market and how these macro forces related to the patterns of critical engagement.

ACTIVITY COMPONENTS AND ANALYSIS

This section discusses the activity system that shaped the patterns of engagement by addressing the following components that were part of the class activity system: goal, subject, mediating tools/signs, community norms/rules, and division of labor. It also touches on the processes of production, consumption, exchange, and distribution as outlined by Engeström (1999). Because these components work together as a system of activity, we do not isolate them into subheadings, but instead discuss them as a relational whole.

From a broad perspective, the overall goal of the course was to use various digital literacies in order to foster students' ability to become critical consumers of media in a global world. Students transitioned from being consumers of texts (for example, books, films, photographs, news articles) to being producers of creative, academically oriented work, which had alternating goals of being descriptive and activist in nature.

In considering the nexus of practice, however, a secondary desired outcome would be for courses such as this one to raise the status of the school. Students talked about feeling special for having more access to technology than many other schools in the district and about wanting their media productions to be public so that others would understand that EHS is a good school with serious students. They felt responsible for the technology they were charged with and for the image of their school.

The most significant mediating tools (beyond language) in Ms. Vasich's class were the laptop computers and Web 2.0 technologies. Laptop computers were used almost daily, with Ms. Vasich often starting class by asking students to "grab a laptop" from the cart, which was always positioned in the front of the classroom.

Various Web 2.0 technologies allowed students to carry out specific tasks related to production, critique, reflection, analysis, and research. Web 2.0 tools included wikis, blogs, online databases, Glogster, Comic Life, Ning, YouTube, Garage Band, Photobucket, Delicious, and Google Presentation. Technology tools beyond laptops included iTouch devices, headphones, digital cameras, and digital voice recorders.

Ms. Vasich encouraged students to "play" with the technology when they were stuck and waiting for her help. "Just play with it," she would say, in order to encourage students to learn through experimentation rather than step-by-step procedures. When she instructed students in the use of new tools, she did so quickly and then moved into coaching mode, helping students in the process of trying the tool. "Does anyone want help with that Delicious thing I just did?" she asked, after a quick demonstration on the affordances of the tool.

Notably, many students did not have access to a computer and/or a fast Internet connection at home. Of the four focal students for this chapter, for example, only Chevy had regular access to a computer. Cody had one computer at home, but shared it with other family members; Perla had no computer or Internet at home and could only access computers at friends' houses, a community center, or the library; and Serena had occasional access to her sister's computer—the only computer at home—but her sister was moving out, thus ending Serena's computer access.

Thus, the everyday access to technology tools that this class afforded students was monumental for some members of the classroom community. Even something as commonplace as learning how to send an attachment represented an accomplishment for students like Perla, who noted that the first time she sent a document to her teacher she copied it into an email and was surprised to learn that she could send the document as an attachment. In general, students' overall feeling of competence increased throughout the course of the year, particularly related to technology use for students who had little access outside of school and related to the ability to act as critical consumers and activist producers.

Ms. Vasich viewed students as knowledge producers. She held high expectations for students and communicated these expectations regularly. She often spoke of college, explaining to students what would be expected of them. For example, when Perla asked if she should take notes in class one day, Ms. Vasich said that students needed to decide for themselves what is important because professors don't tell their students what to write down.

The primary community norm held that the students were knowledge producers, collaboratively and individually. Many students expressed their belief that Ms. Vasich genuinely cared about their learning. When Ms. Vasich addressed the class, students were most often attentive and respectful. In the same way, Ms. Vasich respected each student's individuality and idiosyncrasies. Yet several students perceived more participation in this class than in their other classes.

One student told us that in other classes, the "same three kids" talk, but in "digital media, everyone says something really different." Another student mentioned that the class discussions are interesting, so that "you want to join the conversation and say your opinion." As the class progressed, students seemed to build a concept of themselves as researchers, as much of their discussions centered on the quality of sources and documenting data. In addition, students self-identified as both "producers" and "consumers" of digital media.

Ms. Vasich set broad learning objectives and planned activities for reaching them, but students were individually responsible for carrying them out and shaping those activities to fit their personal interests. Many students reported feeling a sense of autonomy in the class, relating that they were in charge of learning tools (digital media and Web 2.0 technologies) and outcomes. A good indicator of this agentic position with regard to division of labor was Cody's comment:

> with the digital media curriculum *we've set up* [emphasis added] . . . basically, what we do whenever we do big group projects is everyone will come to the table with an idea. . . . And, I mean, we'll have people who came up with completely different ideas working together and blending their topics together in ways that we hadn't thought about at first.

Not only does Cody focus on the importance of the collective, but he also revealed, through his use of "we," his sense that students played a central role in how the class was organized or "set up." In most activities, students worked in groups arranged according to students' topic interests. Students commented that focusing on topics rather than friendships when establishing collaborative groups resulted in affiliations across racial, ethnic, and other identity-related lines. From an AT perspective, "labor" progressed through teamwork and commitment to group and individual tasks.

At times of production, the class was run using an apprenticeship model. That is, Ms. Vasich labeled students as apprentices in a relevant field (for example, photojournalists, citizen journalists) as she helped to apprentice students into the roles they were to inhabit. At the beginning of the year, many students had little experience with technology beyond Facebook or MySpace, which they accessed at community centers and libraries. Some had trouble simply learning to log on to use the various tools such as "Blogger."

However, by November, Ms. Vasich could request that students upload their photos to iMovie or Photobucket without any student questions. Perla noted that in other classes technology is used by the teachers but not the students. In this class, production occurred with a degree of creativity, as students learned about the visual and audio qualities of media projects, and students themselves placed importance on aesthetic components of wiki pages, blogs, or photo portfolios.

Students were free to exchange ideas with one another and Ms. Vasich at any point in the production process. A sense of audience was a central feature of production in this class as students were often given opportunities to present their work to others. During the photojournalism presentations about food consumption, students critiqued one another using a rubric, and this feedback was later made available to students.

Perla felt that this feedback made her see her work differently, with an eye toward revision. She preferred having an audience of peers rather than just handing things in to her teacher. Exchange also took place in digital realms. For example, Ms. Vasich frequently wrote notes to students in the "comments" section of their blogs and wiki pages.

Exchange was also connected, in Bourdieu's (1977) terms, to a kind of capital in the classroom, with students able to exchange their creative and aesthetically pleasing media creations for admiration and social capital, at times resulting in academic capital. For example, Serena, an adept Glogster user, used the program to create an interactive poster related to McDonald's, the focus corporation for her collaborative corporate watch project. Her poster, discussed in more detail in the next section of this chapter, was as artistically thoughtful as it was critical of the McDonald's corporation.

Cody, one of Serena's group members, explained what he learned from her:

> One of my group members actually showed me this website called Glogster, I think it was, and how you can kind of create—she created our whole front page in this really really just sort of deep and meaningful fashion. And she made a mural . . . for our front page . . . and it sort of gets to the heart of what we were trying to say with our project.

Here Cody explains the connection between creativity, aesthetics, and disciplinary learning. Glogster was not just a cool program, but also a vehicle for communicating an important message to others. Serena's talent in using the program artistically leveraged not only social capital in the form of admiration from friends, but also academic capital.

This Bourdieuian concept of exchange is also central to the kind of cultural and academic capital that students felt the DigMe program afforded. Serena referred to a job that her mother mentioned that required strong computer skills. Serena felt that once the employer would see her participation in the Digital Media Studies program, "they're gonna be like whoa, we can just sign her up!" Others talked about the program preparing them for college based on all the analytical work involved in reading and interpreting print and visual texts.

Student work was frequently made available to audiences beyond the classroom as well. For example, student videos and photographs were displayed in a DigMe installation at Mosaic, an annual celebration of the school's diversity. Corporate watch wikis, student blogs, and photojournalism projects were publicly available online. Ms. Vasich promoted the idea that products are not finished but constantly under revision as students learn new things and receive feedback. The front page for the corporate watch unit stated, "Research isn't linear. It's constant and evolving."

Students expressed their awareness of larger audiences on many occasions. Chevy said that she wanted to be "respectful of her viewers." Serena said that she was upset when she was not able to share her propaganda spoof poster with a larger audience. Cody acknowledged that he wanted to effect change with a video he co-created the previous year on gay rights. These quick student snapshots represent the general feeling among students that they preferred to have their work distributed outside the classroom.

As this activity system analysis reveals, the patterns mentioned earlier— social justice, production, circulation, identity, and counter-narrative—were all present with components of activity working together to produce an environment conducive to critical engagement. The next section focuses primarily on students' engagement in social justice and social action.

SOCIAL JUSTICE AND SOCIAL ACTION

I love the digital media program, especially this year with Ms. Vasich, and my writing has improved so much, unbelievable! And now I can't even visit a site without analyzing it and finding the embedded values in it. (Chevy, May 2010)

Naturally, Chevy's claim that reading and interpreting websites will never be the same for her was music to our ears as literacy researchers. Rather than drop the class mid-year in order to join an AP English class as planned, Chevy decided to stay for the year in Ms. Vasich's class. Ironically, Chevy's comment about how much she has learned about writing in a class on media analysis and production is not a view that matches the perceptions of some teachers outside the DigMe program.

For example, Serena shared with Ms. Vasich that one of her teachers was ranting that teachers don't teach writing anymore or assign enough essay assignments, instead giving students "free time" on the computer. This struck Serena as misinformation about DigMe, which she described in an interview as a program that asks students to "dig deeper" than what's on the surface. "And it makes you think. Think hard. Sometimes it gives you a headache, but other times it's awesome."

These student responses align with the goals that Ms. Vasich makes explicit to students. "In this class, we're shaping responsible citizens," she told one student. During the consuming food/consuming culture unit, she prompted students to remember the media scholar Sut Jhally's video promoting media awareness, and told students "Your photos are a form of activism/ advocacy of media empowerment."

Critical Engagement through Entextualization

To illustrate what Ms. Vasich meant when she referred to activism and advocacy, we will return to the Glogster poster that Serena created for the front page of her group's corporate watch wiki on McDonald's. Glogster is a tool for creating interactive posters that include moving images, audio, and other features.

The downloaded and pasted version (figure 9.1) shows Serena's artistic vision and searing critique of McDonald's. The images included are meant to represent McDonald's poor nutrition, questionable ethics related to animal rights, and dangerous appeal to children. On the actual wiki, the eyes move from side to side to emphasize the corporation as big brother watching the consumer to know our habits, and attract our desires and money. Also on the wiki, the black lips (that eat the food) drip black blood, creating a dramatic effect.

Blommaert (2005) builds on the work of Bauman and Briggs (1990) and Silverstein and Urban (1996) in discussing the processes of decontextualization, recontextualization, and entextualization. This process involves a text that is removed from its context (decontextualized) and placed in a new context (recontextualized) in order to produce a "preferred reading" (Bauman & Briggs, 1990, p. 73) that others will take from what has become a new text (entextualization). This process, we argue, is central to digital media production and, more importantly, to what we are calling critical engagement.

In this case, Serena's Glogster poster serves the process of entextualizing McDonald's iconography (the golden arches), so that the initiating text is removed from its interactional setting (different websites containing McDonald's ads and iconography) and placed in a new context. This new context includes one with an apparatus of other wiki pages providing further information about McDonald's questionable ethics. Thus, recontextualized images are entextualized as a new text with a "metadiscourse" that stipulates how it should be interpreted (Blommaert, 2005, p. 47).

This work exemplifies what we mean by critical engagement through production. In order to complete the poster, Serena needed to read and interpret articles and websites about McDonald's corporate actions, as well as analyze the persuasive appeal of McDonald's advertising, iconography, and toys. In creating the poster, Serena deploys McDonald's own golden arches icon for her own purposes—to disrupt the icon that has become so naturalized in our lives as to seem benign rather than dangerous.

She fractures the arches and sets them against a splash of fiery red to address viewers, asking us to view McDonald's in a new way, interrupting commonplace notions of what the corporation stands for. The same fiery red is engulfing the McDonald's purple toy and, along with black, seems to signify death and fire. The "speaker" seems coerced to state "I love McDonald's" because McDonald's is always watching us, regulating our desires and sustaining our addiction to fast food.

Through fieldnotes and transcripts, Serena strongly conveyed that aesthetics is an important component to the work that she does in the class. She was effusive when showing one of us photos of McDonald's advertisements around the world (many of them from a website she found), examining hundreds of photos, and saying often "I'm in love" with this or that photo.

Figure 9.1. Serena's Critique of McDonald's

She discussed the importance of color as a feature that attracts her to web-sites, and often exclaimed the brilliance of Glogster as a tool for expressing her artistic vision.

The pleasure she took in sharing critical perspectives with artistic finesse was available to her through this assignment and many throughout the year that fed students' combined interests in critique and aesthetics. This is the kind of immersion that exemplifies the move from critical literacy to critical engagement.

We end this section with another example of entextualization as a mode of critique in production. Students who worked on the corporate watch wiki focusing on Kraft created a spoof of a Kraft commercial for which they took a commercial for Kraft American cheese from YouTube and replaced the real audio with a voice-over track. The commercial includes a little girl who shares half of a grilled cheese sandwich with her dad, all the while explaining to him the health benefits of Kraft cheese. The students' voice-over created an alternative sound track for the commercial that proclaimed the connection between Kraft and Philip Morris (Marlboros), as well as between Kraft and McDonald's. Ms. Vasich and others were wowed by the effectiveness of the end result.

Here again the students have decontextualized the original commercial and recontextualized it within a new context—that of an academic wiki devoted to discussion of Kraft's ethics violations for an audience of peers who are all immersed in this kind of critical stance. This process of recontextualizing results in a new product, entextualized to construct a preferred reading of the corporation. This preferred reading used humor to achieve a powerful critique.

Perla was also a member of the Kraft wiki group, and although she did not create the spoof commercial, she appreciated its effects. As she put it:

> [Our spoof] was actually the truth so people—our classmates at [EHS]—could actually know what was going on with Kraft instead of like, the little girl [in the commercial] . . . saying all these lies about Kraft and how it's all healthy and—when it's really not.

Perla also learned that corporations don't always want to share information with the public.

When students wrote to Kraft representatives, they were told that the information they were seeking was unavailable. However, they found information that was surprising and significant to Perla—that Kraft recruits immigrants at the border to hire them to work at Louis Rich poultry processing plant. This was a fact that connected to Perla's identity as an immigrant from Mexico, and a fact she remembered and included in her section of the wiki.

We asked students to complete task-specific engagement surveys for particular units. For the wiki unit, all but two out of thirteen students checked "agree" or "strongly agree" for the following statement: "The activity or project allowed me to communicate a message to an audience of readers/

viewers for a purpose I believe in." Two students checked "agree somewhat," but no students checked "disagree" at any level. Chevy wrote the following in her paper reflecting on the unit: "I was really forced to match up my actions with the ethics of my decisions." The project, we argue, engendered the kind of critical engagement we defined at the start of this paper.

Identity Affiliations

Ms. Vasich's class fostered connections between students' identity affiliations and the development of their critical perspectives, just as we saw in the examples of Serena and Perla. Students learned quickly that representing identity would be a running topic throughout the class, a fact that was established early on when their teacher started the year with a unit on identity representations in the media.

The main focus of this unit was race, beginning with a clip from the television show *Black/White*, in which a black family is made to look white and a white family is made to look black, with each family living their lives, for a time, from within a new racial identity. Students were very engaged with this media material along with the other videos and texts that deepened their learning. In the following quotation, Chevy got to the heart of this experience:

> But it's pretty cool to be able to share my thoughts with the teacher about things that, like, no other teacher has been able to ask me. Like, what are my thoughts about race representation in the media? What are my thoughts as an African American woman?

Chevy found an outlet to discuss topics of interest in her DigMe class that would have been taboo in her other classes. When the interviewer asked if she was surprised that the teacher was focusing on issues of race, class, and gender, Chevy said this focus was, indeed, surprising, and caused her to invest in the class right from the start in ways she had not expected.

Despite this openness, topics related to race remain fraught with complexities. For example, students created spoof propaganda posters using Photobucket and Comic Life in ways that used humor and satire to communicate critical messages about topics of central interest to the students. Serena pointed to a complex irony about the process of producing these propaganda posters.

> It was interesting because while making spoof propaganda we kept running into propaganda itself. We were like, we were on the computer [creating] spoof propaganda in quotation marks—not real propaganda—and it would still take us to real propaganda. It was really weird and awkward.

Serena was grappling with a perplexing problem that arises in satire, especially when the satire deals with stereotypes. In the process of using satire to dismantle racism, the work of satire sometimes serves to reinscribe it, especially for readers whose lived experience may make the words hard to accept with an ironic "wink and a nod."

Serena, it seems, understood some of that complexity, which shows how engaged she was in thinking not only about critique (she was critiquing racial profiling in her poster), but also about its consequences. As someone who has family members who are "Mexican, Latino, white, Puerto Rican, African American," she and her family had experienced racial profiling, making her especially aware of its consequences.

The consuming food/consuming culture unit provided ample opportunities for students to combine identity affiliation and critique for critical engagement. For the final project, students were asked to choose a topic related to the unit (hunger, fast food, global food economy, production, distribution, consumption, and waste related to food) and create a photojournalism portfolio of ten to fifteen photos that tell a story or communicate a thesis about the topic. These photojournalism portfolios were presented through Photobucket, during which they received rigorous feedback from fellow students, who served as the initial audience.

Perla's photojournalism project included a close-up of a tortilla package with the words "A Taste of Mexico" on the package. A second close-up of the same package showed that the tortillas come from Georgia. Perla talked about how people in Mexico, her first home, make their own tortillas, so the company's claim for authenticity is absurd from the start. Add to that the fact that the tortillas are made in Georgia, and the absurdity was so clear to her that she decided to make it central to her project.

When she presented her collection of photos, the two tortilla photos generated much discussion about the advantages and disadvantages of globalization versus local food and culture. By pulling from aspects of her identity, the class project seems to have refined Perla's artistic and critical voice.

The same was true for another student from Mexico who was a member of the corporate watch wiki group that focused on the Nestlé Corporation. Nestlé is ubiquitous in Mexico as a maker of baby formula, but not without some controversy related to contamination of the water. The student was highly invested in completing the wiki, in part due to her background with Nestlé.

In her reflective paper, she wrote about how the corporation's ethics violations are related to the movie *Flow* that students had watched in class, a film about water as a resource that is scarce due to contamination and privatization. In all of these examples, students used their identity affiliations to take up critical stances and meet the norms and expectations related to classroom interaction and knowledge production.

CRITICAL ENGAGEMENT AS A NEXUS
OF GLOBAL AND LOCAL PRACTICES

As already discussed, EHS lacked status in the district due to negative perceptions often imposed on urban schools that serve students from families with few material resources. Standardized test scores were low and school enrollment was decreasing. The school's free and reduced-price lunch percentage rose every year, as did the population of English Language Learners. The school was located in a mostly white lower-middle-to-middle-class neighborhood that had a history of pride as a neighborhood school.

At the time of this research, few neighborhood families sent their children to EHS, yet its more illustrious history figured prominently in the language and lore surrounding the school. Such was the history within which DigMe existed. Teachers and students alike were hopeful that DigMe could return EHS to some version of its glory days (albeit a newly conceived version).

This hope for DigMe resonated in the words of many of the students we interviewed. Cody, for example, pointed out that he didn't know if he should attend the school because he had heard "bad stories about it." But he did not want to follow everyone else to another school in this urban district where more of the white students, like Cody, chose to go.

Four years later, as a senior in Ms. Vasich's class, Cody focused his citizen journalism essay on the richness of diversity at EHS. He claimed much school pride and was close with his teachers and with students of different races and ethnicities. Serena also depicted EHS's low status in contrast to her own perceptions of the school:

> I love EHS. I don't like what people say about EHS—like EHS is full of a bunch of hoes and all this stuff. And the bad publicity. That just kind of makes me so mad. . . . Most of us, we're good. We're all gravy.

Neoliberalism sets up school choice and competition as desirable, wherein schools like EHS that serve low-income, racially, ethnically, and linguistically diverse families are losing this game. The mobility of the affluent to choose schools results in the confinement of the poor (Bauman, 2007) to particular schools that the affluent choose not to attend. Whether or not the school offers innovative curriculum and excellent teaching, as was the case at EHS, hardly matters, because the affluent determine which schools have value.

These local institutional contexts and histories of participation create locally manifested ways of being, producing, and interpreting that are shaped by global spheres, such as neoliberal notions of school choice and international assessments of student achievement. Perceptions and enactments of

DigMe at the program and classroom levels were very much shaped by these distal factors, as can be seen in the previous sections.

Students wanted their projects to reach wide audiences so that others would see that the students at EHS were worthy of their respect. Teachers like Ms. Vasich regularly referred to college and to the opportunity this program provided for students without technology access to gain access and be prepared for academics in the twenty-first century.

Pennycook (2010) discusses two seemingly conflicting effects of global forces on local practices. On the one hand, globalization demands homogenization. It demands a "standard" for what a school should look like in multiple localities in the form of standardized achievement scores, graduation rates, and so forth. On the other hand, globalization also generates what Pennycook calls "worldiness"—a site of resistance and rearticulation.

It is this side of the global market—this side of school "choice"—that DigMe is leveraging. Keying into the popular discourse of twenty-first-century skills, DigMe is a site of resistance to the perception of EHS as a "default school," as one teacher put it. Moreover, it is a site that rearticulates the meaning of rigor—the rigor of critical engagement in digital media production anchored in identity representation and emotional investment.

The four focal students we have discussed, and others, who followed Ms. Vasich's instructions to "grab a laptop" at the start of most classes, used Web 2.0 technologies to engage with and confront complex problems in our world, and within their own hyperlocal environments. In contemporary times, English as a subject should build students' repertoires to include the analysis, interpretation, critique, and production of a wide range of signs or texts. Our chapter has made explicit the possibilities for rethinking English education in this way and exploiting the affordances of the media age.

REFERENCES

Bauman, R., & Briggs, C. L. (1990). Poetics and performance as critical perspectives on language and social life. *Annual Review of Anthropology, 19*, 59–88.

Bauman, Z. (2007). *Liquid times: Living in an age of uncertainty*. Cambridge, U.K.: Polity Press.

Blommaert, J. (2005). *Discourse: Key topics in sociolinguistics*. Cambridge, U.K.: Cambridge University Press.

Bourdieu, P. (1977). *Outline of a theory of practice*. (R. Nice, Trans.). Cambridge, U.K.: Cambridge University Press. (Original work published 1972.)

Burbules, N. (2004). Rethinking the virtual. *E-Learning, 1* (1), 162–83.

Carrington, V., & Robinson, M. (Eds.). (2009). *Digital literacies: Social learning and classroom practices*. Los Angeles, Calif.: Sage.

Comber, B. (2012). Foreword. In K. Pahl & J. Rowsell (Eds.), *Literacy and education* (2nd ed.) (pp. vii–xi). London: Sage.

Engeström, Y. (1999). Activity theory and individual and social transformation. In Y. Engeström, R. Miettinen, & R. Punamaki (Eds.), *Perspectives on activity theory* (pp. 19–38). Cambridge, Mass.: Cambridge University Press.

Fabos, B. (2008). The price of information: Critical literacy, education and today's Internet. In D. J. Leu, J. Coiro, M. Knobel, & C. Lankshear (Eds.), *Handbook of research on new literacies* (pp. 839–70). Mahwah, N.J.: Lawrence Erlbaum Associates.

Hill, M. L., & Vasudevan, L. M. (2008). *Media, learning, and sites of possibility: New literacies and digital epistemologies*. New York, N.Y.: Peter Lang.

Holland, D., Lachicotte Jr., W., Skinner, D., & Cain, C. (1998). *Identity and agency in cultural worlds*. Cambridge, Mass.: Harvard University Press.

Hull, G., & Katz, M. (2006). Crafting an agentive self: Case studies of digital storytelling. *Research in the Teaching of English, 41*, 43–81.

Jacobs, G. E. (2009). *Adolescents and instant messaging: Literacy, language, and identity development in the 21st century*. Saarbrücken: VDM Verlag.

Janks, H. (2002). Critical literacy: Beyond reason. *Australian Educational Researcher, 29* (1), 7–27. Retrieved from http://www.unisa.edu.au/hawkeinstitute/cslplc/documents/Beyond.pdf.

Kaptelinin, V., & Nardi, B. A. (2006). *Acting with technology: Activity theory and interaction design*. Cambridge, Mass.: MIT Press.

Kellner, D. (2004). Technological transformation, multiple literacies, and the re-visioning of education. *E-Learning, 1* (1), 9–37.

Kraidy, M. M. (1999). The global, the local, and the hybrid: A native ethnography of glocalization. *Critical Studies in Mass Communication, 16* (4), 454–67.

Lankshear, C., & Knobel, M. (2006). *New literacies: Everyday practices and classroom learning* (2nd ed.). New York, N.Y.: Open University Press.

Lewis, C., Enciso, P., & Moje, E. B. (Eds.). (2007). *Reframing sociocultural research on literacy: Identity, agency, and power*. New York, N.Y.: Routledge.

Lewis, C., & Fabos, B. (2005). Instant messaging, literacies, and social identities. *Reading Research Quarterly, 40*, 470–501.

Lewis, C., & Tierney, J. D. (2011). Mobilizing emotion in an urban English classroom. *Changing English: Studies in culture and education, 18* (3), 319–29.

Misson, R., & Morgan W. (2006). *Critical literacy and the aesthetic: Transforming the English classroom*. Urbana, Ill.: National Council of Teachers of English.

Morrell, E. (2008). *Critical literacy and urban youth: Pedagogies of access, power, and liberation*. New York, N.Y.: Routledge.

Nystrand, M., Wu, L., Gamoran, A., Zeiser, S., & Long, D. (2003). Questions in time: Investigating the structure and dynamics of unfolding classroom discourse. *Discourse Processes, 35*, 135–96.

Pennycook, A. (2010). *Language as a local practice*. New York, N.Y.: Routledge.

Peters, M., & Lankshear, C. (1996). Critical literacy and digital texts. *Educational Theory, 46*, 51–70.

Rogers, T., & Schofield, A. (2005). Things thicker than words: Portraits of youth multiple literacies in an alternative secondary program. In J. Anderson, M. Kendrick, T. Rogers, & S. Smythe (Eds.), *Portraits of literacy across families, communities, and schools: Intersections and tensions* (pp. 205–20). New York, N.Y.: Routledge.

Rogers, T., Winters, K., & LaMonde, A. M. (2010). From image to ideology: Analyzing shifting identity positions of marginalized youth across the cultural sites of video production. *Pedagogies: An International Journal, 5*, 298–312.

Sannino, A., Daniel, H., & Gutierrez, K. D. (Eds.). (2009). *Learning and expanding with activity theory*. New York, N.Y.: Cambridge University Press.

Scollon, R. (2001). *Mediated discourse: The nexus of practice*. London: Routledge.

Silverstein, M., & Urban, G. (Eds.). (1996). *Natural histories of discourse*. Chicago, Ill.: The University of Chicago Press.

Wohlwend, K. E., & Lewis, C. (2011). Critical literacy, critical engagement, digital technology: Convergence and embodiment in glocal spheres. In D. Lapp & D. Fisher (Eds.), *Handbook of research on teaching the English language arts* (3rd ed.) (pp. 188–94). New York, N.Y.: Taylor & Francis.

Chapter Ten

(Digital) Literacy Advocacy

A Rationale for Creating Shifts in Policy, Infrastructure, and Instruction

Troy Hicks

In English education we have been talking about digital literacy for quite some time. Given the number of books, blog posts, wiki pages, curricular documents, interactive websites and highly touted reports that have been published in the past decade—and the fact that our very definition of "publish" has changed, too, because of these many web-based tools—there is no doubt that we are teaching English in an era much different from even the turn of the twenty-first century.

Moreover, we have insights from modern youth about their lived lives; from countless status updates and photos through the careful research of dedicated scholars across disciplines (Ito et al., 2009).

There are criticisms of these so-called digital natives or millennials, no doubt: inattention and a tendency to swim in "the shallows" of our information-driven world (Carr, 2010); the fact that we can feel "alone together," connected to so many people on a surface level and yet feel increasingly isolated from them in terms of deeper emotions (Turkle, 2011); or, in perhaps the most scathing commentary, we could be raising "the dumbest generation" (Bauerlein, 2008).

Yet there are also possibilities.

Sara Kajder (2010), in *Adolescents and Digital Literacies: Learning Alongside Our Students*, argues that our work today as English teachers "is about openings, creativity, ingenuity, and rethinking our practice. But it is also about proceeding in intentional and deliberate ways" (p. 3).

This correlates with a broader conversation about how creativity happens, indeed what conditions must be present for creativity to happen. Ken Robinson (2011), in *Out of Our Minds: Learning to Be Creative*, connects the ideas of creativity and intention:

> Being creative involves *doing* something. It would be odd to describe as creative someone who never did anything. To call somebody creative suggests that they are actively producing something in a deliberate way. (p. 142)

The study of English—from drama, literature, and poetry to composition and rhetoric, to film and multimodal literacies—is a study of deliberate, literate action. How do we employ language to construct our identities? We attempt to understand what writers (as well as actors, photographers, filmmakers, and web designers) have created and, in the best possible scenario, teach our students to create something uniquely their own in the process.

The possibilities for us as English teachers come in the moments in which we invite our students into literacy practices, encourage them to understand what others have created, attempt to try on language for themselves, and to communicate with a broader audience. We want our students to have the basic abilities to read and write, listen and speak, view and visually represent. These skills have never been separated from technology, be it parchment, pens, or pixels.

Thus, this chapter begins with two premises:

- As English teachers, we are inherently advocates of literacy, across all forms of text.
- Being "literate" and being "digitally literate," if they ever were separate, are now one and the same.

In this chapter, the author elaborates on these premises. English teachers have historically been advocates for equal access to all forms of text. We do this for a variety of reasons: the appreciation of literature, the right to free speech, and the goal of creating informed citizens who can think critically and communicate effectively, for example.

To do these same tasks now and in the foreseeable future, we must begin with the clear understanding that English teachers no longer have the luxury to say things like "technology is not my job" or "my students just don't have access" (Hicks & Turner, 2013). Instead, we need to redouble our efforts at becoming literacy advocates, in all senses of what it means to be literate.

For now, then, the parenthetical term "digital" will be kept in front of all mentions of literacy in this chapter, simply to show how much "digital" permeates the ways in which we produce and consume texts. It offers a reminder that we, as English teachers, are responsible for all forms of (digital) literacy, and that three specific areas—policy, infrastructure, and instruction—require our immediate and vigilant attention.

Even though specific tools, applications, and websites will continue to change, the author argues that these three core elements are now and will remain central to our advocacy efforts. The times and tools will change, but our focus on policy, infrastructure, and instruction must remain. For each, a few resources will be offered to help guide readers' (digital) literacy advocacy efforts, and to guide us as we create shifts in thinking at all levels of education, from our classrooms to the halls of Congress.

The intent is not to overwhelm. Indeed, (digital) literacy advocacy is a multifaceted topic, one that requires all of us to work collaboratively in order to achieve our goals of universal access and ubiquitous learning. Whether you are an English teacher born of the baby boom, or Gen X, whether you consider yourself a digital native or immigrant, and whether or not there is a smart phone in your pocket, *you* must become an advocate for your students and their (digital) literacy.

Students' academic and professional lives, not to mention their very understanding of what it means to be (digitally) literate in the world, depend on our deliberate attention to this task.

SHIFTING POLICIES: FROM ACCEPTABLE
USE TO AUTHENTIC USE

As networked computers have entered our schools, many of us have signed Acceptable Use Policies (AUPs). Whether signing for ourselves as school faculty or as parents, we read these documents that outline what can and should happen as users engage in activity on the school's network, generally forcing us to comply with usage limits, copyright law, filtering policies, bans on downloading and installing programs, and any other aspects of being allowed to use school computers.

In a legal sense, these policies are appropriate and necessary so that school districts are in compliance with laws such as Child Online Protection Act (COPA) and Digital Millennium Copyright Act (DMCA), as well as to maintain eligibility for E-Rate funding.

However, the unintended consequences of AUPs are both humorous and troubling. We have all heard a story similar to this: a student who searches for the term "breast" in relation to "cancer" gets blocked from her search results and automatically kicked off the network. We have also likely heard of numerous students who have been sent a cease and desist letter, along with the threat of a fine, from the Recording Industry Association of America (RIAA) for file sharing and a violation of copyright law.

In these two examples, we have one student who has attempted to use the Internet for genuine inquiry; she made a mistake that triggered a filter. The other attempted a crime, even if his own ethical standards led him to believe it was okay. Yet as urban legend has it, both were kicked off the network for violating the AUP.

In short, here's the dilemma: yes, schools must institute policies that prevent students from engaging in illicit online behavior; yet school is also the place where we want to teach students how to use technology in ethical, productive, and responsible ways. Acceptable use policies—and the related filtering and outright blocking that they employ—work against these goals. We conflate the act of learning by making legitimate mistakes, with the potential for misbehavior or criminal acts, all caught in a filter—literally and figuratively—of school policies.

Hence, our first act of advocacy for (digital) literacy: we must support our students and their ability to access and use language, especially language that is shared in the (digital) spaces related to school. We must work with our administrators, technology directors, and communities to shift from acceptable use to *authentic* and fair use.

This approach requires us to 1) understand what our school's current approach to acceptable use is as well as 2) to better understand educators' and students' rights under fair use provisions of the U.S. Copyright Law. Partner these understandings with 3) the stances of our professional organizations, and we have three powerful ways to begin our advocacy efforts.

1. Acceptable Use Policies

The Consortium for School Networking has created a guide, *Acceptable Use Policies in the Web 2.0 and Mobile Era*, that outlines the qualities of AUPs that are "based on the premise that children need to learn how to be responsible users" and "that students need to acquire the skills and dispositions of responsible Internet usage and to be held accountable for their behavior" (2013).[1]

Instead of beginning with a policy that locks students out of web resources, ultimately leading them to frustration and attempts to subvert established policies through hacking or other work-arounds, we should create policies that invite them in, helping them understand when and how to use Internet resources in appropriate ways.

Inviting stakeholders, especially parents, into conversations about how to revise and implement AUPs would be a good way to discuss many issues, such as privacy, cyberbullying, social network participation, and appropriate websites and tools for learning. Coupled with efforts at parent outreach, focusing our (digital) literacy advocacy on AUPs can help us articulate a vision for shared governance over technology resources, entrusting these tools to students, not merely tolerating students as they learn how to use the tools.

2. Copyright and Fair Use

Copyright is complicated, and in her book *Copyright Clarity: How Fair Use Supports Digital Learning*, Renee Hobbs (2010) articulates the ways in which teachers and students are allowed, even encouraged, to exercise their fair use rights under U.S. Copyright Law. Built on her work with a team of other scholars who created *The Code of Best Practices in Fair Use for Media Literacy Education* (2009), Hobbs elaborates on many of the ideas present in the code, most notably that *"The effective use of copyrighted materials enhances the teaching and learning process"* (p. 5, italics in original).

On the companion website,[2] Hobbs and her colleague Kristin Hokanson have created a thinking guide for "Supporting the Fair Use Reasoning Process."[3] This guide helps students work through the "four factors" that contribute to decision making related to fair use:

- First, understanding your *purpose* for the use in relation to the original copyright holder's purpose.
- Second, the *nature* and, third, the *amount* of your use in relation to the entire copyrighted work.
- Fourth, whether or not your use of the material was *"transformative"* in the sense that you are creating new work from the original copyrighted material.

Closely related to questions of fair use are the issues of copyright-friendly materials, and materials available in the public domain. Another pair of useful resources for these issues is the Creative Commons website (http://creativecommons.org/), which provides links to materials that are licensed for collaborative work, and Joyce Valenza's "Copyright Friendly" wiki (http://copyrightfriendly.wikispaces.com/), which points to a variety of copyright-free or public domain resources. Both understanding and exercising your fair use rights—all while employing copyrighted materials in purposeful ways—is an act of (digital) literacy advocacy.

3. Understanding the Ethical Stances That Our Professional Organizations Hold

Many position statements and policy briefs released over the past decade from the National Council of Teachers of English (NCTE) describe the organization's stance on "twenty-first century" and "multimodal" literacies. Other organizations, such as the International Society for Technology in

Education (ISTE), have released curriculum documents and statements about how to "effectively leverage technology for learning."[4]

These are but two of many professional organizations that have such documents and, either implicitly or explicitly, these documents promote a specific ethical stance toward technology use and (digital) literacy skills. The ways in which we either welcome or forbid access to the Internet will determine, in large part, the ways our students use it.

As an example of one that is explicit, the NCTE *Literacy Learning in the 21st Century Policy Brief*[5] states that English teachers must "Attend to the ethical responsibilities required by these complex [technological] environments." ISTE outlines a call for "Policies, financial plans, accountability measures, and incentive structures" that support technology use.

When it seems as though no one else in the building or district is listening, we can use these free, web-based resources as a way to start a conversation about how our policies either support, or impede, teaching and learning. As (digital) literacy advocates, we can rely on the stances taken in these broader professional communities to make a case for our students. As we rethink the policies, we will also need to consider the resources that students have available to them to enact (digital) literacies.

SHIFTING INFRASTRUCTURE: FROM BANNING DEVICES TO BRINGING DEVICES

As English teachers, especially as teachers of reading and writing, we should be fascinated by, not appalled by, our students' uses of language in relation to mobile tools and web-based applications. Described by Kristen Turner as "digitalk," this is a unique form of language use, and students should understand how to code switch depending on the context (Turner, 2012).

In many ways, the argument about whether we should allow students to use cell phones, tablet PCs, laptops, e-readers, or other such devices in school comes down to a power struggle. Because we as English teachers (and our administrators) may not be entirely familiar with the devices, or how they are used, and because there is still a sense that many of us must control our students' learning, we aim to ban the tools.

This approach to supporting a technology infrastructure misses the point entirely. Let me illustrate. Take a case in which a student uses a pencil to write a nasty note about a classmate or teacher. Certainly we take the note away (either to defuse the situation or provide evidence for a disciplinary procedure, or both). Yet we rarely, if ever, would think to take the pencil. If a student sends an offending text message or picture, it begs the question as to whether or not we should take away the phone.

Granted, many of these devices are connected to the Internet and that raises an additional level of security and threat that moves beyond the example with the pencil, yet there are also many reasons why we would want students to have their mobile devices in class, not the least of which would be to provide them with opportunities to read and write.

This leads to our second act of advocacy: moving from a policy that bans students' own technology to one that embraces them bringing their own technology (often referred to as "BYOT" or "BYOD," using "technology" or "device" at the end of the acronym, respectively). Many districts, and individual teachers, are adopting this approach, one that shifts the focus to how we can more effectively employ mobile devices in our instruction activity.

There are at least two interrelated points that you, as a (digital) literacy advocate, can make about the growing use of mobile devices as you talk with colleagues, administrators, parents, and your community. Even though not everyone will acknowledge the inevitable conclusion of this line of argument, you can present them with a variety of evidence that shows, without a doubt, that mobile devices will become a key component of schooling within the next five years, like it or not.

1. Easing, Although Not Entirely Erasing, Concerns about Equity

Sadly, the truth about our nation is that inequality exists in our society and our schools. However, we cannot fall back to this as an excuse, as a reason for why we should not be advocates for digital learning. No English teacher would suggest that we stop promoting our efforts to bring books into the lives of children, nor would we ignore the teaching of writing.

As my colleague Bud Hunt[6] has reminded me in talks about the digital divide, it is terrible that some children come to school without having breakfast, a change of clothes, or any idea where they might sleep the next night. Still, we educate the vast majority of children knowing that they may have limited access to these resources, sometimes even no access.

As advocates for (digital) literacy, we must now take the same approach with Internet access. Even though we can point to a student in each of our classrooms who does not have regular access to the Internet, the Pew Internet and American Life Project's latest demographic reports (2011) for teens show that 95 percent of them do.[7] Moreover, three quarters own a cell phone or a computer. Our students are online, whether they admit to it or not. Whether we like it or not. The question then becomes: How soon will it be before they bring these devices with them to school?

What amazes me, however, is the fact that when the latest and greatest mobile device comes out, millions are sold in the span of days. Where did the millions of devices that were replaced by this new gadget go to? How might this help provide productive ways to support students' (digital) literacy inside and outside of school?

2. Mobile Devices Are Coming to School

Now that we have proof that teens are using the Internet ubiquitously, and mobile devices in an overwhelming majority, we must consider the implications of this for school. One group, the New Media Consortium, considers questions like this every year when they release their annual "Horizon Report."[8]

In 2009, with the first edition of the K–12 Horizon report, they had predicted a two- to three-year window in which cloud computing and mobile devices would be adopted. This was only two years after the release of the iPhone. Then, in the 2012 version, they predicted that the time for broad adoption of mobile devices and tablet computers to be less than one year, noting, "Students have ever-increasing expectations of being able to work, play, and learn on these devices whenever they want and wherever they may be."

Regardless of whether students *expect* to be able to "work, play, and learn" on their own devices, there is solid evidence to suggest that they *should*. Recent professional books such as Nielsen and Webb's *Teaching Generation Text: Using Cell Phones to Enhance Learning* (2011) and Liz Kolb's *Cell Phones in the Classroom: A Practical Guide for Educators* (2011) offer many possibilities for how this can happen. Also, websites like Cool Apps for Schools[9] have emerged, offering constantly updated lists of the latest apps that would be useful across a variety of subject areas.

Parallel to the research of the New Media Consortium, Mark Warschauer reports in his latest book, *Learning in the Cloud: How (and Why) to Transform Schools with Digital Media* (2011), that there are a number of key elements that create a successful one-to-one laptop integration program with demonstrable gains in student achievement.

Warschauer characterizes the successful program as having well-defined goals and planning, a thoughtful integration of curriculum, teaching, and assessment, adequate physical infrastructure and an online environment to support student learning, a staged rollout with program evaluation, and perhaps most importantly a strong professional development component for teachers.

Whether the school provides these devices, or whether students are on the BYOD plan, it is clear that the adoption time frame is coming soon, and as (digital) literacy advocates we need to acknowledge this fact and, in combination with considering the policies noted above, think about how we can work to develop our school infrastructure in order to handle this influx.

While I understand that school budgets continue to be stretched, I also wonder, based on the amount of junk our children bring home each week in their Friday folders, how much our school spends on paper and ink, and whether that budget easily be converted to cover the cost of a tablet. In order to make this shift possible, we need to also consider how we might better organize our curriculum and instruction, the final piece of our (digital) literacy advocacy plan.

SHIFTING INSTRUCTION: FROM CONTENT CONSUMPTION TO CONTENT CREATION

Since the mid-1990s and the dawn of the web browser, computer engineers have been trying to design content management systems that allow teachers to create optimal learning experiences for their students, both as a supplement to face-to-face instruction and as an opportunity for fully virtual instruction.

Of the many systems that have been developed, both commercial products such as Blackboard as well as open source alternatives such as Moodle, the defining features of these interfaces generally include many teacher-centered tools such as an announcement board, discussion forums organized by threads, spaces to post assignments, online quizzes (with automatic multiple-choice scoring), and grade books.

On the one hand, these content management systems do allow us, as educators, to integrate technology into our teaching. Students are reading, writing, and interacting in online spaces, thus using literacy and technology to engage in conversations with one another and the world around them. Yet on the other hand, these systems are systemic, and reflect all the poor elements of schooling that education reformers have been pushing against for decades.

While these systems make it easy for teachers to manage content, they do not make it easy to facilitate student interaction or invite students to create their own content in ways that move beyond typical "teacher prompts/students respond" interactions. In fact, many of the features of such systems are punitive, including plagiarism detection software and locked-down web browsing for test taking.

In short, the content management systems themselves reflect a model in which teachers control the materials for the lesson, prompt students to engage in semi-scripted and surface-level conversations, and assess knowledge through questions that are easily acceptable in multiple-choice format. Claiming that students are "more engaged" because they are online and traceable does not mean that they are truly engrossed with their reading, writing, and overall literacy learning in substantive ways.

Thus, a third point for us to consider as (digital) literacy advocates: we need to move students into roles as content creators, not just content consumers. We also need to do this for ourselves through critical and creative professional development.

In the ever-widening expanse of services and applications, such as social bookmarking, audio and video editing, collaborative word processing, and contributing to wikis, blogs, or other web-based spaces, both teachers and students are well positioned to use their mobile devices and existing computers to create content that can be shared and accessed through cloud-based services.

This shift is significant in the sense that teachers would both honor the ideas that students discover and develop on their own and through collaboration, as well as the fact that they would be ceding some control over the content that gets presented in class. The idea of a "living textbook," as well as collaborative inquiry, critical reflection, and creative expression, all hold new possibilities as students think about how best to work together across time and space.

For instance, teachers may have to set up groups of students in a particular web-based service such as Diigo (http://www.diigo.com/), Scoop.it (http://www.scoop.it/), or Google Docs (http://drive.google.com); then students could work together to contribute content through those services.

Students engaged in a collaborative research project could use Diigo to share interesting websites within their private group, Scoop.it to then annotate and display those websites in a public page, and then Google Docs to collaborate on a final report. Thus, we need to consider what a (digital) literacy advocate does both for her own professional learning, and for her students.

1. Create a Personal Learning Network

Amongst tech-savvy educators, and even the U.S. Department of Education,[10] the idea of a using a social network as a means for professional development has become quite popular. Often dubbed "personal learning network" (Richardson & Mancabelli, 2011), or PLN for short, the concept centers on the fact that teachers can use Facebook and Twitter—as well as blogs, wikis, podcasts, and other web-based tools—to stay in touch with one another, share resources, and invite participation into traditional and nontraditional professional development events.

While teachers may go about this task in different ways, creating a personal learning network provides individual educators with an opportunity to share what they know as well as to learn from the experience of others. For instance, popular among thousands of educators are social networks such as Classroom 2.0[11] and the English Companion Ning.[12] These are two of the most popular examples of how educators can use the social networking platform to build community, share stories, invite response, and take action. Some educators are creating smaller groups within Facebook, Google+, or other larger social networking tools.

Also popular are various educational "chats" that take place on Twitter using "hashtags." For instance, each Monday night at 7 p.m. EST, English teachers from around the nation and the world get together for synchronous conversation using the "#engchat" hashtag (http://www.engchat.org/). There are numerous other educational conversations happening on Twitter, ranging from discussions of the Common Core Standards to special education to literacies. Retired educator Jerry Blumengarten (@cybrarman1) offers an ever-expanding list of such chats. [13]

Another way to gain insights from a professional learning community is by subscribing to various RSS feeds. RSS, or "really simple syndication," is the feature that pushes content out from various websites, blogs, and podcasts, thus making it easily accessible from sources other than the main website itself.

First made popular by services such as Bloglines, NetNewsGator, and Google Reader, there are now numerous apps that allow us to quickly subscribe to a variety of RSS feeds such as Flipboard, Zite, and Google Currents. [14] Essentially, these apps allow us to read blog posts, news stories, Twitter feeds, or any other item that can be delivered via RSS in a magazine-style format.

You construct your PLN; you will be able to connect with other (digital) literacy advocates, share ideas with them, and move toward action. They can provide you with other resources, just as you can share resources with them. Over time, as you build your own PLN, you can then develop formal collaborations in order to invite your students to do the same.

2. Invite Students to Create

We should not just be managing content, but also helping students create content. As (digital) literacy advocates, we know and understand the need for an authentic audience. Since publishing to the web has become second nature for most of our students, it is likely that we will not meet much resistance as we invite them to create content.

What might provide more resistance, however, is asking them to think about that content and how it affects their readers, viewers, and listeners that will interact with it. More importantly, we also need to invite students to think about how they are contributing to the broader conversation and responding appropriately to their peers.

To that end, I provide brief introductions to three projects that are worthy of your further attention. I do not have the space in this chapter to fully elaborate on each one, and you will be well served to visit each site to find out how educators are actively promoting (digital) literacy skills in the lives of youth.

Youth Voices[15]

Coordinated by National Writing Project teachers Paul Allison and Chris Sloan,

> Youth Voices is a school-based social network that was started in 2003 by a group of National Writing Project teachers. We merged several earlier blogging projects. We have found that there are many advantages to bringing students together in one site that lives beyond any particular class. It's easier for individual students to read and write about their own passions, to connect with other students, comment on each other's work, and create multimedia posts for each other. Further, it's been exciting for us to pool our knowledge about curriculum and digital literacies.

Digital ID Project[16]

Gail Desler and Natalie Bernasconi, also National Writing Project teachers, have created a project based on digital citizenship and authentic writing opportunities:

> It is our hope that through this project and wiki, we can help students understand and reach their full potential as 21st century digital citizens. We also hope to initiate conversations at sites and districts around the importance of digital citizenship skills being taught as an integral part of the core curriculum, as opposed to a set of lessons or unit taught in isolation.

Student Docs[17]

George Mayo, a middle school language arts teacher from Maryland, has created a project in which his students learn the skills of documentary filmmaking: Student Docs. Over the course of a semester, students do traditional research at the library and on the Internet, and may also contact experts on the topic to conduct interviews, either in person or via Skype. The final films are then shown at the festival and judged by peers and parents. Each film is designed in a documentary style, and students study the art and craft of filmmaking while also engaging in a substantial amount of writing.

These are but a few examples of the many outstanding educators who are engaging in (digital) literacy advocacy through authentic projects that invite students to compose texts across a variety of genres, media, and purposes. Shifting our vision of instruction can be done, and these teachers and their students provide models for how it can happen.

CONCLUSION

(Digital) literacy advocacy, like any form of advocacy, requires vigilance. This action is no longer under the purview, if it ever really was, of technology coordinators or IT staff. These colleagues understand technology, and we need their collaborative efforts to support the policies, infrastructure, and curriculum. However, they do not have the deep knowledge about literacy that we, as English teachers do. It is up to us.

Specifically, we need to shift our thinking, teaching, and outreach to administrators, technology directors, and parents. We would never stand for a school that limited access to pencils, paper, and books. So, too, must we never stand for a school, even in these times of limited budgets, core standards, and ongoing assessments, that would limit access to the Internet, prevent students from using the devices that they already use, or narrow our curricular scope and instructional choices.

As English teachers, we must advocate for (digital) literacy with the same fervor that we have used to stop books from being banned, to encourage a process-based approach to writing, and to integrate multiple voices and cultures into our canon of literature. Sponsors for these literacy causes have long histories from which we can learn. The implications for students' (digital) literacy are far too important for us not to take on this new front as advocates.

NOTES

1. http://www.cosn.org/sites/default/files/pdf/Revised%20AUP%20March%202013_final.pdf
2. http://copyrightconfusion.wikispaces.com/
3. http://copyrightconfusion.wikispaces.com/file/view/Tool+for+reasoning+Fair+Use.pdf
4. http://www.iste.org/docs/pdfs/netsessentialconditions.pdf?sfvrsn=2
5. http://www.ncte.org/library/NCTEFiles/Resources/Magazine/CC0183_Brief_Literacy.pdf
6. http://www.budtheteacher.com/
7. http://pewinternet.org/Trend-Data-(Teens).aspx
8. http://www.nmc.org/pdf/2012-horizon-report-K12.pdf
9. http://coolappsforschools.wikispaces.com/home
10. http://www.ed.gov/technology/netp-2010
11. http://www.classroom20.com/
12. http://englishcompanion.ning.com/
13. http://cybraryman.com/chats.html
14. http://flipboard.com/, http://zite.com/, https://www.google.com/producer/currents
15. http://youthvoices.net/
16. http://digital-id.wikispaces.com/
17. http://studentdocs.wikispaces.com/

REFERENCES

Bauerlein, M. (2008). *The dumbest generation: How the digital age stupefies young Americans and jeopardizes our future.* New York, N.Y.: Tarcher.

Carr, N. (2010). *The shallows: What the Internet is doing to our brains.* New York, N.Y.: W. W. Norton & Company.

Center for Social Media, School of Communication, American University. (2009). *Code of best practices in fair use for media literacy education.* Retrieved from http://mediaeducation-lab.com/sites/mediaeducationlab.com/files/CodeofBestPracticesinFairUse.pdf.

Hicks, T., & Turner, K. H. (2013). No longer a luxury: Digital literacy can't wait. *English Journal, 102* (6), 58–65.

Hobbs, R. (2010). *Copyright clarity: How fair use supports digital learning.* Thousand Oaks, Calif.: Corwin Press.

Ito, M., Baumer, S., Bittanti, M., boyd, danah, Cody, R., Herr-Stephenson, B., Horst, H. A., et al. (2009). *Hanging out, messing around, and geeking out: Kids living and learning with new media.* Cambridge, Mass.: The MIT Press.

Kajder, S. (2010). *Adolescents and digital literacies: Learning alongside our students.* Urbana, Ill.: National Council of Teachers of English. Retrieved from http://www1.ncte.org/store/books/language/130985.htm.

Kolb, L. (2011). *Cell phones in the classroom: A practical guide for educators.* Washington, D.C.: International Society for Technology in Education.

Nielsen, L., & Webb, W. (2011). *Teaching generation text: Using cell phones to enhance learning.* San Francisco, Calif.: Jossey-Bass.

Richardson, W., & Mancabelli, R. (2011). *Personal learning networks: Using the power of connections to transform education.* Bloomington, Ind.: Solution Tree.

Robinson, K. (2011). *Out of our minds: Learning to be creative* (2nd ed.). North Mankato, Minn.: Capstone.

Turkle, S. (2011). *Alone together: Why we expect more from technology and less from each other.* New York, N.Y.: Basic Books.

Turner, K. H. (2012). Digitalk as community. *English Journal, 101* (4), 37–42.

Warschauer, M. (2011). *Learning in the cloud: How (and why) to transform schools with digital media.* New York, N.Y.: Teachers College Press.

Chapter Eleven

"Don't Say Gay"

*Using Action Research to Interrogate Language
Use in the English Classroom*

Susan L. Groenke and Judson C. Laughter

The English classroom is unique; nowhere else is time set aside in school for the direct and specific study of language. Too often, however, this study consists of prescriptive grammar rules or vocabulary terms rather than investigation into the power of language itself: how language shapes our thinking and ways of being in the world; what language makes possible; what it constrains and oppresses; how language nurtures and empowers, or disrupts, or is disrupted. Fairclough (1989) asserted that through language our assumptions are made visible, and assumptions about others, ourselves, and the way the world should be predicate power relationships.

As critical English teacher educators, the authors believe that the English classroom is a particularly suitable place to unmask how power relationships work. In the English classroom, teachers can encourage students to consider how authors use words in particular ways to stir up emotions, to highlight particular ideas about situations, individuals, or groups of people, and to manipulate others. It is in English classrooms especially where students can learn to understand how words are imbued with particular meanings by the cultures in which they live, and how oppression can happen through the labels and discourse styles they use (Johnson & Freedman, 2005).

The southern writer Ellen Gilchrist (1987) said, "We live at the level of our language. Whatever we can articulate we can imagine or explore" (p. 30). This powerful sentiment resonates and informs the work with preservice English teachers discussed in this chapter.

What is the language level of our soon-to-be English teachers? What are they able to articulate, and thus imagine or explore? What are they not able to articulate, and thus not imagine or explore? What is our responsibility in disrupting their language use or giving them language to use? How can we best prepare them to challenge their own students to interrogate the language they use and to possibly learn new languages?

These questions are explored in this chapter through two parallel stories, one set inside the frame of the other. The first is the story of an English education internship program at the University of Tennessee, Knoxville. The second is the story of Casey (pseudonym), a former English education intern in the program. Casey's story provides an in-depth, representative example of how English educators and preservice teachers strive to learn a new language together—the language of social justice. In particular, Casey's story engages the power of language and the power to change people through language.

At the University of Tennessee, the English education program follows a specific path in this language process, which culminates in an original Action Research project. Over the course of a year-long internship, teacher interns like Casey are guided through a process designed to awaken their own critical consciousness in the classroom, connect them with their students, and develop practical methods for making the classroom, the school, and the community a better place.

For those involved, Action Research (hereafter AR) is more than just teacher self-study, more than learning how to develop better classroom management skills or create a better unit plan. Instead, it is a methodology for unmasking and unmaking systemic oppressions that surround the act of teaching itself. Learning to interrogate language and disrupting status quo language use—especially when it oppresses and denigrates others—is part of this process.

The chapter begins with a more in-depth definition of AR to provide a framework for our goals and methods as critical English teacher educators. It then presents a series of assignments that culminate in the action research project and traces Casey's progress through each as representative of the interns in our program. It concludes with reflections on the teachers that interns become and the authors as critical English teacher educators.

WHAT IS ACTION RESEARCH?

AR provides practical solutions to real problems in the classroom. AR allows a teacher to systematically identify a problem, understand a problem, and work toward rectifying a problem. AR is grounded in the real, lived context of the classroom, but maintains the scientific ideals of systematicity and empirical findings grounded in data.

As such, AR is not something that happens behind the scenes, but is a process that engages researcher and participants as allies: "It is important to remember that action research does not involve studies *on* participants (as in positivist human subjects research). Instead, it involves studies *with* participants" (Hinchey, 2008, p. 97, emphasis in original). Everyone in a classroom benefits from the resolution of problematic issues and so AR emerges from within the setting and involves all stakeholders as potential beneficiaries.

Several definitions of AR exist in the literature (see table 11.1), but with the interns, two primary sources are focal: Reason and Bradbury's (2001) *Handbook* and Hinchey's (2008) *Action Research*; the latter serves as the primary textbook for the two-semester sequence.

While listed last by Reason and Bradbury (2001), the emancipatory nature of AR is the foundation of our work; in short, if a project does not engage issues of social justice, then it isn't considered Action Research.

In limiting our definition of AR to "Emancipatory Action Research" (Hinchey, 2008, p. 41), we find our roots in John Dewey's view of teachers as active agents, John Collier's work (as the Commissioner of Indian Affairs) to undo injustices, Kurt Lewin's countering of social discrimination, and Paulo Freire's vision of dialogue and activism. (Hinchey's *Primer* includes an excellent summative history of AR.)

Overall, this project builds on the foundation of Reason and Bradbury's (2001) succinct definition that casts AR as Praxis, the development of new knowledge, and new kinds of knowledge, through action and reflection:

> [AR is] a participatory, democratic process concerned with developing practical knowing in the pursuit of worthwhile human purposes, grounded in a participatory worldview, which we believe is emerging at this historical mo-

Table 11.1.   Action Research Definitions

Hinchey (2008)	*Reason & Bradbury (2001)*
• Conducted by those inside a community rather than by outside experts;	• Starts with everyday experience;
• Pursues improvement or better understanding in some area the researcher considers important;	• Develops living knowledge and new abilities to create knowledge;
• Involves systematic inquiry, which includes information gathering, analysis, and reflection;	• Emerges over time and cannot be programmatic or defined in hard methods;
• Leads to an action plan, which frequently generates a new cycle of the process.	• Is emancipatory, a verb rather than a noun.

ment. It seeks to bring together action and reflection, theory and practice, in participation with others, in the pursuit of practical solutions to issues of pressing concern to people, and more generally the flourishing of individual persons and their communities. (p. 1)

At each step in the AR process, students are encouraged to identify and engage the myriad social issues they see and language use they hear in their own classrooms, schools, and communities.

THE INTERNSHIP YEAR

Teacher education at the University of Tennessee follows a fifth-year Holmes model; interns complete content-area degrees as undergraduates and then come to our department for a graduate degree in general and content pedagogy. In addition to twenty-four hours of graduate coursework, each intern completes a twelve-hour student teaching internship that lasts an academic year. From the inception of this program, negotiations with the graduate school required a research component to the internship in order for students to earn graduate hours for student teaching.

While this may seem a burden, particularly by those interns experiencing their first year as teachers, our two-semester AR sequence provides an opportunity to combine theory with practice in the engagement of social justice issues. Throughout the internship year, the program purposively constructs assignments to foster an awareness of social justice issues and language use in educational settings (and beyond). These assignments are described below.

Social Justice Autobiography

The course begins with the assumption that the desire to become a teacher is somehow rooted in a desire to make the world a better place. Thus, the first assignment of the fall semester asks interns to engage their own educational and personal histories through a summative and critical autobiography. Like other critical teacher educators who utilize narrative writing in their coursework (for example, Clark & Medina, 2000; Dyson & Genishi, 1994), we believe that student-authored narratives can be powerful tools in helping beginning teachers make and understand the complex connections that exist among issues of social justice and teacher identity.

This assignment begins the process of helping beginning teachers consider their own teacher identities, particularly an identity willing to engage issues of social justice:

> You will write a five to seven page autobiography describing your memories and thoughts about how you are coming to see yourself as a potential change agent. You might find it useful to pose questions to your parents, teachers, or

siblings but you should mostly rely on your own memories, thoughts, and reflections about how you came to understand, represent, and develop awareness of social justice issues. The informal oral presentation and written assignment might focus on various stages of personal development and should convey not only a summative report of awareness but should also demonstrate critical thinking about that development and growth. (Syllabus)

Before teachers can come to know and care for their students, they must come to know themselves and wrestle with any pieces of their upbringing that might prove antithetical to seeing themselves as change agents.

As Clark and Medina (2000) explained, autobiographical narratives encourage beginning teachers to make a "critical revision of the life influences that help individuals construct their identity and how that identity relates to the rest of the world" (p. 65). In writing their autobiographies, interns engage in a process of self-critique and revision that catalyzes their initial understandings of who they are, both as individuals and as teachers.

As an intern, Casey engaged in this process of self-critique and revision in the writing of the autobiography. In attempts to understand personal social justice motivations, Casey wrote, "[In my hometown,] I heard loud preaching about the word of God and being good Christians, but I saw racism, widespread homophobia, and judgment. In response to the hate that I witnessed, I tried to distinguish myself from the small-town small-mindedness and actively reject the culture."

In addition, Casey experienced anger and humiliation when matriculating to college and realized only Creationism had been taught in the local high school biology courses. Similarly, while Casey had made good grades in high school, the realization hit that high school had not provided preparation for writing the lengthy, expository essays professors required. Angered once again, Casey vowed to return home as a small town teacher and "avenge the deficiencies in my own schooling."

However, as explained in the autobiography, Casey realized the need to come to terms with "small town culture," and even appreciate it. Casey also realized that these earlier feelings about upbringing and hometown were influencing a desire to work for social justice as a teacher:

Having experienced what it feels like to be written off as unintelligent because I am Southern and because I am from a small town, I feel compelled to be a part of a school that is doing everything it can to give students a chance to succeed in spite of it all. No longer is my philosophy only to expose [future students] to a social justice curriculum, but it is also to be a part of social justice for them. While I still want to combat the culture of racism, homophobia, and anti-intellectualism that can often go unchecked in a small town . . . I want to do it from a position that acknowledges the injustices committed against the students.

As Bruner described, narrative is a way of "world-making" (1994, p. 28), a "speech act . . . whose intention is to initiate and guide a search for meanings among a possible spectrum of meanings" (1986, p. 25). Our students search for meaning—using the language they have—in the life stories they write, and thus make their "level of their language" visible, and what they can both imagine and may need to explore further.

Ultimately, their narratives become dialogical artifacts that provide a space for professor and interns to begin discussing language use, particularly the language used to describe student and educational experiences. As such, autobiographical narratives "help to disrupt preservice teachers' stereotyped conceptions of *others* and interrupt . . . dominant, generalized discourses" (Clark & Medina, 2000, p. 73). In sharing the autobiography with the rest of the cohort, interns begin to see similarities and differences in each other's educational experiences and also begin to recognize the limits and partiality of their perspectives.

Research Question

The next step in the AR process is the development of a strong research question that matches the context of the study and addresses some issue of social justice. Following is a modified version of Dana and Yendol-Hoppey's (2008) list of eight *passions* that emerged from an analysis of over 100 teacher inquiry projects:

1. Helping an Individual Child
2. Desire to Improve or Enrich Curriculum
3. Focusing on Developing Content Knowledge
4. Desire to Improve or Experiment with Teaching Strategies and Teaching Techniques
5. Desire to Explore the Relationship Between Your Beliefs and Your Classroom Practice
6. The Intersection of Your Personal and Professional Identities
7. Advocating Social Justice
8. Focus on Understanding the Teaching and Learning Context

Interns are steered toward projects relating to the first four. Passions 5, 6, and 8 require more classroom experience before they can be engaged meaningfully (although there have been some interns who have pursued such projects).

Course instructors reinforce that passion 7 is not a separate option but something taken up in any project. At first, the insistence that the interns find something in which they are personally interested does not always lend itself to advocating social justice. However, a focus of the assignment is drawing out a social justice issue from even seemingly mundane research questions.

For example, a question centered on how to engage students more effectively can reach into areas of student motivation and the development of students who advocate for their own educational needs. Likewise, a project wanting to examine the practice of literature circles quickly leads to the possibilities of dialogic pedagogy and the development of student voice. Through one-on-one negotiation with each intern, research questions are constructed that are both important to each intern and advocate for social justice at some level.

As indicated in the autobiography, Casey saw social justice as intimately connected to work as a high school English teacher. Casey wrote a desire to "be a part of social justice" for students, and when starting the internship at an urban high school Casey got this opportunity.

On one of the first days teaching independently, three self-identified straight males began calling each other "gay dudes" and using the word "gay" to describe things they did not like. Casey made efforts to challenge their language use, but the students resisted these efforts—sometimes combatively—and asked Casey to give reasons why they couldn't use the word "gay." They claimed to have said it all of the time and that it "didn't matter." "Other teachers" did not care.

As the AR class moved beyond the educational autobiography and into the action research project, Casey saw an opportunity to learn how to effectively address and disrupt the students' homophobic speech in the classroom. In reflecting back on motivations for the action research study, Casey explained that this was a responsibility as the teacher and "authority in the classroom," to be "a visible ally for any students in the classroom who were experiencing discrimination, including LGBTQ youth." For Casey, being a "visible ally" meant challenging students' use of homophobic speech.

Thus, through the AR study, Casey wanted to explore what happened when making such challenges in the classroom. Casey also wanted to "raise student consciousness regarding the use of the word 'gay,'" and wanted to see if dialogue and strong teacher-student relationships could be used to challenge heteronormativity in the English classroom.

Ultimately, too, Casey wanted to "create a classroom environment that was not only safe for but also affirming of sexual minority students." The guiding research question Casey settled on was: How might a teacher use positive relationships with students as a method for stopping homophobic speech and reducing homophobia among students?

Equity Audit

Concurrent with the development of the research question, instructors also provide tools to help interns explore the context in which their AR project will occur. Our primary tool is Frattura and Capper's (2007) equity audit, an eight-page document that presents a series of general and demographic-specific questions that ask interns to quantify certain aspects of their schools, such as status of labeling (for example, "gifted," "at-risk") and number of students receiving free/reduced-price lunch. Other questions focus on social class, race and ethnicity, English Language Learners, ability, and sexual orientation and gender identity (see Groenke, 2010, for more information).

In the English education program, interns in the same schools often work together to find as many of these labels and numbers as they can, and they are encouraged to consider the implications and consequences of the labels used to describe students. The power of the equity audit, however, emerges in class discussion when interns begin to compare schools within the same district.

Interns begin asking questions about why one school has a larger number of English Language Learners but no significant support for their education. They ask why the labels "at-risk" and "gifted" so often correlate with the numbers of "students of color." These discussions often drive the development of the research question, either causing interns to completely rewrite their questions, or to begin to see how social justice issues intersect with real, day-to-day issues in schools.

For Casey, the equity audit helped make how the school had a publicized, school-sponsored Gay Student Alliance (GSA), with both LGBTQ students and straight allies, visible. Casey also used the equity audit as an opportunity to research the schools' bullying and harassment policy, and found that sexual orientation and gender expression were specifically protected in the policy. This emboldened Casey to pursue this line of research.

The Literature Review

From this grounding, the rest of the AR project proceeds like many qualitative studies. The interns perform a review of current research in which we move them away from the format of an annotated bibliography toward a more critical synthesis. They travel to the library and learn how to use the available database and research resources effectively. Interns are encouraged to write a description of their literature review process and develop a review chart in which they organize notes about each article reviewed.

Because Casey was interested in the role of the teacher, teacher-student relationships, and the use of classroom dialogue in preventing homophobia in the high school English classroom, Casey focused the literature review on student homophobic rhetoric and teacher responsibility. Casey used the literature review to find specific classroom strategies teachers had used to combat homophobic speech and to read research by other educators specifically attempting to disrupt the heteronormative culture of schools.

Through the literature review and research, Casey found that the word "gay" used in a negative, pejorative way was the most frequently reported usage of homophobic language in schools (Kosciw et al., 2010). Casey also found that students' homophobic language use in schools is often met with silence from teachers and administrators and, as a result, many LGBTQ students feel unsafe at school.

However, as Casey also found, it is the classroom teacher who is a key factor in how sexual minority students feel about their school experiences. In fact, positive student feelings about the teacher—that the teacher cares about students, that the students get along with the teacher, and the teacher treats students fairly—were the most significant factors in preventing school troubles for sexual minority youth.

While this information was helpful to Casey in that it reinforced and supported the rationale for carrying out this research, it was Zack, Mannheim, and Alfano's (2010) "I Didn't Know What to Say: Four Archetypal Responses to Homophobic Language in the Classroom" that helped determine how to pursue a position in the classroom as a "visible ally" for LGBTQ youth.

Zack, Mannheim, and Alfano (2010) classified preservice and new teachers' responses to homophobic speech into four categories: the avoider, the hesitator, the confronter, and the integrator. Avoiders and hesitators either ignored or were reluctant to address instances of homophobic language in their classrooms. The authors explained reasons for this silence or reluctance as fear of "being accused of being gay by students, encountering religious opposition . . . and feeling pressured to focus on content" (p. 105).

On the other end of the spectrum, an integrator is a teacher who combats homophobia "by integrating homophobia reduction into the curriculum" (Zack, Mannheim, & Alfano, 2010, p. 104). Student teachers in this category planned and implemented full curricular units focused on LGBTQ issues and equality.

The remaining category, confronters, consisted of student teachers that were willing to "take time from the scheduled lesson plan to address homophobic slurs that were leveled against the students" (Zack, Mannheim, & Alfano, 2010, p. 103). Still other confronters intervened against homophobic language even when it did not have a specific target—for example, when students used the word "gay" as a synonym for "stupid" (p. 103).

These teachers did not incorporate anti-homophobia messages into the curriculum, but they also did not let teachable moments pass them by. Another common characteristic of confronters was their belief that their school, administration, and school board would support them in efforts to combat homophobia.

Casey did feel supported by the school and administration, but had another reason for choosing this confronter model:

> I chose this latter archetype, the confronter, as a model for my own teaching because it was compatible with my curricular restraints [Casey, as a student teacher, could not implement a new curriculum], but also allowed me to put my lesson plans on hold at my own discretion. Although this placed me in a reactive rather than proactive position within the classroom, I was able to address instances of homophobic language as needed while also staying on track with prescribed curriculum pacing.

In addition to finding literature that helped Casey better understand how to be a "visible ally" for students, Casey was also able to find useful information on specific strategies for combating homophobic speech in the classroom. Casey found one particular article helpful, Maurer-Starks, Clemons, and Whalen's (2008) study of athletic trainers who were working to disrupt homophobic language use in school athletics.

Casey liked Maurer-Starks, Clemons, and Whalen's (2008) idea of a three-step program for confronting homophobic speech: 1) acknowledgment, or making students aware that you heard the language; 2) education, or teaching students about the weight and consequences of their words; and 3) dialogue, or the willingness to engage students in conversation about their language use. Casey agreed with the authors that "a dismissive reprimand only forces the students' attitudes underground and leaves them unchanged and [thus] they will likely continue their homophobic remarks" (p. 331). Thus, she adopted the three-step program as a framework for how to address homophobic language in the classroom.

Methods

Once a firm foundation in available research is established, interns begin to develop study methods addressing their research questions. The methods include specific information about the study context and participants, an area in which information from the equity audit is often included. The methods also include descriptions of data collection and analysis. Casey decided to focus on interactions and conversations with three male students in particular—Jamal, Wayne, and Robby (pseudonyms).

Casey chose these students due to behaviors that they had demonstrated during class time, particularly their initial outbursts of homophobic language that Casey challenged immediately, as well as one student's persistent, repetitive use of homophobic language even after Casey's challenges and consistent use of the three-step approach.

Casey took personal fieldnotes from class. After class ended each day, she would make observations about what had happened during that lesson and was particularly careful to document instances of homophobic language use, making note of both the content and context of conversations as they occurred between students and teacher. Casey considered details such as how much time had passed in the lesson, the nature of the discussion that preceded the incident, what other students were doing during the exchange, and how teacher and student agreed to move forward.

These observational notes went hand in hand with Casey's second data source, a researcher journal. While Casey tried to remain objective in presenting events in the fieldnotes, the researcher journal was a space and an outlet to reflect on and analyze the events described in the notes. Casey found that reflecting soon after an incident and then again later, after being removed from immediate reactions and responses, was significant in helping to understand her own process for working with the students and responding to their behavior.

The journal also served as a space for reflection. Casey writes, "This journal was also a space for me to critically analyze my role as a teacher, researcher, and adult role model to all of the students who were directly and indirectly involved in my project. It also let me reflect on how I might or could have done things differently than I did in the moment."

Casey's final data source was a thirty-minute semi-structured interview with each of the three student participants described above; they all consented to be participants and took consent forms home with a description of the study. To develop a protocol for the interviews, Casey relied on observational fieldnotes from class.

When wanting students to reflect on their motivation for certain behaviors, Casey went back through the notes and described classroom events in which students had used homophobic language and Casey had worked to challenge it. Casey did this first, and gave students the opportunity to describe how they understood the events. This ensured that she and the students shared an understanding of the classroom events before Casey asked them to reflect on them.

Casey then proceeded in the interviews to ask specific questions: each participant was asked to define what "gay" meant to him, how often they chose it as an insult as opposed to other terms, how long they had been using that term as a pejorative, how they responded to Casey's challenge strategies, and what alternative measures Casey could have taken to be more effective in disrupting their homophobic speech.

Findings

In the spring, as the study methods are put into play, class time is devoted to working on data analysis and practicing the constant comparative method (Strauss & Corbin, 1998). Instructors specifically separate findings from implications. They push the interns to first describe what happened when the study methods developed in the fall were put into practice. This specific separation between asking "What happened?" and "What does it mean?" is important for new researchers who too often want to jump to sweeping claims about what they are seeing in their classrooms or expect a reader to make those jumps for them.

Casey's analysis of fieldnotes and researcher journal revealed patterns in Jamal's, Wayne's, and Robby's use of homophobic speech over time. Predominantly, Jamal and Wayne began autocorrecting themselves and apologizing for "slipping." But Robby continued to resist Casey's attempts to disrupt and challenge his speech. Casey wrote in the journal about one particularly trying day:

> Robby revealed that even though he was trying not to say "that's so gay" in my class, he did not care if people knew that he did not like gay people. This led to more of a confrontation than a conversation on my behalf. In previous conversations, I had tried to demonstrate that I was always open to hearing the participant's side of the dialogue; however, I was not willing to let him justify this statement and further the conversation.

He would later claim that his personal religious beliefs justified his sentiments.

Data collected during interviews confirmed the notes made during observation and reflection. Robby had said in his interview that he was proud to reveal that he would not change his language or feelings about gay people, and there was nothing Casey could have done to change his mind or behavior, even using a teacher's authority to stop him from saying it in the classroom. Robby admitted to having been reprimanded for his language before, but only laughed about it.

During his interview, Casey had Robby compose his own statement, so that he would not be misinterpreted or misrepresented in the study. In response to the question, "What could I or someone else do to get you to change your mind about the offensive nature of calling things 'gay' when you mean bad?" he responded:

> Being very religious I wouldn't care if a "gay" person got mad. The way I mean it, it's taken out of context so if they get mad I wouldn't care cause I know god don't approve of their choice in sin, that's why god destroyed "sodem and gumor."

Casey felt progress in working with Jamal and Wayne, the "G dudes," had been considerably more successful than with Robby. Based on initial observations, Casey suspected that the motivation behind their use of homophobic speech was of a different nature than Robby's. Data analysis revealed that Jamal was self-correcting his offensive speech and language choices far more frequently than Robby. Jamal had even gone so far as to promise Casey that he would try to hold Wayne and himself accountable for not "slipping up" anymore.

Jamal revealed in his interview that he considered the word "gay" to mean weak and admitted to using it as a form of disrespect. However, he insisted during an interview that he was "not really upset with gay people." He explained that Wayne and he were "just playin'" when they said it in class, and eventually continued saying it just to tease Casey. The data Casey collected about conversations with Jamal over time and ongoing reflections about Jamal's statements suggested that he continued to struggle in connecting his use of the word "gay" with actual harm. Two statements from his interview revealed this contradiction in his held beliefs.

First, his assertion that he used the word to put his male friends down showed a connection between being "gay" and being undesirable or weak. However, when asked for his final comments, he wanted Casey to include that he was not "against [being gay]" and would even support legalized gay marriage. In his perception, he was not bullying anyone or intending any harm. However, Jamal and Casey reached a mutual point of respect over the course of the school year. He wanted to stop saying "gay," and he also demonstrated through his promises that he wanted to please his teacher.

Casey's third participant, Wayne, fell somewhere in the middle of the spectrum between Robby's acknowledged homonegativity and Jamal's honest attempts to change his language. Over the course of the year, data analysis revealed that Wayne's use of the pejorative "G dude" remained consistent when Jamal and Robby were making observable efforts to use homophobic speech less and less.

Wayne was also the only student who had been previously written up for using the word "gay" as a pejorative. He was sent to the office, but then "just sat in the office," which was "not that big of a deal." This demonstrated that formal disciplinary measures were not enough to dissuade some students from this habit. When probed about his personal history with this type of speech in his interview, he recalled hearing it from his older brothers as long as he could remember.

Wayne often rationalized his use of the word "gay" as okay because he thought no one in Casey's class was gay. In ongoing observation of his behavior, Casey documented his indifference about the consequences of his behavior. He was not afraid of getting in trouble, and he did not believe that his language was offensive. However, the information he revealed in his interview was a significant contribution to Casey's findings.

When asked about his motivation for continuing to say "gay" and "G dude" despite requests for him to stop, he replied, "about 8/10 times I do it just to bother you." Casey realized from this that, quite unintentionally, the rapport that developed with Wayne had backfired: Wayne's decision to keep saying "G dude" actually became his perceived way of joking with Casey.

Casey concluded that Wayne had not been taking these efforts seriously. When Casey asked Wayne if he would have been more likely to quit using homophobic language if Casey had used formal disciplinary measures instead, he replied that he would have been "less likely to cooperate." Suggested in this answer is his belief that although he continued to say "G dude," he had on some unspoken level been cooperating with Casey's efforts.

Implications

From their analyses and findings, professors push the interns to draw implications from the data both for the field and for their own practice. In short, they invite the interns to think about what they are learning from their project and describe: 1) Why is this important to you as a teacher? and 2) Why might this be important to another teacher?

Ultimately, Casey felt that all three participants exemplified both the homophobia and heteronormative assumptions that pervade school cultures. Casey felt that Wayne, Jamal, and Robby used the word "gay" among straight males as a form of dominance behavior. For Jamal at least, labeling another male as "gay" was intended to indicate weakness and therefore inferiority, while also elevating the status of the labeler in contrast.

Casey described how these behaviors established a hierarchy of power among students that prevented equitable opportunities for engagement and learning within the classroom. These behaviors also served to solidify gender role stereotypes that contributed to the culture of heteronormativity so prevalent in schools.

Even though Casey's high school provided institutional and visible support for LGBTQ students, this "symbolic" support did not guarantee LGBTQ equality. Casey felt that the fact that each participant thought nothing of using the word "gay" in front of a teacher was telling; none of the students were afraid of being disciplined for using homophobic speech. For Casey, Wayne's revelation that the administration did not punish him for his previous offense only further confirmed the importance of the teacher's responsibility to confront homophobia uncovered during the literature review (Kosciw et al., 2010; Maurer-Starks, Clemons, & Whalen, 2008; Zack, Mannheim, & Alfano, 2010).

This only strengthened Casey's resolve: "The only way to ensure that students confront their ideas is to engage them in a dialogue about the consequences of their language, even if they do not perceive how it is causing harm." Casey also felt strong in the conviction that being a "visible ally" for LGBTQ youth in schools required curricular integration of literature and current events to raise awareness of human rights issues.

Being an ally required a teacher's willingness to consistently confront homophobic speech and actions. Developing relationships with students and providing opportunities to dialogue about typically taboo subjects helped Casey in direct challenges and confrontations of students' homophobic language use.

As Casey wrote in the final report of the study, "Homophobia and heteronormativity disrupt the possibility of safe and equitable learning conditions for all students. . . . As a teacher, I had a responsibility to demonstrate caring and support for all of my students. . . . Through the committed use of personal relationships and ongoing dialogue, I was able to make small gains in addressing prejudicial beliefs and expressions."

Casey remained hopeful that other teachers might learn from this research and take up the practice to address and challenge homophobia and hate speech. She did understand, however, that larger, more systemic attention needed to be given to fighting homophobia in schools: "Ultimately, more substantial progress and success in the fight against homophobia will require a change in the larger culture and institutions of our nation as a whole."

CONCLUSION

Casey's experience as described here—from a burgeoning understanding of social justice motivations, to a study of ways to address homophobic speech in schools, to the active and courageous fight to confront and interrogate homophobic language use—evidences the fact that AR is a powerful and necessary process for beginning teachers. Social justice-oriented AR, as described by Hinchey (2008) and Reason and Bradbury (2001), pursues improvement or better understanding in some area the researcher considers important, develops living knowledge and new abilities to create knowledge, and actively pursues an emancipatory agenda.

Through AR, Casey accomplished these goals, learning how to be an ally to LGBTQ youth and how to challenge and disrupt homophobic speech in the classroom and school setting. The authors are proud and encouraged by the fact that Casey now teaches full time and continues to pursue this work.

Casey's AR project also confirmed the importance and value of centering the study of language as power in both the English classroom and English education program. Casey's story shows that people use language for multiple and varied purposes, and one cannot always assume to know what those purposes are. As Casey found, students used homophobic speech for different reasons—some to police masculinity, some to denigrate others or others' perceived lifestyles, and still others just to irritate the teacher.

Merely calling such language "inappropriate" or sending students to the office for using such language without interrogating students' understandings and purposes of the language does not help move beyond the current "level of our language." Such practices might serve as temporary (and certainly necessary) solutions, but they do not help to explore the motivations behind current language use, or to learn new language to use, and thus new ways of being in the world.

Critical English teacher educators must continue to help beginning teachers to understand that the English classroom can be more than a place to read classical literature and learn grammar rules and vocabulary terms. The English classroom can also serve as a site for new "world-making," and Action Research can help beginning teachers imagine and explore such worlds.

REFERENCES

Bruner, J. (1986). *Actual minds, possible worlds.* Cambridge, Mass.: Harvard University Press.

Bruner, J. (1994). Life as narrative. In A. H. Dyson & C. Genishi (Eds.), *The need for story: Cultural diversity in classroom and community* (pp. 28–37). Urbana, Ill.: National Council of Teachers of English.

Clark, C. T., & Medina, C. L. (2000). How reading and writing literacy narratives affects preservice teachers' understandings of literacy, pedagogy, and multiculturalism. *Journal of Teacher Education, 51* (1), 63–76.

Dana, N. F., & Yendol-Hoppey, D. (2008). *The reflective educator's guide to classroom research: Learning to teach and teaching to learn through practitioner inquiry* (2nd ed.). Thousand Oaks, Calif.: Corwin Press.

Dyson, A. H., & Genishi, C. (Eds.). (1994). *The need for story: Cultural diversity in classroom and community.* Urbana, Ill.: National Council of Teachers of English.

Fairclough, N. (1989). *Power and language.* New York, N.Y.: Longman.

Frattura, E. M., & Capper, C. M. (2007). *Leading for social justice: Transforming schools for all learners.* Thousand Oaks, Calif.: Sage.

Gilchrist, E. (1987). *Falling through space: The journals of Ellen Gilchrist.* New York, N.Y.: Little, Brown & Co.

Groenke, S. L. (2010). Seeing, inquiring, witnessing: Using the equity audit in practitioner inquiry to rethink inequity in public schools. *English Education, 43* (1), 83–96.

Hinchey, P. H. (2008). *Action research.* New York, N.Y.: Peter Lang.

Johnson, H., & Freedman, L. (2005). *Developing critical awareness at the middle level: Using texts as tools for critique and pleasure.* Newark, Del.: International Reading Association.

Kosciw, J. G., Greytak, E. A., Diaz, E. M., Bartkiewicz, M. J., & Gay, L. (2010). *The 2009 National school climate survey: The experiences of lesbian, gay, bisexual and transgender youth in our nation's schools.* New York, N.Y.: Gay, Lesbian and Straight Education Network (GLSEN).

Maurer-Starks, S. S., Clemons, H. L., & Whalen, S. L. (2008). Managing heteronormativity and homonegativity in athletic training: In and beyond the classroom. *Journal of Athletic Training, 43* (3), 326–36.

Reason, P., & Bradbury, H. (Eds.) (2001). *Handbook of action research.* Los Angeles, Calif.: Sage.

Strauss, A., & Corbin, J. (1998). *Basics of qualitative research: Techniques and procedures for developing grounded theory* (2nd ed.). Thousand Oaks, Calif.: Sage.

Zack, J., Mannheim, A., & Alfano, M. (2010). I didn't know what to say: Four archetypal responses to homophobic rhetoric in the classroom. *The High School Journal, 93* (3), 98–110.

Chapter Twelve

Practitioner Research in English Education

Patricia Lambert Stock

As a participant in what has been described as the teacher research movement in K–12 education and the scholarship of teaching movement in postsecondary education, for more than thirty years, along with others in the field, I have studied literacy teaching and learning from the perspective of the practicing teacher (for example, Anderson & Herr, 1999; Cochran-Smith & Lytle, 1993, 1998a, 1998b, 1999; Fleischer, 1994; Hatch et al., 2005; Huber & Morreale, 2002; Hutchings, 1996; Hutchings & Shulman, 1999; Smith & Stock, 2002a, 2002b; Stock, 2005; Shulman, 1993, 2000).

Particularly, I focus attention on what I call overlooked and underexamined genres of practitioner research (Stock, 1993, 1995, 2001). In this chapter one of those studies is referenced—an inquiry into the sources, conduct, defining characteristics, and impacts of the teacher inquiry workshop (TIW) that is at the heart of the invitational summer institutes of the National Writing Project (NWP), a highly acclaimed, forty-year-old professional development project.

Attention is drawn to several kinds of multimethod research that those of us who think of ourselves as practitioner researchers in English education have been developing and applying to beneficial effect for the last half century.

Although I did not realize it at the time that I wrote the following words at the conclusion of an article published in the journal *English Education* (2001), with them I proposed this research project that my earlier work had prepared me to undertake.

In highlighting the anecdote and the workshop, two genres in which I have observed reflective practitioners shape and share their knowledge, I mean not only to draw attention to the forms and forums in which reflective practitioners work but also to raise questions about the nature of research that stands to benefit teachers and learners and research that is positioned to legitimate and authorize the research of the corps of reflective practitioners who are teacher researchers. It is not that I disagree with the claim that research must be intentional, systematic, purposeful, and made accessible for peer critique and community use, it is rather that I believe there has been little systematic study of the genre of research that reflective practitioners have used and are using to build the base of knowledge about teaching that they distribute for review in their professional community, although the possibility for such systematic study surrounds us, if professional researchers in education are moved to undertake it. In the corps of teacher consultants of the National Writing Project, for example, there exists an extensive community of reflective practitioners who employ the genre of research and publication I have described in this essay as well as other genre yet to be identified. Might we not have much to learn from systematic study of the forms and forums of research in which these professional practitioners work? (p. 111)

In this chapter, after describing a multimethod research project that I—a university-based practitioner in English education—designed as a means of studying those forms and forums, I discuss one case study conducted within the project for two reasons.

First, to draw attention to the subject of the study—the sources, conduct, distinguishing characteristics, and impacts of the teacher inquiry workshop (TIW)—a practitioner research genre developed in the NWP. Second, to draw attention to why and how reflective practitioners conduct teacher research, how and where they publish their research for peer review and community use, the uses to which they put the findings of their research, the scholarship of teaching practice that their research is building, and the significant, for the most part unacknowledged, impact of their research on American education.[1]

THE RESEARCH PROJECT

All teachers who apply and are invited to participate in NWP summer institute's conduct teacher inquiry workshops (a.k.a., demonstrations, teaching workshops), and most, as NWP teacher consultants, continue to conduct workshops afterward in NWP continuity programs, various professional development programs, and professional conferences.

Simply put, in these workshops, NWP teacher consultants engage participants in classroom-tested teaching practices, framing the engagements as an inquiry of some kind. In the process, workshop leaders "publish" productive teaching practices for peer review and community use and engage colleagues in inquiries grounded in those practices.

The study described here, in which I have been and remain engaged for more than thirty years, is a qualitative, multimethod exploration of four broad questions: 1) What are the sources of these workshops?; 2) How are the workshops conducted?; 3) What are the defining characteristics of the teacher inquiry workshops developed in the National Writing Project?; and 4) What are their impacts? To conduct this inquiry, I have engaged in three sets of activities.

First, I have worked as a participant-observer in five NWP sites, all of which serve diverse communities of learners. In 2005, I was a fully participating observer in the summer institutes of three of these sites; in 2006, in a fourth, and from 2007 to 2010, as director of the project in a fifth.[2] In addition, I have been a participant-observer in group interview sessions for the summer institutes in two of the sites, in orientation sessions for institutes in four of the sites, and in continuity programming for summer institute fellows in all of the sites.

I have also participated in and observed workshops that summer institute fellows, now teacher consultants, in all of the sites, have offered in regional, state, and national conferences since 2005.

Following the summer institutes in which I participated, I conducted: 1) observations in classrooms at all levels of instruction (elementary, middle, secondary, college) of fellows who have adapted practices they experienced in summer workshops to serve their own various curricular goals and requirements; 2) follow-up interviews with individual summer institute fellows; and 3) focus group discussions with summer institute fellows during continuity session reunions of them.

Second, to learn more about the development of the genre of the TIW across the years, I have been conducting interviews with NWP site directors who are themselves observers of TIWs and part of whose responsibility it is to describe these workshops to university colleagues, school district administrators, and teachers applying to participate in summer invitational institutes.

I have also conducted focus group discussions with site directors who have been associated with the writing project for fifteen or more years, and I have read reports, articles, memoirs, and print descriptions of the TIW that have been distributed in handout form over the years to summer institute applicants and fellows.

The third avenue of inquiry in which I have engaged is one I am able to pursue because I have been associated with the NWP in a variety of ways, as both an insider and an outsider, for more than thirty years. Across these years, I have had occasion to participate in and observe a substantial number of TIWs in a number of writing project sites and writing project conferences.[3]

In the context of my study of the TIW in the NWP, I decided to revisit several workshops that have influenced my teaching and my research in order to add a historical dimension to the study, a dimension that has enabled me to explore the impacts of NWP teacher inquiry workshops over time. To revisit these workshops, I have interviewed (in person, in telephone conversations, and in email exchanges) the teacher consultants who conducted them and others who participated in them, and I have collected all extant artifacts related to them that I have been able to locate.

The case study approach I have pursued to learn about the impacts of these workshops has provided me multiple data sets for examination and cross-examination (that is, interviews, email exchanges, documents of various kinds produced at the classroom, school, school district, state, and professional levels).

A CASE STUDY WITHIN THE RESEARCH PROJECT

In this chapter, for two important reasons, I feature the work of Laura Roop, school research relations coordinator at the University of Michigan's School of Education and outgoing director of the Oakland (Michigan) Writing Project, also at the University of Michigan. First, Roop's work allows me to narrate a case in point of the sources, conduct, defining characteristics, and impacts of a TIW in multiple contexts, and multiple networks, over time.[4]

Second the case reveals the multimethod inquiries in which practitioner researchers engage for the purpose of their own and one another's professional development and their students' learning in settings in which education is conceived as professional—not bureaucratic—work. In effect, this essay is the story of an organic, inquiry-based approach to research and teaching embraced in the field of literacy education in the second half of the twentieth century that has been developed in communities of practice like the NWP and the National Council of Teachers of English.

Laura Roop was a high school English teacher in Oakland County, Michigan, in 1985, when she was selected to be an invitational summer institute fellow in the Oakland (Michigan) Writing Project. Her work as a teacher consultant in the project and in Oakland County began almost immediately thereafter.

That fall, Aaron Stander, founding director of the Oakland Writing Project and language arts coordinator of the Oakland Intermediate Public Schools District, a state-funded education agency providing professional development and service for the twenty-eight diverse school districts located just west and northwest of the city of Detroit, arranged for Roop to conduct a countywide teaching of poetry series for middle school and high school teachers.

In part because she was an outstanding teacher in her home school district and in part because she was now a teacher consultant in the writing project, Roop was also invited to "model teach" and "coach" in classrooms in her home school district. Over the next five years, Roop earned a reputation in Oakland County and beyond in the state of Michigan as a talented teacher who approached her work as a learner for and with her students, and as a valued teacher consultant who approached that work as a co-learner for and with colleagues and their students. [5]

Sources of a Teacher Inquiry Workshop

When Stander retired in 1990, Roop was selected to succeed him as the Oakland Intermediate Public Schools language arts coordinator and as director of the Oakland County Writing Project. Early in her tenure as Oakland County's language arts coordinator, Roop was approached by Julie Casteel, language arts coordinator in the Waterford School District, with a request for help. Administrators in Waterford's schools were concerned about the quality of elementary school students' writing in the district.

In an email correspondence to me as part of our ongoing effort to reconstruct the sources and impacts of a teacher inquiry workshop Roop conducted in which I participated, Roop described the problem for which Casteel was seeking help: "From [district-level administrators'] perspective, students were writing a lot, but the writing produced wasn't very good overall. Lots of personal narratives, characterized by 'this happened,' followed by 'and' and the next item on a list" (email, February 23, 2007).

Approaching the problem as a practitioner researcher, Roop met with Casteel to plan how they might begin to address it. She describes the meeting this way:

> Julie and I got together and brainstormed our questions and wonderings about this situation. I wondered whether teachers were modeling writing for their students, whether they felt comfortable writing, and whether they were making connections between the features of the texts kids were reading and their writing. (Email, February 23, 2007)

Roop's simply-put description of her first meeting with Waterford's language arts coordinator reveals much about her work and the work of NWP teacher consultants: when asked to shape professional development programs for teachers in particular settings, these practitioner researchers do not assume the role of visiting expert who arrives with already-prepared answers to the challenges facing the teachers involved in them. Instead, they assume the role of knowledgeable co-workers whose first step toward problem solving is working with colleagues to determine the problem's nature and dimensions.

Conceiving their work to address the challenge they had been presented from the perspective of co-inquirers into it, Roop and Casteel invited teachers in the district's elementary schools to join them in a study of how best to help elementary school students become the most effective writers they might be. Teachers in three of the district's fifteen elementary school buildings took up the invitation.

Roop describes how she, Casteel, and the teachers engaged in the study shaped it cooperatively:

> [Teachers in the three elementary school buildings] selected the genre of "fiction" to focus on (undoubtedly realizing that their classroom libraries and basals were full of examples). Julie and I engaged in a kind of inquiry you might expect: I gathered texts on genre. . . . We found lots of examples—for children, for adults, with a special focus on fiction, and the characteristics of fiction.
>
> We arranged for me to collect samples of student work, interview students and teachers on videotape, etc. . . . [Teachers brought] examples of student fiction (a student struggling, a typical text, and a top example writer)—for reflection and description in an after school workshop. (Email, February 23, 2007)

Going on to describe her approach to her work as a teacher consultant in the Waterford schools, Roop gives voice to the manner in which teacher consultants in the NWP often work in the sustained, inservice professional development programming that the writing project advocates: "[T]his is the way I often work when 'consulting'—I'm inquiring into a topic on behalf of a group of practitioners, and then I am co-designing opportunities for practicing teachers to inquire" (email, February 23, 2007).

Roop, Casteel, and teachers in three Waterford schools conducted their inquiries in meetings like those typically conducted by teacher research/ teacher inquiry groups in the NWP community, that is, as workshops, by which I mean that in such groups, one or another member usually leads the meeting (the "shop") in which the group "works" with the materials the leader brings for study for the purpose of "developing" or "making" something(s) (for example, literacy lessons, writing assignments, assessments of student work, understandings of various kinds).

In this case, teachers read and discussed the literature Roop gathered to inform their study, and they read and discussed "student work" that teachers brought to the meetings in order to examine their writing assignments and the student writing composed in response to those assignments, the effects of their responses to students' writing, etc., and they studied videotaped teacher-student interviews that—in effect—all brought to the meetings for study.

Roop notes:

> [By the end of the school year,] we had a district-wide meeting where it became clear that the three schools we had worked with had made much more headway than the other schools in the district—as in, the teachers at those schools felt they understood more about genre and coaching writing as a result of our work together—and that became apparent to the other teachers, who didn't feel like they had made much headway at all. (Email, February 23, 2007)

As a result of this meeting, a team of teachers—including some who had not been part of the first year's study—began to work together with Roop and Casteel to plan and design a district-wide professional development initiative for the next year, one that built on the first year's work. The plan called for Roop to offer a course for all interested elementary and middle school teachers and administrators. Roop recalls that sixty teachers and administrators enrolled in the course entitled "Quality Literacy," which she describes this way:

> [W]e began with district exit outcomes, then looked at extra-institutional and school day learning opportunities, to see what kinds of opportunities K-12 learners had to engage in high quality, intensive experiences that would permit them to achieve the outcomes. There was a "genre" aspect to "Quality Literacy"—I remember sessions on "making" high quality anything—art, furniture, scientific theories, etc. We emphasized the exploration and process one needed to do to get to "quality." And then, sessions on particular genres—both reading and writing. There was a "mini-case study" dimension to the whole thing—so we had people gathering work from one student, etc. I remember showing DaVinci's sketches, then finished inventions, etc. (multimedia before it was easy—I remember having two overheads and a projector or some crazy thing). (Email, February 23, 2007)

At the same time that she was teaching the "Quality Literacy" course, Roop developed and offered a teacher inquiry workshop for some seventy elementary and middle school teachers in Waterford. As it happens, this workshop figures as a precursor to the one I wanted to revisit for the purposes of my broader study of the sources, conduct, distinguishing characteristics, and impacts of TIWs developed and conducted in the NWP.

The workshop about which I write here grew out of the part of the professional development inquiry project that Roop was conducting with Sharon Martens Galley, a fourth- and fifth-grade teacher in Haviland Elementary School, whose students read and wrote a variety of genres, composed portfolios, and—in interviews conducted by Roop—reflected critically and comparatively on the work of authors they read, as well as on their own writing across the school year.

When Roop first offered the teacher inquiry workshop, inspired by Galley's literacy curriculum and based on the data they were collecting to document it, Galley herself was a participant in the workshop. Galley (1996) describes her experience of that workshop in these words: "When Waterford elementary teachers watched and listened to video [tape recordings of my students reflecting on their reading and writing] for the first time, the room grew hushed. No one graded papers. No one shuffled or whispered. Faces displayed complete amazement" (p. 250).

Galley also notes that she herself was taken by surprise, not surprise at how her students talked about their writing—after all, she'd been talking to them about their writing all year—but surprise at her colleagues' responses to how substantial her students' discussions of their writing were. Reflecting on her response, Galley (1996) writes:

> It took me a while to get it. After the initial interviews, I was so busy defending Zach and Melissa, insisting they were normal kids (almost any student in my room could talk about writing and reading in the same terms) that I failed to see the big picture. The big picture was the power of the evidence that the taped interview provided—evidence that even the most unwilling skeptic, the teacher who doesn't think kids can, has to accept. Since I had been hearing students talk like this in the classroom for a while, I thought it was normal and routine. . . . It took those interviews to prove it wasn't commonplace. What seemed ordinary was indeed extraordinary. (p. 252)

Furthermore, as she watched the tapes in Roop's workshop, Galley decided that she had much to learn about teaching from her students' discussions of their learning. She began to see her students' conversations about their reading and writing as evidence of their and her own ongoing internal literacy journeys. She too had learned to read and write and to become a critical thinker in conversations about reading and writing. Inspired by her discovery, Galley began a teacher research study of her own.

She began to videotape interviews with her students, interviews conducted along lines inspired by Roop and by the conversations she herself liked to have about books and writing. As Galley reviewed the videotapes, she did so through the eyes of her students' teacher. She writes: "I remember my reaction when I first saw Andrea and Ryan on video. I applauded their connections, but I moaned their lack of insight on revisions. . . . I began to assess my own practices" and to change them (1996, p. 253).

What began with an invitation to an NWP teacher consultant to work with a language arts coordinator in a large school district to create inservice opportunities aimed at helping teachers improve the quality of elementary school students' writing took shape as a professional development initiative that engaged teachers and administrators, individually and collectively, across the school district in collaborative inquiries into their practice and their school district's literacy curriculum over a period of three years.

It also led several teachers who engaged in the project to go on to conduct systematic inquiries into their teaching and to publish those inquiries in juried journals, to become teacher researchers in their own right.[6]

What is of particular interest to me is what my research to trace the sources of the teacher inquiry workshop Roop offered and in which I participated in 1993 revealed about how Roop's inquiry-based approach to the "consulting" she was invited to do benefited the quality of professional development, curriculum development, and instruction in the Waterford Public Schools.

Conduct of a Teacher Inquiry Workshop

Each January in the early 1990s, teachers associated with Michigan's writing projects came together to teach and learn from one another and to hear from a well-known researcher in composition studies in a conference that was called *The Michigan Writing Projects Leadership Conference*. In the 1993 conference, I planned to attend a breakout session in which Laura Roop was to conduct a workshop addressing issues in writing assessment.

After welcoming some twenty-five of us who gathered for the workshop and inviting us to introduce ourselves to one another, Roop introduced the workshop, telling us that we were going to spend the time we had together studying the work of two fifth-grade students with whom she and her colleague Sharon Martens Galley had been working that year as part of a project with elementary and middle school teachers in the Waterford Public Schools.

Roop initiated our inquiry by projecting on a screen at the front of the room the Michigan Educational Assessment Program (MEAP) scores of two students with whom she had been working. She asked those of us participating in the workshop to write briefly in response to this set of questions: What do you know about these children and their literacy from this information? What do you infer? What can't you see?

After we wrote and discussed our responses to the questions based on numerical test scores, one of which was stronger than the other, Roop projected before us report cards that indicated their teacher's evaluations of these students' work in the language arts (reading, writing, speaking, and listening). Once again, she asked us to take a few minutes to write and then to discuss what we now knew about these children and their literacy from the information we now had, what we inferred, and what we were unable to see.

Discussion revealed that the teachers' grades and comments were not exactly what we might have expected in light of the students' MEAP scores. Our curiosity piqued, Roop followed our discussion by projecting single samples of each student's writing, asking us once again to write and discuss our responses to them in term of the set of questions framing our inquiry.

As we studied the two students' writing samples, we noted what we thought we now knew, inferred, and could not say about the students' competencies as writers. When we discussed what we were noting—students' vivid use of language, mature syntax, engagement with the subjects they were writing about, etc.—we observed changes in our original hypotheses about the writing ability of the students whose literacy we were investigating in the workshop.

Following this discussion, Roop asked us to gather in groups of three or four. She distributed to each group packets containing excerpts from the students' literacy portfolios. Once again, she asked us to examine the artifacts in the packets and to respond in writing and discussion to the set of questions guiding our study.

After examining, writing about, and discussing the two students' portfolios, which included reading responses, a log students kept about the books they read, and multiple samples of their writing, our responses to the set of questions was not only considerably more complicated than our first responses to them, but they also called our previous judgments into question.

Finally, Roop played videotapes of interviews she had conducted with each of the students. In each interview, Roop and the student sat at a table with the student's portfolio before them. During the interviews, students discussed books they had and were reading, their writing, their composing processes, their goals for their writing, and their assessment of their work in progress in response to questions like these that Roop asked them:

- Can you tell me about the best book you've read this year?
- Were you inspired by that book to write another piece?
- Is that a work in progress?
- Can you choose one of the pieces that you've brought along from your portfolio and read it aloud?
- When you're working on a piece, how do you know what to revise? How do you know what to change in your piece?
- When you look at the pieces that you have done, how do you see yourself changing as a writer over the course of the year?
- Do you learn anything about yourself as a writer when you write with other people?
- How do you think the authors of these books put together their works? (Galley, 1996, p. 254).

The interviews revealed students who were engaged and enthusiastic about their reading and writing and able to talk, thoughtfully and analytically, about published texts and their own compositions. The tapes also revealed similarities and differences between the literacy practices, competencies, interests, and proficiencies of these two fifth-graders, a boy and a girl.

These similarities and differences led us to question whether there was a relationship between gender and patterns of literacy learning and development, a question some participants began to investigate with their own students after the workshop, one that has become the subject of much research and publication since.

After viewing the videotapes, those of us in the workshop responded a fifth time in writing and discussion to the questions Roop had posed at the beginning of the workshop. Not surprisingly, our responses to Roop's questions grew richer and deeper and more complex with each new piece of data we examined.

Our study of a number of these students' literary artifacts and discussions of their reading and writing led us to discover that both students were strong, purposeful readers and writers, who deserved to be described as critical readers of published texts and whose analyses of their own compositions were insightful, drawing attention to purposeful choices they made in their writing, occasions when they used their reading as "mentor" texts, examples from their writing that they thought were effective, and pieces in need of work.

As Roop drew the workshop to a close, participants reflected on how impressed we were with these students' discussions of their reading and writing as well as the interrelationships between them and with how our judgments about the quality of the students' literacy developed and changed with each new piece of data we examined. We left the room talking about the students, their writing, and the teaching that enabled students to be able to talk so insightfully and confidently about what they knew how to do and what they had to work more to learn how to do.

In effect, the workshop Laura Roop conducted that January morning in 1993 constructed an argument: meaningful (valid) assessment of student writing requires evaluators to look at multiple pieces of students' work composed for different audiences, purposes, and in different circumstances. It also argued to the teachers in the room for the value of engaging students in self-assessment and in discussions of their reading and writing with their teachers and others, discussions like the ones Laura modeled with students in the videotapes.

Defining Characteristics of a Teacher Inquiry Workshop

Based on the teacher inquiry workshops I have studied to date—whether in summer institutes or in subsequent continuity programs like the one in which Roop conducted the workshop I have just described—I have observed five characteristics that distinguish them.

First, in these teaching workshops the conduct and publication of inquiries are not discrete activities. Instead, in these workshops, the conduct and publication of experiments in teaching and learning are fluid, mutually dependent, holistically realized activities. Furthermore, this all-at-once, altogether conduct and publication of research is neither accidental nor a flaw of the work. It is, in fact, intentional, generative, and demonstrably productive.

Roop's 1993 workshop on the assessment of student writing published her research for peer review and community use of those of us in the workshop. As it engaged us in teaching practices and in assessing particular students' work, it also asked us to entertain the implicit question underlying the workshop: What information must be examined to produce valid assessments of students' writing?

Second, I have observed that when these workshops make arguments, whether for generative classroom teaching practices or about broad issues of concern to educators, as this one did, those arguments are constructed jointly in the "work" of all workshop participants, not by the workshop leader alone. In this case, Roop, the workshop leader, brought to the workshop study data about and samples of students' writing as well as videotaped interviews of students discussing their writing.

She also planned activities in which participants would examine the data and questions to guide the inquiry. Participants in the workshop studied the data, developed, refined, and revised understandings, and reached communally constructed responses to the inquiry questions. In those communally constructed responses, the argument of the workshop was constructed.

In this case, the third, fourth, and fifth characteristics of the genre that I have observed develop in the NWP—its immediate impact on practice, its contribution to the scholarship of teaching practice, and its contribution to the discourse about issues of concern to practicing educators—are best illustrated in a discussion of the impact of the workshop to date.

IMPACTS OF A TEACHER INQUIRY WORKSHOP

When I began to interview Roop to learn more about the impacts of the teacher inquiry workshop in which I participated in 1993, some of what I learned, I expected to learn. Roop's work had influenced the practice of teachers beyond Waterford, just as it had influenced the work of teachers in Waterford, for whom it was becoming customary to inquire into their students' learning and adjust their practice responsively (for example, Casteel, Roop, & Schiller, 1996; Galley, 1996).

For example, Kathleen Hayes Parvin, transported Roop's multipurpose practice of asking open-ended questions for interviewing students about their reading and writing and the interrelationships between them back with her to her home school district (Southfield, Michigan) to use and study with her students and colleagues.

However, I was unaware of the full extent to which Roop's widely admired professional development work coupled with her scholarship of teaching practice published in print (1995, 2002, 2006) made her what Lieberman and Friedrich (2007) call a "turn to" person in the state of Michigan for projects that required deep knowledge of literacy studies and literacy pedagogy, imagination in working with teachers, and an unflagging commitment to all students' learning.

Roop's leadership in two state-level projects and influence on a third suggest the reach of the teacher inquiry workshop in which I participated and her inquiry-based professional development work 1) on development of curriculum, instruction, and assessment of writing in a number of school districts across the state of Michigan, 2) on the development of English language arts standards and benchmarks in the state, and 3) on practitioners' work to continue to beneficially influence the practice of English language arts instruction in an era that equates testing with learning.

The Frameworks Project

A project that made extensive use of the work Roop led in the Waterford schools and the teacher inquiry workshop she conducted at the Annual Michigan Writing Projects Leadership Conference was the Frameworks Project, a state-wide curriculum development project in Michigan for which Roop served as a co-developer in the early 1990s.

In the Frameworks Project, Michigan State University's Educational Extension Service, working with partner organizations, including intermediate school districts like the Oakland Intermediate Public Schools, designed professional development activities and reading experiences that local school districts might use to respond proactively to a complex education reform package passed by the Michigan legislature in 1990 (Public Act #25).

The reform package required all school districts to do one of two things: 1) adopt core curriculum outcomes developed at the state level or 2) proactively develop their own core curriculum outcomes while engaging in the professional activities and readings developed by the Frameworks Project.

At early planning meetings in the Frameworks Project, the co-developers agreed that it would be important to create professional development activities that purposefully and productively related instruction, curriculum, and ongoing assessment in the English language arts to one another.

Roop recalls that when the planning group began to discuss the professional development activities they would develop and readings they would gather to address issues related to assessment in language arts, she immediately thought about Sharon Galley's class and the kinds of artifacts, including videotapes, that she and Galley were continuing to collect and make.

Roop reports that by the time this discussion took place in the Frameworks Project, she, Casteel, and Galley were already thinking about how to develop assessment processes and rubrics that would help classroom teachers like Galley know what "kids understood, had dispositions toward, and habits for" when they were engaged in complex literacy acts in a rich integrated language arts curriculum (February 23, 2007).

Roop thought of Galley's classroom for the Frameworks Project for two additional reasons: First, Galley and her students were accustomed and willing to be interviewed and videotaped and, second, Galley was teaching at a transition point. Her students were about to move to the middle grades, which meant that workshops focused on her students would be of interest to both elementary and middle school teachers.

After the Frameworks Project's co-developers studied videotapes and work samples from Galley's classroom, they decided the materials were the kind they wanted to use in the professional development sessions they were designing. As a result, a version of the teacher inquiry workshop in which I participated that grew out of Roop's classroom research with Sharon Galley in Waterford became the English language arts assessment workshop that was published in the Frameworks Project's English Language Arts Professional Development Kits used by workshop leaders in settings across the state.

This version of the workshop did not engage participants in writing about and discussing what they knew about two children and their literacy, what they could not see, and what they wanted to know as they examined accumulating examples of the children's writing; instead it asked them to write and discuss descriptive reviews of various samples of Galley's students' writing.

After attending sessions in which they were prepared to do so, a corps of teachers from Michigan school districts that opted to develop their own core curriculum outcomes while engaging in professional activities designed by the Frameworks Project conducted Roop's teacher inquiry workshop for colleagues in their home districts. Following these workshops in which participants wrote descriptive reviews of Galley's students' work, participating teachers brought samples and wrote descriptive reviews of their own students' work in follow-up workshop sessions.

In addition to samples of student work, videotapes, overheads, and step-by-step workshop procedures for using the materials, the Frameworks Project's English Language Arts Professional Development Kits that Roop and other co-developers designed included books and articles. Some years later, the kits were among the materials that Karen Smith and Linda Crafton studied to develop the National Council of Teachers of English's Reading Initiative, a professional development initiative adopted, among other places, by the entire state of South Carolina.

The Michigan English Language Arts Frameworks Project

Even as she was working to develop the Frameworks curriculum development project and even as her scholarship of teaching practice was shaping professional development across the state of Michigan in that project, Roop was invited to become a member of the management team and co-designer with Richard Koch and Karen K. Wixson of professional development within the Michigan English Language Arts Framework Project (MELAF).

One of several projects conducted at the state level to promote standards-based reform through Goals 2000, the MELAF Project (1993–1996) was supported with competitive grant funding awarded by the U.S. Department of Education to the Michigan Department of Education and the University of Michigan.

Because MELAF's leaders were convinced that inquiry-based, sustained professional development lay at the heart of reform, they designed the project as an extended professional development initiative to take place in diverse school districts to enable individual teachers to explore the implications of standards for their own classroom practice and school districts to determine the role standards would play in their local educational reform (Dutro et al., 2002). Four school districts, selected to represent the range of districts in Michigan, were chosen to serve as demonstration sites for the project.

In an article they published in *Teachers College Record* in 2002, Roop, Koch (co-director of the Oakland Writing Project and professor of English in Adrian [Michigan] College), and Wixson (then professor and subsequently dean of education at the University of Michigan), together with colleagues who joined them in analysis of the MELAF project—Elizabeth Dutro and Maria Chesley Fisk—describe how the NWP influenced the shape of the project's professional development work from the outset:

> One external network in particular influenced our design of MELAF professional development: the National Writing Project, a federally funded network [of] . . . university-school collaborations offering literacy-related professional development influenced by constructivist and developmental educational concepts. . . . Consistent with this conceptual base, the MELAF professional development program attempted to enact the following principles: First, educator-participants must "be" what we want them to help students become— that is, they must experience the kind of teaching and learning that students are to experience in classrooms. Second, participants must adopt habits of study (reading, writing, discussing, reflecting) and inquiry. Third, a community of educators must work collaboratively over time if substantive change in schooling is to occur. Fourth, expert mentoring, grass roots development, and administrative support are all necessary parts of the process. Fifth, professional

learning occasions must offer multiple invitations or support structures for
learning: intensive summer workshops or institutes, school year classroom
implementation, and follow-up problem-solving. Finally, all parties involved
must be conscious of the fact that the roles of individuals and groups within
the community will change at different points and that this movement will
itself be an important part of the change process. (Dutro et al., 2002, p. 789)

In their work to establish language arts standards and benchmarks in the
state of Michigan, MELAF's leaders were themselves committed to the development of practitioner researchers. To accomplish these multiple goals,
Roop, Koch, and Wixson, together with other members of the project's management team, co-designed and co-facilitated professional development
workshop activities undertaken by teachers and administrators from the four
demonstration districts in MELAF team meetings and in multiple-week summer institutes.

In these workshops, participants explored standards, teacher research,
curriculum, and assessment. In turn, teachers and administrators who participated in these workshops, together with Roop, Koch, Wixson, and management teams members, conducted similar professional development workshops for colleagues in their home school districts.

The teacher inquiry workshop in which I participated in 1993, the thread
running through this case study of practitioner research as professional development in and beyond the NWP, also figured in the MELAF project. In this
project, it was redesigned once again to engage participants in looking at
student work through various lenses, including the Prospect School's Descriptive Review of the Child (Kanevsky, 1992) and the standards and benchmarks the project was developing.

Following work done in the MELAF project to produce standards and
benchmarks, teachers and administrators from the four demonstration sites
engaged 200 of their peers from across the state of Michigan in discussion of
those standards and benchmarks and in some of the activities that produced
them in a conference, "From Paper to Practice: Creating a Living English
Language Arts Curriculum" (1996).

In addition to producing these standards and benchmarks and gaining
broad "ownership" of them from educators across the state, a number of
teachers who participated in the MELAF Project took on leadership roles in
their home schools and school districts. A group of teachers in one of the
demonstration sites proposed to the district's administration that they build
on the work they had been doing in a year-long, district-wide program of
inquiry-based professional development activities.

Another school district opened its doors to teachers who were attending a
national conference in the area and wanted to learn more about how state
standards and benchmarks were being enacted in a school district that partici-

pated in their development. A number of individual teachers who participated in the project took on leadership roles as principals, language arts coordinators, curriculum directors, and one as an associate superintendent. Teachers from all four districts wrote for publication.

Reflecting on the positive outcomes of the MELAF project, in the article they published in *Teachers College Record*, Roop and her colleagues recognized several implications of the work accomplished within the project, among them these two related ones:

> [T]here may well be strategic points in a school system's development for investing large sums of monies in professional development. And it may be strategically effective to invest resources in districts with a core community of teacher leaders who are willing to share their learning with others, and to invest more heavily in these teachers' professional learning. (Dutro et al., 2002, p. 808)

In other words, the positive outcomes of the MELAF Project led its assessors to conclude that there are substantial benefits to nurturing practitioner researchers to become teacher leaders in local communities, leaders who will introduce and engage colleagues in professional development that is ongoing, inquiry-based, and focused on student learning.

The reach of the MELAF project extended beyond the state of Michigan as educators in other states and researchers in education examined published reports of the standards and benchmarks for teaching the English language arts and the means by which they were developed in Michigan.

In this report, *Statewide and District Professional Development in Standards: Addressing Teacher Equity*, which was widely disseminated as part of the NWP monograph series, Koch, Roop, and Setter (2006) present the model developed in the MELAF Project for practitioner-led, inquiry-based development of state-level standards for English language arts teaching and learning.

After MELAF

Like most states, Michigan has developed subsequent standards for student learning in the English language arts in the years since the MELAF work. Although these projects have not braided inquiry-based professional development with standards development, practitioners were well represented on the committees that shaped the Michigan High School Content Expectations in the English Language Arts (2006) and Michigan's more recently adopted Common Core Standards (2010).

At the same time, the consortium of NWPs in Michigan, the National Writing Projects of Michigan (NWPM) has continued to develop and refine the work that Roop and her colleagues in the Waterford schools began together—some twenty years ago—to productively integrate inquiry-based professional development with the development and assessment of curriculum, instruction, and learning.

They have continued this work in classrooms, schools, school districts, and in state-level initiatives, and they have published their ongoing work for peer review and community use in writing project programs, local, state, regional, and national conferences, and in print.

Cases in point of this ongoing work may be found in *The Portfolio Guidebook: Implementing Quality in an Age of Standards* (2000), a book reporting on a three-year-long, school-district-wide portfolio research project, written by Richard Koch and Jean Schwartz-Petterson, a teacher in the Adrian Michigan Public Schools. At the practical level, the book provides the rationale and apparatus for implementation of a K–12, system-wide use of portfolios for instruction and assessment.

In case studies, the book also offers substantial evidence of students' growth and development over time and teachers' collaboration across levels of instruction for the purpose of their professional development and their students' learning. Finally, *The Portfolio Guidebook* raises questions emerging from the study, questions like those that have continuously led to the development of the practitioner research illustrated in this essay.

More recently, in 2009, in the Michigan Portfolios Project (http://www.michiganportfolios.org), the National Writing Projects of Michigan under Koch's leadership, has initiated another effort to purposefully reconnect teachers' professional development with instruction, and student learning. In a December 2, 2011, email correspondence, Roop described the impetus for developing the website.

> There came a moment, several years ago, when Dick [Koch] was presenting about portfolios, along with folks from Kentucky, at the National Writing Project annual meeting, when Mary Cox [Detroit school teacher and writing project director] turned to me and said: WE HAVE TO BRING BACK PORT-FOLIOS. We thought that the fact that MI was rolling out New Tech High Schools and International Baccalaureates (both models rely on portfolios) and that the NCLB writing tests were being cut back due to a lack of funding meant maybe we should focus on digital portfolios as a statewide network. So last summer, Troy Hicks [associate professor of English Education in Central Michigan University] and Dick Koch led a three-day workshop for site leaders on digital portfolios . . . and we're going to keep this conversation going over the next several years.

The NWPM website that keeps the "conversation going" features, among other things, video clips of teachers interviewing their students about work in their students' portfolios. These interviews are very like those that Roop shared with participants in her 1993 workshop. The Michigan Portfolios

Project website has now, in effect, made the practices for which Roop's 1993 workshop argued available worldwide and surrounded them in Richard Koch's texts and remarks with theory supporting the practices.

CONCLUDING THOUGHTS

Studies in education like the one that is the subject of this chapter are uncommon for two reasons. First, as I noted in the essay that led me to this research project, the genres of practitioner research have been largely overlooked and undervalued in American education. Second, researchers are under pressure to conduct and publish their work "in a timely fashion"—which usually means within a year or two, and which usually determines the kinds of studies that can be conducted as well as what those studies are able to reveal.

For this reason, thickly descriptive studies—like ethnographic case studies conducted over time—are rare. The research reported in this essay was undertaken for the purpose of providing a thick description of the sources, conduct, distinguishing characteristics, and impacts of the teacher inquiry workshop (TIW), a genre of practitioner research developed in the NWP.

Because I have participated in various roles in NWP sites for some thirty years, at this point in time, I have participated in hundreds of these TIWs, and because I was supported with a grant from the NWP and a research leave from Michigan State University, I had the opportunity to trace the origins and impacts of dozens of them. The case in point that I have described here demonstrates the complexity of such an enterprise.

I chose to present the story of Roop's 1993 workshop in this chapter because it highlights so much of what my research has revealed more generally about one of the underexamined, largely overlooked genres of practitioner research in education. Recent readers of this essay, like former NWP site directors—Cathy Fleischer and Sheridan Blau—whose suggestions have improved it have mentioned name after name of other teacher scholars about whom I might also write to illustrate the richness of the sources, conduct, distinguishing characteristics, and impacts of the genre of practitioner research—the teacher inquiry workshop.

If Ann Lieberman and Linda Friedrich's vignette studies and the NWP's legacy studies initiated by Paul LeMahieu reveal the tip of an iceberg of the NWP's productive work in education, case studies like Roop's shed light on its reach.

AND ONE LAST WORD

Three years after Shirley Brice Heath published her award-winning study of language learning and use in *Ways with Words* (1983)—a long-term ethnographic study that revealed what had been overlooked until her remarkable work—I had the pleasure of coordinating a working conference sponsored by the School of Education and the Office of the Vice President for Academic Affairs and Provost of the University of Michigan.

The conference, aimed at influencing conversations about teacher education underway in the United States at the time, brought together a group of outstanding scholars interested in American education. Heath was among them. In a pre-conference position paper, Heath argued that the best hope for the beneficial reshaping of teaching education in America and, by extension, American education might be achieved if teachers were prepared to become learners for and with their students (1986, 1).

The story of Laura Roop's teacher research—of the research that is conducted and published in NWP teacher inquiry workshops—reveals teachers learning for and with their students as surely as it reveals the nature and value of a previously overlooked and underexamined genre of practitioner research that was developed for the purpose of building a scholarship of teaching practice.

NOTES

1. I wish to thank the National Writing Project (NWP) and Michigan State University, respectively, for the grant and research leave with which they so generously supported the research I describe here. I also wish to thank a group of remarkable colleagues in the NWP for their advice, insights, and encouragement at every stage of this work: Richard Sterling, executive director emeritus; Judy Buchanan, associate executive director; Elyse Eidman-Aadahl, Joye Alberts, Tom Fox, Mary-Ann Smith, directors; Paul LeMahieu and Linda Friedrich, former and current directors of research in the NWP; and Sherry Swain, research associate.

2. One of the sites serves primarily rural communities in the northwest; a second serves the rural communities and middle-sized cities in the northeast where it is located. The third, fourth, and fifth, located in large metropolitan areas on the east coast and in the southwest, serve urban, suburban, and rural communities.

3. In the early 1980s, I participated in the summer institute and served as a consultant for the Oakland Writing Project (Michigan) as it was becoming established in Oakland County (Michigan). From 1990 to 1993, I served as an outside "researcher in the field of composition studies" on the National Advisory Board to the NWP. In 1993, I co-founded the Red Cedar Writing Project located at Michigan State University. From 2000 to 2010, I participated in and observed TIWs in the South Coast Writing Project (California). In 2007, I co-founded the writing project in the University of Maryland, College Park, and served as its director through 2010. The various ways in which I have been associated with the work of the NWP for the past thirty years, as an insider and an outsider, have enabled me to "tack," as Clifford Geertz argues that all interpretative researchers must, between experience-near and experience-distant concepts and perspectives. I find the dialectic between these two ways of looking at the data I have collected to be generative (Geertz, 1983, 57).

4. In the multiple roles she has fulfilled in the University of Michigan's School of Education and as director of the Oakland (Michigan) Writing Project located at the University of Michigan, Roop has engaged in countless outreach activities that have allowed her to circulate her explorations of the scholarship of teaching practice.

5. In the NWP vignette study, Ann Lieberman and Linda Friedrich (2007) have observed these characteristics of leadership in the work of a number of NWP teacher consultants.

6. As it happens, these teachers also went on to become NWP teacher consultants. Both Julie Casteel and Sharon Martens Galley were 1993 summer institute fellows in the Oakland Writing Project.

REFERENCES

Anderson, G. L., & Herr, K. (1999). The new paradigm wars: Is there room for rigorous practitioner knowledge in schools and universities? *Educational Researcher, 28* (5), 12–21, 40.

Casteel, J., Roop, L., & Schiller, L. (1996). "No such thing as an expert": Learning to live with standards in the classroom." *Language Arts, 73* (1), 30–35.

Cochran-Smith, M., & Lytle, S. (1993). *Inside/outside: Teacher research and knowledge.* New York, N.Y.: Teachers College Press.

Cochran-Smith, M., & Lytle, S. (1998a). Relationships of knowledge and practice: Teacher learning in communities. *Review of Research in Education, 24,* 251–307.

Cochran-Smith, M., & Lytle, S. (1998b). The teacher research movement: A decade later. *Educational Researcher, 28* (7), 15–25.

Cochran-Smith, M., & Lytle, S. (1999). Teacher research: The question that persists. *International Journal of Leadership in Education, 1* (1), 19–36.

Dutro, E., Chesley, M. F., Koch, R., Roop, L., & Wixson, K. (2002). When state policies meet local district contexts: Standards-based professional development as a means to individual agency and collective ownership. *Teachers College Record, 104* (4), 787–811.

Fleischer, C. (1994). Researching teacher-research: A practitioner's perspective. *English Education, 26,* 86–124.

Galley, S. M. (1996). Talking their walk: Interviewing fifth graders about their literacy journeys. *Language Arts, 73* (4), 249–54.

Geertz, C. (1983). Blurred genres: The refiguration of social thought. *Local knowledge: Further essays in interpretative anthropology.* New York, N.Y.: Basic Books.

Hatch, T., Eiler White, M., Raley, J., Austin, K., Capitelli, S., & Faigenbaum, D. (2005). *Into the classroom: Developing the scholarship of teaching.* San Francisco, Calif.: Jossey-Bass.

Heath, S. B. (1983). *Ways with words.* New York, N.Y.: Cambridge University Press.

Heath, S. B. (1986). The education of a teacher: Shaping a creative tension between general and professional education. In *Tension and dynamism: The education of a teacher.* A Collection of Pre-conference papers. Ann Arbor, Mich.: The School of Education.

Huber, M. T., & Morreale, S. P. (Eds). (2002). *Disciplinary styles in the scholarship of teaching and learning: Exploring common ground.* Washington, D.C.: AAHE.

Hutchings, P. (1996). *Making teaching community property.* Washington D.C.: American Association for Higher Education.

Hutchings, P., & Shuman, L. S. (1999). The scholarship of teaching: New elaborations, new developments. *Change, 31* (5), 11–15.

Kanevsky, R. D. (1992). The descriptive review of the child: Teachers learn about values. In J. Andrias (Ed.), *Exploring Values and Standards: Implications for Assessment* (pp. 41–61). New York, N.Y.: Teachers College National Center for Restructuring Education, Schools, and Teaching.

Koch, R., Roop, L., & Setter, G. (2006). *Statewide and district professional development in standards: Addressing teacher equity.* Berkeley, Calif.: National Writing Project.

Koch, R., & Schwartz-Petterson, J. (2000). *The portfolio guidebook: Implementing quality in an age of standards.* Norwood, Mass.: Christopher-Gordon Publishers, Inc.

Lieberman, A., & Friedrich, L. (2007, April). Changing teaching from within: Teachers as leaders. Presentation at the annual meeting of the American Educational Research Association, Chicago, Illinois.

Shulman, L. S. (1993). Teaching as community property: Putting an end to pedagogical solitude. *Change,* 6–7.

Shulman, L. S. (2000). From Minsk to Pinsk: Why a scholarship of teaching and learning? *Journal of Scholarship of Teaching and Learning, 1* (1), 48–52.

Smith K., & Stock, P. L. (2002a). Current trends and issues and future directions in the teaching of the English language arts. In J. M. Jensen, J. Flood. D. Lapp, & J. R. Squire (Eds.), *Handbook of research on teaching of the English language arts* (pp. 114–30). Hillsdale, N.J.: Erlbaum.

Smith, K., & Stock, P. L. (2002b). Teacher research in language and literacy. In B. Gazzetti (Ed.), *Literacy in America: An encyclopedia of history, theory, and practice* (pp. 643–46). Denver, Colo.: ABC Clio.

Stock, P. L. (1993). The function of anecdote in teacher research. *English Education, 25* (4), 173–87.

Stock, P. L. (1995). *The dialogic curriculum.* Portsmouth, N.H.: Boynton/Cook-Heinemann.

Stock, P. L. (2001). Toward a theory of genre in teacher research: Contributions from a reflective practitioner. *English Education, 33* (2), 100–114.

Stock, P. L. (2005). Practicing the scholarship of teaching: What we do with the knowledge we make. *College English, 68* (1), 107–21.

About the Contributors

Lauren Causey earned a Ph.D. in Curriculum and Instruction: Literacy Education, from the University of Minnesota–Twin Cities in 2013. Her research interests include critical media analysis and production, activity theory, and the set of issues concerning diversity in children's and young adult literature.

Jerica Coffey is in her thirteenth year of teaching in public schools in both south Los Angeles and southeast San Francisco, and is a founding member of The People's Education Movement, a grassroots teacher-led organization that is engaged in struggles for educational justice in Los Angeles.

Jose Paco Fiallos is a teacher of world literature and creative writing at Lincoln High School in Tallahassee, Florida. He has served as a beginning teacher mentor and has designed and facilitated professional development sessions at the local, state, and national level.

Antero Garcia is an assistant professor in the English department at Colorado State University. Prior to moving to Colorado, Antero spent eight years teaching high school English in South Central Los Angeles.

Susan L. Groenke is an associate professor of English education and advises the English education program at the University of Tennessee. Her research interests include the development of critical thinking skills through the reading of young adult literature and effective strategies for democratic dialogue in the classroom.

Dr. Troy Hicks is an associate professor of English at Central Michigan University and directs the Chippewa River Writing Project, a site of the

National Writing Project. Hicks is the author of the Heinemann titles *Crafting Digital Writing* (2013) and *The Digital Writing Workshop* (2009), as well as a co-author of *Because Digital Writing Matters* (Jossey-Bass, 2010) and *Create, Compose, Connect!* (Eye on Education/Routledge, 2014), in addition to numerous journal articles and book chapters.

Latrise P. Johnson is an assistant professor of secondary English language arts and literacy at the University of Alabama. Her past experiences as a middle and high school English teacher in Atlanta public schools inform her current work with preservice teachers, current practitioners, and underserved student populations.

Judson C. Laughter is an assistant professor of English education and teaches courses on sociolinguistics and action research. His research interests include multicultural teacher education and culturally relevant pedagogy.

Cynthia Lewis is Professor of Critical Literacy and English Education at the University of Minnesota, where she holds the Emma M. Birkmaier Professorship in Educational Leadership. Her current research examines the role of emotion in urban classrooms, focused on critical media analysis and production. She has published widely on the intersection of social identities and literacy practices in and out of school.

Danny C. Martinez is currently an assistant professor of adolescent literacy at the University of California, Davis. Martinez's work is informed by the youth he worked with as an English and ESL teacher in both San Francisco and Los Angeles. His research examines the sociocultural language and literacy practices of black and Latina/o youth in learning settings.

sj Miller, an award-winning author and associate professor of secondary literacy at the University of Colorado Boulder, has published widely in journals and presented at national conferences on a variety of topics related to teaching young adult literature, anti-bullying pedagogy, undervalued student literacies and identities, challenging the gender binary, multimodal applications of popular culture in secondary classrooms, and cultivating socio-spatial justice dispositions with secondary preservice English teachers. sj is a member of the CEE Executive Committee, AERA Division K: Section 4 co-chair, and series co-editor of *Social Justice across Contexts in Education,* with Peter Lang Publishers.

Ernest Morrell is the Macy Professor of English Education and Director of the Institute for Urban and Minority Education at Teachers College, Columbia University. He is also the president of the National Council of Teachers of English and a Fellow of the American Educational Research Association. Ernest has taught English at every level from eighth grade to graduate school and he also loves to write fiction and coach youth sports.

Dr. Leslie S. Rush is Associate Dean for Undergraduate Programs in the University of Wyoming's College of Education. Previously an English teacher and English teacher educator, she is the co-editor of the journal *English Education.*

Lisa Scherff teaches English and reading at Estero High School (Florida). Formerly an English teacher educator and chair of the National Council of Teachers (NCTE) of English Assembly for Research, she is the co-editor of *English Education* and chair of the Joan F. Kaywell Book Award committee.

Patricia Lambert Stock is Professor Emerita in Michigan State University and a past president of NCTE. She has written more than fifty books and articles about literacy teaching and learning, curriculum, practitioner research in education, and the scholarship of teaching.

Maisha T. Winn is a professor of language and literacy and the Susan J. Cellmer Chair in English Education in the Department of Curriculum and Instruction at the University of Wisconsin-Madison. Her program of research examining language, literacy, and youth justice has appeared in *Race, Ethnicity, and Education; Pedagogies: An International Journal; International Journal of Qualitative Studies in Education;* and *Research in the Teaching of English.* She is a former elementary school teacher and high school English teacher.